P9-EDW-107

Planning Japan's Economic Future

Planning Japan's Economic Future

Kyoko Sheridan

First published 2005 by
PALGRAVE MACMILLAN
Houndmills, Basingstoke, Hampshire RG21 6XS and
175 Fifth Avenue, New York, N. Y. 10010
Companies and representatives throughout the world

PALGRAVE MACMILLAN is the global academic imprint of the Palgrave
Macmillan division of St. Martin's Press, LLC and of Palgrave Macmillan Ltd.
Macmillan® is a registered trademark in the United States, United Kingdom
and other countries. Palgrave is a registered trademark in the European
Union and other countries.

ISBN-13: 978–1–4039–47779–6   hardback
ISBN-10: 1–4039–4779–1   hardback

This book is printed on paper suitable for recycling and made from fully
managed and sustained forest sources.

A catalogue record for this book is available from the British Library.

Library of Congress Cataloging-in-Publication Data
Sheridan, Kyoko.
   Planning Japan's economic future / by Kyoko Sheridan.
      p. cm.
   Includes bibliographical references and index.
   ISBN 1–4039–4779–1 (cloth)
      1. Japan–Economic policy–1989– 2. Industrial policy–Japan. I. Title.
HC462.95.S524 2005
388.952–dc22   2004056897

10   9   8   7   6   5   4   3   2   1
14   13   12   11   10   09   08   07   06   05

Printed and bound in Great Britain by
Antony Rowe Ltd, Chippenham and Eastbourne

Contents

Preface   vii

Part I   Background   1

1 Formulating a Strategy for Economic Development   3
   Establishment of economic society   3
   Industrialization through people   10
2 Planning of the National Economy   15
   Keizai Hakusho, 1947–2004   15
   In praise of growth and efficiency once again   22
   Observation and lessons   31
3 Plans to Improve Living Standards   44
   Capital-scarce labour-surplus economy   44
   Economic development evaluated   50
   The transformation of the economy   54
4 Planning for Improved Living Standards   59
   The overall picture of the economy in the post-World   64
   War II years
   Planning experience   66
5 The Spirit of Japan's Political Economy   82
   Study through interviews conducted 1994–2005   82
   Interview surveys   84
   Preliminary findings, 1994 and 1995   86
   Koeki (in the public interest)   89
   Characteristics of officers   91
   Characteristics of Japanese public administrative officers   91
      through my interviews
   In search of an effective 'economic objective'   98
   Emerging types among the 'young recruits'   104

Part II   Case Studies of Economic Bureaucrats   109

6 The Society-consulting Public Administrator: Mr M.,   111
      Type C Officer
   Family, schooling and university days (1938–60)   111
   Career path   113

Work experience	117
Post-Ministry career in business (*amakudari* appointment)	123
7 The Intellectual Public Administrator: Mr N., Type D Officer	131
Career path	132
Administrative guidance evaluated	144
8 The Intellectual Planner: Mr K., Type A Officer	152
Career path	152
Observations made in Asia	162
Writing industrial policy	166
9 The Society-consulting Planner: Mr O., Type B Officer	169
Personal background	171
The *Jitan* proposal	174
The reduction of working hours, 1994–2004	182
Part III Conclusions	**191**
10 Economic Development and People's Satisfaction in Life	193
How contented are the Japanese today?	195
Quality of life and life satisfaction	201
11 Planning the Future	211
Reasons for failures in the economy and society in 2004	211
Life purposes and economic objectives post 1945	213
In search of proposals for the future	223
Exploration into a new frontier	224
Notes	233
Bibliography	248
Index	255

Preface

There are many questions to be asked about the Japanese economy. What is its fundamental nature? What are its objectives? On what principles does it operate? What is its management style and driving force? And how have the Japanese maintained its effectiveness?

In my book entitled *Governing the Japanese Economy* (1993), I addressed these questions. In this book the focus of my study is government-planned activities of the economy. I want to see how government in Japan has organized its planning activities to promote the industrial and social development of the country. In the mid-1980s the economy was fully developed with large prospects for its future. Yet a decade later this highly productive and most robust economy began its sudden deterioration – the national economy became depressed and business hesitated to make new investments. As economic growth rate fell, so planners lost their way, losing confidence, trying to find new directions, and studying models on other economies, most notably America. Instead of assessing the worth of their accumulated assets – economic and intellectual – so that they could develop strategies for the future, they have busied themselves revising, reforming or abandoning the old systems that have brought the country development and prosperity.

The economy ailed for some time as business hesitated over new investment and people began refraining from consumption: many businesses faced bankruptcy, lost management control and ownership to more active foreign companies, and the workforce shrank, creating unemployment across all ages and skills, something the country had not experienced for a long time. This was the result of the collapse, at the end of 1991, of the speculative boom that developed in the late 1980s. The boom was enormous and so was the damage it wrought.

Today, more than ten years after the collapse, the economy is still trying to recover. Many economic policies, including a Keynesian public spending programme, deregulation to introduce restructuring of the industry, and the reform of work practice in business, were formulated to activate the economy. None, however, brought the expected effects.

The sudden collapse of the boom is blamed for creating the economic difficulties that face Japan today, but a close examination shows that the economy had reached a stage in its development where previous approaches were no longer relevant. Rather than bringing about a decline in the economy, the end of the boom marked the arrival of a new stage. The attempts of developed economies in the West to sustain an active economy into a post-industrial, affluent society reveal how problematic it has been to move such a society into its next stage. The Japanese economy is today said to have reached that difficult point.

However difficult it is, I see in it an opening on to a new future. What exactly the new stage brings and what problems are experienced will differ from economy to economy and culture to culture. Rather than drawing on ideas and solutions from the troubled West, the Japanese must define the nature and extent of their own problems so as to develop strategies to counter them.

We need to see the shape of the emerging economy so that we can brief economic planners, business strategists and social reformers. This book is concerned with that briefing.

So why, despite their previous success in industrialization, are the Japanese now experiencing difficulties? What has caused the 'troubled state'? How can the economy be freed? What reforms will be required to rescue the economy and to guarantee its continued development?

And what is the future direction of the economy? The Japanese must explore new directions so that they can build a society in which they can truly 'better' themselves. How can this be done? What new management principles and skills will be required to provide for people's happiness and satisfaction? How can Japan make wise use of its accumulated economic resources and the skills and experiences of its people?

The study of the Japanese economy is now more important than ever because, in Japan, the problems and difficulties have emerged so quickly and with such serious implications that it is a matter of urgency to find ways to sustain people's living standards and quality of life.

In 2004 the Japanese economy has been in a gravely 'depressed' state – unable to bring growth – for nearly a decade. But it would be wrong to call this period 'the lost decade', as many do. I want to argue that 'Why the failure?' and 'Has the economy permanently lost its past dynamism?' are the wrong questions. What we should be asking now is 'What is actually developing in the economy and people's lives?' Before looking at how to stimulate growth and expansion we must assess whether it is necessary, given the economic stage of development in the country and the affluence of the people. Perhaps it would be more useful to look at how to build a 'dynamic' society, one that is progressive in ways different from those that only generate growth in the GNP.

For a long time the Japanese economy has no longer been oriented towards high growth. More than two decades ago we saw signs of a turn in the economy. In 2004 ordinary people in Japan, having noted the improvement in their *material* standards of living, are now looking to the economy to help them reach a better *quality* of life. Japan's political leaders, however, who still look to make Japan the top world economy, do not share this sentiment.

To improve quality of life, a new system with a different structure must be developed. It should be designed to serve people's welfare and the quality of their lives – and certainly not as a matter of vanity or national image.

The issue is not about finding new markets and new products, or restructuring industries and reallocating industrial resources, but about building a new system that is based on a reassessment of why people work and what they need to satisfy them.

The discussion of political economic thought can take various directions. We could start by asking how the Japanese developed their economy through public planning and policy. And what were the objectives of that planning, with what role was government entrusted, how was the plan conducted and on what principles, what activities and policy devices have been experimented with and developed, and which approaches have been formulated and practised?

Academics will need to ask what conceptual frameworks and assumptions researchers rely on to evaluate economic activities and find their working logic.

Business and community leaders will need to decide the preferred strategies for building growth so that corporate managers can organize and operate workplaces, invest, engage with employees and business competitors and save and distribute profits; and when they wish to establish their business in society as good citizens, how and what contribution they wish to make.

People in the general workforce will need to look at their career expectations, including education and training for them and their children, and their general expectations of life.

In this book I study the working of business (economic planners, policy writers and public administrators). With this aim I met and had in-depth discussions with 71 selected bureaucrats working in the Ministry of International Trade and Industry (formerly called MITI, now called METI) in Tokyo from 1994 to the end of 2003.[1] I conducted interviews with them to discover their professional approaches, individual beliefs in how to carry out their duties, and views on the economy and society; I also tried to understand their personalities and attitudes to life. Some of them welcomed me and showed interest and support, and I visited these people several times to understand how their approach and skills had developed and to discuss the economic activities and business of the time, evaluate the previous record of industrial development in the light of public plan efforts, and see what future image of the country could be explored. From these discussions I wanted to learn what the Japanese are capable of and what mistakes they have made so that I could make recommendations for the future.

I have a working hypothesis: the formation of a new economic system for Japan will emerge from the accumulated wisdom of the post-industrial economy. The new system will reflect most closely the country's technical and industrial knowledge and public administrative and business management skills, which have been formulated and tested for effectiveness for many years.

I believe the new system will emerge as a child of the old. The old system has been built on the basis of what people felt comfortable with, and were good at, so it makes sense to select parts from it for the new system. That the old system has survived for so long should be taken as proof that it does 'make sense' and is acceptable to people. It has the support of the culture, customs and habit.

What is 'new', then?

The new system pursues a new objective, which is about quality of life. It will replace the old, which was about raising the material standards of living. To make it work, the new system must be sought by, and its realization achieved through, initiatives by the people. Under the old system, provisions were handed out to them by the economy. Under the new system, people will need to take the initiative to understand what they want and how to use it, and economic and social planners will be asked to develop the understanding and skills to respond to their needs.

In this way, the job of economics will move beyond its traditional concern with effective allocation of resources to how it can be used to help people find satisfaction in a wider arena. The value of various forms of social engineering and the workability of accumulated economic development strategies will be tested in making a move in this direction.

Kyoko Sheridan

Part I
Background

1
Formulating a Strategy for Economic Development

Establishment of economic society

Introduction

There are two important and characteristic features of industrial development in Japan: 1) the Japanese willingness to plan and, 2) the development and use of man-made resources. The first emerges from my general observation that Japanese people are frequently ready to organize themselves and make plans in conducting economic activities. Given the unfortunate economic conditions of the shortage of economic resources under which Japan had to promote its industrialization this willingness has led them to explore various ways to develop the work force into highly productive human resources. Individual workers made initiatives to become productive workers and effective operators at offices and factories, with objectives that went beyond making simple efforts to work hard to acquire educational and professional work skills. They made social engineering efforts so as to build man-made resources to counter the paucity of economic resources. This willingness to plan for the better construction of the economy and society and the large effort to build human resources in the economy has developed in to the driving force of the building of economic society in Japan.

I must hasten to note that the Japanese were not the only people who experimented with social engineering activities for the development of their economic society. However, the effort to develop human resources is in many ways unique. The Japanese have developed various approaches and devices of their own to make effective use of the developed human resources in a co-operative and human networks oriented economic environment. The purpose of this study is to examine the making of this driving force, in order to understand how the Japanese built their economic society, and to examine with what logic and work mechanisms the Japanese have achieved the goal of high economic productivity and output. I wish to examine the strength of men working together in a community-based economy as an alternative to the merits of individual champions competing in free market economy. This has come about. Today they face a challenge in the need to make progress towards a higher purpose. The previous traditional approach must be reformulated. In this book I present my examination of the nature and logic of those two characteristic features with the aim of seeing what direction the economy should take in the future.

The economic history of the country tells how the Japanese decided to begin industrialization when confronted with the challenge from advances in the West. Fears arose that the nation would lose political independence, which led the country to decide to promote rapid industrial development. *Fukoku kyohei* – to build a thriving industry and strong economy that would maintain an independent Japan – was the national aim. The decision was not made according to the kind of economic logic that would have predicted the impossible nature of the task. There were few economic resources needed for industrialization. Something had to be devised to make this politically conceived task work under the impossible economic conditions, and it was sought through labour.

This process began as a result of the need for a programme of rapid industrialization towards the end of the nineteenth century during the Meiji Restoration. But the willingness to plan began in a much earlier era, which suggests that the reason for its emergence lies in the country's social culture. If this is the case, it will not be readily replaced in today's market-oriented business environment. I expect the importance of those two characteristic features of the economy to continue. Their roles, however, will take different forms as the economy develops in further post-industrial and affluent directions.

Early experience

Since feudal times, Japanese people of all social standings have wanted to make better provisions and opportunities for their families. This was not unique to Japan. In any society people make efforts to improve their way of living and to secure a better standard of living for their children. What differentiates the Japanese, however, is that the efforts have been made in a systematic and organized way to the extent that 'plans' and 'programmes' for the economy could be seen as the characteristic feature of society.

This should surprise us in view of a conventional reading of feudal society where most people existed in a passive state with little chance for improvement at home or in the workplace. Ordinary people in the lower classes were forced to live under rigid rules and regulations imposed on them by the ruling lords and their administrative retainers. The official records of the feudal government show how commoners in cities were forced to comply with a set of arrangements for all aspects of their lives and how peasants in villages were forced to follow regulations in such a stifled manner as to determine what and how much, and in what ways, and by when, to produce goods to best serve the economic needs of the ruling lords. They were expected to be contented with the status of a lowly law-abiding taxpayer.

In some Japanese economic history texts, the authors claim that there has been no history of economic thought in Japan.[1] When reviewing the development of economic thought in the country from the early seventeenth century to the present, historians argue that the Japanese only developed the management of the economy from the viewpoint of the country's leaders. According to this view, ordinary people were left to work as passively as livestock for four hundred years. But such a view does not make sense. We have to ask if people, feudal or modern, are really so inhibited in expressing their desire for a better life. Granted that in the feudal system there was ubiquitous policing of the activities of working commoners, I regard it as a gross underestimation of their abilities.

With this feeling of doubt I read books to see how the development of economic and social thought took place in Japan. In feudal Japan, before the official industrialization by the Meiji government, I found rich material about how people had assessed activities such as farming, trading and money-lending. Some dreamt of a better economic society. Others wrote about their dreams in books, or gave lectures, or led discussions to share their ideas. Others put into practice new schemes to begin reform of the system.

Even in feudal Japan, people were sufficiently *economically minded* to plan for more productive farming, to conduct efficient industrial and merchant activities, to organize their workplaces, or to work more effectively by themselves or in groups.[2]

To support my argument, I would like to look at some of the initiatives that people in Japan made at different times and places to alter the economic structure in which they found themselves and the terms of work under which they operated.[3]

Najita's examination of the research and educational activities of Kaitokudo, a merchant academy in Osaka from the mid-sevententh century to the Restoration period, illustrates how ordinary merchants located under the ruling *samurai* class on the social ladder of the time had developed ideas of reform.[4] They established the academy with their own money on the understanding that merchants, as much as their ruling *samurais*, needed to be educated so that they could think deeply enough to articulate their ideals. The merchants were pragmatic and initially made attempts to practise their ideals in daily trading, with the hope that their success would persuade others to see its value and incorporate it in political, economic, business and commercial fields and in this way begin the reform of society.

Najita writes that the intellectual enquiries at the academy expanded and were conducted widely in the fields of the social and natural sciences as well as the arts. By adopting such a wide interdisciplinary approach they aimed to relate their activities in trading and finance to all human activities and subsequently to find a better way to live.[5]

There are many records of the activities of peasants at about the same time. They wanted to improve farming methods to increase the yields of their crops. They experimented with the organization and layout of their villages and took into consideration the physical ability of every member of the household, including the old, the sick, and babies and small children, so that they could increase their total output while maintaining houses, pathways and other facilities. Such efforts were indeed made, although they were forced to work within the fields and paddies allotted to them and under rules set down by lords for their own convenience and economic benefit.[6]

There are also many examples of industrial activities within various local *han* governments. Economic historians call them *buiku*, industrial policy, and study the way *samurai* public administrative officers away from the ruling central Tokugawa government made individual and *han*-based efforts to gain economic and financial understanding and develop industrial policy skills. With these, they were able to establish *han*-owned and -financed public plants where they could produce goods such as textiles, clothing, timber products, salt and camphor, among other things.[7] These local initiatives aimed to establish and promote industrial activities to supplement the steady rice and other farm income as much as possible. Saving wealth within the *han*'s own coffers was seen as necessary to cushion it against unexpected natural disasters like the failure of crops and to follow their economic principle of *keisei saimin* (governing people by economic means to bring order and peace to society).[8]

In all those cases the idea was devised and the work carried out by people who wished to improve, in whatever way, and to whatever extent, their own living conditions and those of the people around them. The initiative came from the people and was not part of any grand public design or directed to a greater national purpose.

Two messages emerge: people must acquire an understanding of the importance of improved living standards; and this knowledge must develop at the same time as living standards observably grow, however small and gradual the growth is, to cement their conviction that the effort to improve living conditions brings results.

Are we able to read in these observations a sign of the emergence of economic development in the old feudal society before the Meiji Restoration? If so, did it come in a specific Japanese form, reflecting cultural and economic needs? To give substance to this speculation let us make some further observations drawn from the history of agrarian Japan.

Adam Smith tells us how at the dawn of the Industrial Revolution in the middle of the eighteenth century people in England began to transform themselves. They tried to improve their living standards by taking part in industrial activities and participating in markets. In the process we observe that they transformed themselves from passive farmers and artisans, contented with life as it came to them, into modern citizens.

What do these stories from economic history tell us? It would be easy to make too much of them, drawn as they are from scattered pieces of evidence. But they do lend substance to the view that people did not simply accept the economic environment in which they found themselves. The ruling class lived well. The rest of the people had to live and work in an economic and social system that did little for their well-being. They developed a critical view of the system and the habit of thinking of reform.

Establishment of economic society

Economic historians estimate that, in Japan, there was a steady growth in GNP (with increase in population, cultivated farm land and net yields from the land) and a rise in labour productivity that gave people in general some positive improvement in their living standards throughout the seventeenth century.[9]

To supplement the ability to plan, inherited from the pre-industrial society, the Japanese sought and formulated an industrialization strategy to overcome the difficulties imposed by unfavourable economic conditions.

Traditional economic theory of the time argued that, to industrialize, an economy must have an adequate amount of natural resources, capital and modern technology. They were regarded as three essential resources – the sources of strategic advantage. When an economy is able to combine adequate resources with good management skills, the resulting economy develops a competitive advantage over others in the world market and begins industrial development.

At this time, before the rise of multinational enterprise, there was little investment in building a basis for production in the less industrially developed parts of the world.[10] It was a time when multinationals were not so adventurous as at present in going out to explore business opportunities beyond national borders. It was also before the time of foreign aid programmes. Japan could expect no outside source to help it build an industrial basis beyond its national frontier. To make the task even harder, Japan had to accept a most difficult trading condition, known as 'unequal treaties'. Japan had been forced to operate, from the time of the Restoration in 1868 to 1911, without the right to control tariffs, so that imports from the industrial West came to Japan virtually free.[11] Industry in the world economy at the time was conducted without charity.

By way of compensation, what Japan had at that time was an abundant source of labour. Many developing economies chose to build labour-intensive industries first, in the hope that modern industries would later be established on the back of them. Japan did not follow this model.

So it was natural that Japan's leaders in the country sought strategies for the economic and industrial development of the effective use of labour. The problem, however, was that available labour was peasant labour in villages. These people had few relevant industrial skills and knowledge, which made this labour, though available in large numbers, of little value for industrial employers. Education and training had to be provided before this labour force could contribute to the programme of industrialization.

To educate and train workers is not a new strategy. Any industrializing country directs its national effort to the task. With Japan, however, the strategy took a different form, with a different emphasis from educational strategies elsewhere.

The effort to educate and train peasant labour was conducted with the aim of improving the quality of the people themselves. Their training and education were not primarily directed at making them skilful machine operators or plant managers, but at making them workers or managers who understood the difficulties that arise out of the need to industrialize a backward economy without good economic resources.

This is where the specific Japanese approach to economic development and business management practices originates. When we trace the way that industrialization was promoted in Japan, we see how the human role is appreciated and relied upon by strategists. Workers are expected to make contributions to the objective – whether it is the growth of the national economy or the cost competitiveness of international corporations. This attitude has become the most important guiding principle in implementing economic strategies.

From this basis the essence of the Japanese management style grew. Simply stated, it is that *people*, not machines, techniques or theories, are the central concern of management. How people work together and share a common goal was the most important consideration, and it became deeply ingrained in the Japanese management philosophy.

To see how government economic planners turned unskilled working people into industrial resources, let us follow the approach practised by Ookubo Toshimichi (1830–78), the supreme commander in the Meiji government, at the beginning of industrialization in Meiji. His approach illustrates how the government effort to give workers technical training brought not only a technically skilled workforce but also modernization and the acquisition of the industrial mind.[12]

Ookubo decided to modernize existing industries and workplaces first before building large-scale modern plants. The industrial activities in Japan at the time were conducted in cottage-based plants that operated using traditional work skills. His policy was to replace old facilities, traditional production skills and management practices in those small, labour-intensive and inefficiently managed places with modern facilities and skills. What is unique about Ookubo's approach is that he began plans for industrialization in the cottage industries. He decided to allocate government funding exclusively to them instead of allocating public funds to new plants.

His aim was clear. He wished to create workers with an understanding of modern methods. He claimed that building a modern model plant is an effective way to lead people to learn about what is modern and how it operates. But he thought the best and fastest way to modernize the country and the people living and working in it is to expose as many of them as possible to things modern. In his view, reading about modern industries or hearing of modern plants built in cities some distance away was a slower way. What was urgently needed, he thought, was to renovate those cottage industries and install modern machines as quickly as public funding would allow. He hoped these direct work experiences would transform those traditional workers into modern industrial employees with scientific knowledge and skills to operate machines.

Under his plan, those cottage industries were quickly mechanized (through the use of electricity, for example) from a level of 20 per cent to 54 per cent within a decade and up to 80 per cent by 1930.[13]

Corporate historians record many cases of the way cooperative efforts began between workers and their supervising managers on the shop floor in the course of modernizing industries. Learning how to operate machines and tools imported from the West was an equally new experience for workers and managers and the experiments were eagerly shared. To save the cost of importing the equipment and to satisfy their intellectual curiosity, they searched for ways to redesign them, substituting Japanese traditional tools for parts of the Western machines to make a convenient hybrid machine. In some cases, they also made various efforts to reorganize the work schedule and work layouts on the factory floors and in offices to supplement the capital-intensive production methods with available labour.[14]

Despite all these efforts, perhaps most practices up to this stage may be viewed as little more than 'makeshift' devices that serve only to supplement with labour the missing gap created by the shortage of capital.

It is important to note, however, that if this exploration of replacing and supplementing capital with labour had remained at the state of implementing 'makeshift' devices, there would not have been any strategic development of human resources in the Japanese economy. A modern industrial state would not have emerged in Japan.

Industrialization through people

In search of Japan's own approach

Further efforts followed to develop the supply of man-made resources out of the simple work of educating and training labour. The effort did not stop at just creating a skilled and educated workforce. It progressed further with the aim typically to 'develop labour' into human resources in the true sense. Let me explain this argument further.

Official statistics record that in 1920 industrial production exceeded that in the agricultural sector. The date may be taken as marking Japan's successful 'take-off'. The growth rate of manufacturing industry increased continuously from 4.4 per cent in 1878–1900 to 5.4 per cent in 1901–20 and further to 6.5 per cent in 1921–38.[15] By the mid-1920s manufacturing industries became the major driving force of the growth of the national economy.[16] Inside the industrial sector, the growth of modern production activities was considerable. Heavy and chemical industries grew fast to replace the importance of light industries such as textiles in the national economy. They were to contribute nearly two-thirds of the growth of GDP.

The importance of heavy and chemical industries was the highest during 1956–76. The high-speed growth of the Japanese economy is said to have been brought by the growth of these industries. They were estimated to dominate by contributing 79 per cent of the total industrial activity. So it is surprising to see that the level achieved by the heavy and chemical industries in the 1920s was already not much behind that of the heyday of the industry. Given the achievement, it is understandable that people saw in this a success of industrialization. People saw the fast growth of heavy and chemical industries as proof of the appropriateness of their economic plan and business approach. They came to be convinced that if labour were trained effectively and employed in a well-organized work environment, it would become a new resource for industrial development.[17] The subsequent strategy for economic growth and industrial development was built on this conviction.

Building of man-made resources

The search brought its own answer. An effective direction emerged from the cooperative working of the two forces – the willingness to plan and to build human resources in industries, with the national aim of fast industrialization of the country.

Banno Junnji reports that workers in a Pilot pen factory organized on their own initiative as early as 1933 a study group to find ways to improve their operations on the shop floor.[18] The move came from their wish to make a contribution to the employer, and started when individual workers began to see that there were many ways in which they could improve production procedures. They believed these would bring savings in production costs and improvement in the quality of output.

The initiative came directly from the view that it is as much the responsibility of employees as of employers to seek ways to reduce costs and improve the quality of products. Many meetings took place at the factory until the workers came to see the importance of fully understanding the corporation's activities, which they believed was essential if they were to have a role in the working of the company. In this way they could relate their job to the work of the company as a whole. And from this understanding employees would be inspired to see how and where they could make a contribution.

This example is a good reference point for locating the origin of Japan's 'QC' (quality control) activities four to five decades later. Many studies show how this initiative among the Pilot pen workers subsequently influenced the evolution of 'lean' production methods in the automobile and electronics industries in Japan.

Late in 1987 Koike observed some new patterns in the behaviour of Japanese workers, particularly among blue-collar workers.[19] He noted that many Japanese workers operating on the shop floor possessed intellectual work skills and work attitudes similar to those of 'white-collar' technicians and engineers: they used their skills and attitudes effectively to deal with the unexpected problems that interrupt routine operations on the shop floor in a similar manner to managers and supervisors. He characterizes this behaviour as the 'white-collarization of blue-collar workers' and says it is one of the most remarkable characteristics of Japanese industry in its attempts to build human resources.[20]

Kumazawa noted a further development. He said that employees worked hard for the growth and profitability of the company specifically to share the work value and the corporate objectives of the employers. It is this willingness to work for the company, he argues, that has brought growth and efficiency to Japanese corporations throughout the 1970s and 1980s.[21]

These observations by Koike and Kumazawa are well known, and many business scholars accepted them as a useful explanation of the Japanese management system and employment practice during the 1970s and 1980s.

In search of sources for economic growth, Arthur Lewis noted differences in people's willingness to take up economic and business activities, observing that people in some societies generate more economic activities than others.[22] People in one society are busy allocating much of their personal and professional time to economic and commercial activities. Those who prefer to live outside the material world build a less economically active society.

He says there is a difference in the degree of the 'will to economize' in people's minds and argues that this is what creates the difference in economic growth performance between countries and between societies. Some societies have a strong drive to economize while others lack it and he finds the reason for the disparity in the different cultural and historical traits in different societies.

A traditional force in Japanese society – which could be labelled the spirit of self-help – guides and encourages people to make themselves active and industrious in work and life. Such a force has been observed in Japan throughout its period of modern industrialization. Kimmoth, for one, observed in the emergence of a middle class in Japan a sign of people's urge for self-advancement. He argued that self-advancement had been sought by many young people throughout generations in Japan, especially in efforts to obtain a high level of education and subsequent good employment.[23] The forms of education and employment differed between individuals depending on their family background and their economic means. But in general this desire to improve themselves through education was based on a belief that people should support themselves and their family through work and individual effort so as to become a force for economic development and modernization.[24] The major source of economic growth in Japan can be found in the accumulation and effective use of this spirit of self-help.

We have examined how businesses developed their growth strategies along with their effort to build human resources in the workplace. It was, to begin with, the government's ability that led people to see the importance of building industrial skills and knowledge. It was government planning that led people to see a need to develop their own inner resources in order to conduct industrial activities effectively and efficiently. Having found the approach effective, they have made a continuing effort to increase their productivity without further use of capital and technology.

This approach brought results in the form of economic growth and cost-competitive industries.[25] It was not only on production lines where the building of human resources was promoted. The same approach had been applied to management skills and business practice in the search for the most effective way to build human resources. The structure of the employment system and workplace arrangements were formulated to build Japanese management techniques. The will to economize characterizes the style of economic management.

Two forces in the Japanese economy, planning and the determination to build human resources, have worked effectively to bring about industrialization. Both worked together well for the purpose of supplementing what was lacking in economic resources. The logic was accepted by the people, who showed their support through hard work. The nation has been successfully industrialized as planned.

But will it continue in the future?

The economy has solved the problem of a shortage of economic resources. It was on the understanding of this problem that Japan's economic development strategy was formulated and under the pressure of this problem people made a huge effort.

After a century-long national effort to counter the difficulty, the problem has been solved. There is no longer an obvious shortage of economic resources. What we see today is that the strategy remains with the people in the economic management of government, business strategy and the household. The strategy to build productive industry and the work effort asked of people to achieve the goal now seems to have lost its relevance.

But the Japanese are not much happier today than before, despite solving the problem, achieving the goal, and accumulating economic resources to allow them to live in affluence.

With this understanding I will examine the Japanese economy, its structure and logic, and look at a possible future for the economy that should give people a contented life.

2
Planning of the National Economy[1]

Keizai Hakusho, 1947–2004

The structure and work mechanism

In this chapter I want to look at *Keizai Hakusho*, the Economic White Paper (hereafter the White Paper or the Paper) produced by the Keizai Kikaku-cho, the Economic Planning Agency (EPA) now incorporated into Naikaku-fu.[2] The Paper is published annually in August or around this time as an official government report on the economy. It is the product of the approach developed by the Japanese government in an effort to understand the nature and the working of the economy, and has been published annually for many years.

The result is a comprehensive picture of Japan's economic activities. It shows the government's evaluation as well as providing a review of the working and the effect of government economic policy.

I must caution readers against arriving at a superficial impression of the function of the Economic Planning Agency. The EPA is not a government organization established for the purpose of economic planning. It is a government agency that prepares for planning but does not actually draw up plans. The agency is not meant to write policy programmes but to provide others in government and business as well as the general population with an overall basic picture of the economy.

The Paper is a view in 'prospect and retrospect' of the national economy. It presents the EPA's analysis of economic performance in the previous year, consolidates the government's understanding of the country's economic condition, and comments on future trends. The agency's publicly projected view is that its analysis and understanding of the national economy will help people to hold sound and well-informed economic discussions.

The publication of the White Paper began in 1947 and has continued to the present. There are, thus, 57 volumes available for examination. The report is a short-run analysis with its perspective extending roughly over three to four years.

Officially the Paper is not intended to offer policy statements. Such tasks are entrusted to other ministries such as the Ministry of Economy, Trade and Industry (formerly MITI, now METI),[3] the Ministry of Health, Labour and Welfare, the Ministry of Culture, Sports, Science and Technology, and so on, which write policies for specific industrial sectors. Government ministries and agencies also publish findings in various forms in order to give people guidance on the efficient economic management of the country.

In addition to publishing policy documents, the EPA conducts many surveys and public enquiries to see where, and to what extent, government policy attention is required. A good example is the agency's effort to understand people's perception of economic development and their level of satisfaction with the economic provisions available to them. I give a discussion of this in Chapter 10 below.

Referring closely to the Papers, I will examine how Japanese people view their own economy, what economic experience they have and, most important, what picture of the economy they want to have.

The Paper is written by the head of Naikoku Chosa-ka, the research department of domestic economic activities in the EPA and is widely read by people in business as well as by the general public.[4] Lively discussions often follow immediately after publication, suggesting that the White Paper is taken seriously by many, reflecting the extent of people's interest in economic matters and how much they value it as an accurate and comprehensive guide to the macroeconomy.

The Paper is called the annual report of the economy, with various subtitles that indicate the issues for economic planning of the year. Special care is given to the wording of the White Paper's titles and subtitles so that they convey at once the gist of the message. Something of a *haiku* master's skill is demonstrated. In Table 2.1, I give the subtitles of the Papers for the 57 years between 1947 and 2004 in my own translation to try to capture the content and message of the Papers and the spirit in which they were written.[5]

Column A of the table should give readers a good understanding of the content of the Papers. Their chronological listing should show, *pari passu*, the development of the economy and public thinking about it.

I read all 57 volumes to see how, in 'retrospect and prospect', the government's economic thinking developed over the period; how the government communicated with the people; and what message it conveyed.[6]

It is fair to comment here that at least during the high growth in the economy – up to 1973 – the Papers built people's trust in them as a useful and reliable source of economic information and might justly claim to have provided a more positive service to Japan than counterparts published elsewhere. I observe a clear view of the function of planning through the presentation of the economy in 'retrospect and prospect' each year and across the whole period. Let me explain.

I need to begin by clarifying what I mean by planning. In a 1975 paper Kirschen and others made a comparative analysis of public policy in various free capitalist and planned socialist countries in Europe.[7] To do this they followed the development of policy from identifying aims and selecting policy agendas (economic objectives) for policy formulation to the formulation of actual economic measures.

To understand the meaning of the function of planning in Japan's government I reformulated Kirschen's method as follows. What distinguishes the Japanese planning approach from other economies is that their economic planning begins with the efforts of planners understand the overall state of society. After the planners have conceptualized any problems or pitfalls in the society, they turn their attention to the economy. Only then does the effort to draw up economic plans begin.

To demonstrate how this develops I have summarized the process in Table 2.1. In this table I first give the official terms of reference in column A, and progress to the structure: the initial state of social enquiry (Bi), the economic objectives (Bii), instruments (Biii) and measures (Biv) so as to begin economic planning work (see below).

In the second stage, the planners conceptualize these problems and concerns in economic dimensions in terms, for example, of a certain level of unemployment, economic growth rate and price stability, most of which can be quantified as an economic objective towards maximized targets.

In the third stage the search is directed into areas where government can effectively influence the activities of the economy. These areas are most commonly investment and management of public corporations, public research institutions and economic and social infrastructure facilities, management of income policy, control of imports and borrowing and investment from abroad, public financial and monetary decisions on interest rates, and regulations of industries and business laws and so on.

The fourth stage proposes policy tools. For some years the White Paper did not include this stage, the government only making suggestions about policy instruments and refraining from specifying actual policy measures and tools. In this way, the agency acts within the terms of the Paper to report on the facts and figures alone.

The 57 years from 1947 to 2004 shown in Table 2.1 cover almost the entire post-war years of the country. In the first period, 1947–72, the economy achieved historically phenomenal growth. In the second, 1973–91, which sees three cycles of changes of policy approaches (I refer to them under 'policy cycles' below), 1971–77, 1978–85 and 1986–91, the economy transformed itself and followed a more stable growth path by maintaining moderate growth in the economy. There have been many problems, new and old, in the economy in the years post 1992. Questions were asked about how the trouble developed and why there was such a persistent failure to find solutions. A careful examination of the Papers in this troubled period compared to those in the preceding two periods should guide us to the answers.

The story of how the economy grew from its semi-industrial state to a world industrial power is already well documented. The annual Economic White Paper witnessed this development and recorded the process of economic growth and industrial development.

Through a careful reading of the subtitles of each paper (see column A, Table 2.1) I want to examine how public thinking progressed. The aim is not to review the discussion in the Papers but to trace how policy writers changed their views through the stages. Column B shows how such an exercise in planning developed.

I attempted to classify the key words in the titles and subtitles into four categories – aims, objectives, instruments and measures – to locate the development of government thinking on policy. I did this by asking, for example, if a particular Paper was about 'understanding' or 'evaluating' the economic condition, making it part of stage one; whether it tried to identify objectives, taking its policy thinking to stage two; if the discussion in it was developed to the stage where an attempt could be made to find economic policy instruments; or if it went further to that final point when actual policy measures and tools were identified.

Policy cycles

Just as we take the pulse to confirm the presence of life, so we verify in policy cycles the dynamic power of capitalism at work. I identified nine different policy processes that traversed the four stages.[8] Those nine processes together demonstrate how the Japanese economy made its way from a less developed state to an advanced one through a process of problem solving that was both upwardly spiralling and cyclical.

The 1947 Paper began with the memorable opening statement: 'The Japanese economy in national debts, government, business and household is all running in entire debit.' So the subtitle reads: 'The economic report, the real image of the national economic crisis, urgency in finding counter-measures.' Thus the first policy cycle emerged, revealing the government's understanding of the nature and the extent of difficulties in the national economy in 1947. The government was clear that the shortage of supply in the economy was causing extreme instability and disrupting industry's attempts to begin production. An effort was made in the 1948 White Paper to show the present state of the nation's economic problems in 'retrospect and prospect' and to locate the cause of the shortage of goods and services in a distribution system in which black marketeers prospered. (In column Bii the need to regain the normal economic conditions is urged as an economic objective.)

The government used the Paper of 1949 to explain the importance of bringing stable and fair market arrangements into the economy. It explained that productivity would return to the economy once the black market was destroyed and there was a resultant return to economic stability. The message was articulated further in the context of the emerging peacetime free market.

On this understanding the 1949 and 1950 White Papers discussed the need to stop inflation as the economy's priority, including introducing various anti-inflationary policy measures to control the money supply, limit wage and price rises, and establish a fixed exchange rate. For 1950, those anti-inflationary policy measures are suggested as economic measures in column Biii. To recapitulate, the first cycle emerged across the nine years between 1947 and 1955. In the first period, 1947–49, the government spent the time making an effort to understand the economy in the chaos of the immediate post-war years. The economy was struggling to resume its peacetime activities, and a clear picture of the facts and figures of production and distribution activities were crucial to begin any new plans. The Papers presented essential information on where the rebuilding of production capacity had been achieved.

This led to an analysis of the economy's behaviour from 1950 to 1952. The government examined the nature and extent of the problems in the economy at this difficult time and concluded that economic stability was the priority.

During the 1953–54 period, the government was in a position to contemplate how the economy should be directed to begin peacetime economic activities.

In 1955 the government was able to state with confidence that production facilities in factories must be modernized, as must management skills in corporate boardrooms. Innovation through imported technology is proposed in column Biv as an economic device. Government and business organized many missions to the USA to learn production techniques and management skills that could be transplanted to Japanese industry. The White Paper introduced a new term 'innovation', expressed in English, which had not been used in Japan. It became a popular word to guide investment and management activities.

At this time many of Japan's traditional employment systems and other business practices, which were regarded as pre-modern and unscientific, were evaluated stringently based on US standards and practice.

The 1955 White Paper signalled that Japan's economic survival depended on the people's capacity to promote and use modern technology and to acquire a high level of managerial and administrative skills. At this stage, the Paper recommended the active importation of technologies and knowledge from the USA, supplemented by European knowledge, if needed, to produce an efficient and productive economy.

The 1956 White Paper took up this aim to modernize production. It began further cycles in 1956–60, 1961–72 and 1976–77 to guide the economy towards rapid growth, despite operating under a difficult international economic environment with oil crises in 1973 and 1978.

Growth towards a welfare economy

The concern of the Papers during these policy cycles was to ensure that the economy promoted growth.

As early as 1968 the White Paper began to propose that Japan, on the strength of its accumulation of economic assets and advanced technology, should build a welfare economy. It voiced the proposal despite the economic difficulties brought on by the oil crises in 1973 and 1978. It made several specific proposals as economic measures, as we see in Table 2.1, column Biv. Through the 1970s and the early 1980s the White Paper expressed its concerns about a negative side of economic growth that appeared to take place in various forms in society and spoke clearly of the need to build a welfare-oriented economic society. It invited the population to see the need to build a welfare economy and argued that the economy had reached an advanced stage in its development with an adequate accumulation of economic assets to begin such a task.

Between 1973 and 1977 the authors of the Papers made an effort to provide an understanding of the welfare economy. They explained why the economy needed to alter its orientation from growth and efficiency to economic stability, equity and quality of life, and showed that it was within Japan's capacity to aim for an increase in the well-being, rather than the wealth, of individual people. In the Paper the notion of 'quality of life' was introduced for the first time and argued strongly for the role of government in directing and generating the nation's economic activity towards this end (Table 2.1, column Biii lists general expansion of the public-sector economy in 1972 so as to provide social welfare and equality to everyone in the country).

The subsequent seven publications of the papers in 1976–82 discussed ways to build an economic system that would achieve slow (4 per cent GNP growth, that is, half the average rate of the preceding two decades) but steady economic growth through careful guidance. In this period the White Paper frequently referred to Japan as an 'advanced nation' so as to secure people's understanding that Japan had indeed become an advanced country, leaving behind its approach of catching up to the West by means of growth.

In 1981, however, the White Paper noted the emerging policy direction in the USA and UK, which was to reduce the size and role of government. The remark appeared to be a casual one, but in hindsight it did suggest that the bureaucrats had already begun to think about a move to smaller government. At this stage the White Paper did not comment on the desirability or otherwise of a similar change for Japan. Until this time, the Japanese economy had not accumulated much public deficit despite the increase in public welfare spending in the decelerated economy. But in 1982 the Paper proposed that, for the sake of the economy, Japan needed to move to small government.

At the beginning of the 1980s, the Japanese saw that the historical task of catching up with the West had finally been accomplished. Many spoke in celebration of the successful end of the post-war (post-World War II) years and the prospect of a new prosperity ahead. As if to confirm the promising outlook, within five years they saw that the economy had not only caught up with the advanced economies but also stood at the forefront of industrial and affluent states in the world.

It had the capacity to generate the world's second largest GNP, the highest (measured by the official exchange rate) level of income per head for their people and large and growing asset holdings overseas. The feeling of achievement and the confidence in their way of working seemed to be endorsed by outside observers, who dubbed[6] 'Japan as No. 1' or spoke of 'the Japanese superstate', or 'the Japanese miracle'.[9]

In praise of growth and efficiency once again

Japan as No. 1

In reality, inside Japan, people were not as optimistic as the outside observers. They knew how hard it had been to overcome the oil crises, and how real had been the challenge from Asian countries in industries such as ship-building, steel-making, and electrical, electronic and chemical manufacturing. The high-growth economy, which had recorded a 10 per cent or higher rate of expansion every year, was now moving to a slow growth path.

It is true that the consensus was to pursue slow but steady growth in the economy. Yet with the slow growth now as low as 4 per cent, people began to worry that this rate might be further reduced in the future, given an ageing population, further deterioration in the environment and limited resources and food internationally. Exacerbating Japan's concerns were mounting trade and political pressure from outside, particularly from the USA, to refrain from exporting and balancing its external accounts (that is, pressure to reduce its trade surplus). The unease was reflected in the 1983, 1984 and 1985 White Papers with 'continued growth', 'internationalization' and 'new growth' – now key phrases in the titles – raising questions about how to maintain economic growth and how Japanese exports and overseas investment could be carried out without meeting a harsh response in the global economy.[10]

As I have said, throughout the 1970s national economic debates were held to assess people's understanding of, and support for, the economy to operate in a slow and stable mode in order to focus on the quality of life and move away from the previous growth orientation. But towards the end of the 1980s government, business and most of the working population reverted to their traditional solutions to economic problems.

The leading view in the EPA followed the national trend so that it quickly abandoned any progressive thinking. We read in the 1983 to 1985 White Papers how the government tried to understand the emerging economic environment, its scale and nature, and focused on stage one of the planning process. To spend as long as three years on this stage of the planning process should be justified, given that the Paper was entrusted with the task of reviewing the economy's performance. What was regrettable was the repeated questioning of how to sustain growth, globalize the economy and find new directions for economic growth in the subsequent five years until 1991, thereby letting the economy plunge into boom and bust.

We saw how the Japanese economy began building a welfare economy following the proposal in the White Paper in the 1970s and how the economy began to develop many of its own welfare measures, introducing various new and progressive systems and economic and social practices. The White Paper should have reviewed this development and made suggestions about how to develop the proposal. Instead it joined the popular trend of growth promotion as the way to solve problems, economic and social. Why?

Speculation boom, mid-1980s to end of 1991

The period between 1986 and the end of 1991 was the time when the economy lost its way and fell into an uncontrollable speculative boom. People read praise from abroad about the management of the economy and corporate business as endorsing a programme of continuous growth and expansion. They were convinced that Japanese management had found the ultimate way to employ economic resources. In this mood of confidence and preoccupation with wealth, a large number of people, first in business, but soon more widely across society, began to speculate, looking for fast and high-return investment opportunities.

The rising value of the Japanese currency overseas also acted as an additional force to drive the investment expansion offshore. There are many accounts of how and why the boom came to Japan and in what ways people were affected.[11] This is not the place to go into them.[12] There is, however, one important observation that should be made. I argued that the importance of the White Paper was in its ability to project the desirable direction of the economy. The Paper performed well, sustaining that ability up to the mid-1970s. After that time, however, it began to fail to suggest an economic objective that would realize the national aim. It failed to grasp the national aim (Bi) and how to achieve the aim via economic means (Bii). As Table 2.1 indicates, it could not advance from Bi to Bii, but only recommend deregulation of the economy and a reduction in the size and responsibility of government, without adequately explaining why this recommendation should be followed at this particular time under these particular social and economic conditions. The authors could not project a new economic future and failed to connect Bi to Bii as noted above because they did not understand how people live, or the condition of society or economy, or how it should be reformed. In this they failed to act as economic planners. Or, perhaps, the role of economic planning had altered.

What was the national aim at this time? We see that people wanted to maintain the economy on its growth path in order to secure a continuous rise in incomes and living standards. If this was the aim, I must object that it is not the task of economic planners. They have an obligation to bring improvements to people's lives beyond the smooth operation of daily economic activity, which is the job of public administrators. With this mission in mind, economic planners should have evaluated the worth and acceptability of the continuous economic growth as the national aim.

When growth and efficiency became the national aim once more, there was ready support for deregulation of the economy and reduction in the size of government. The logic of this was more technical than related to 'ideals' such as the desire to construct a sound economic society for the welfare of the people. The superficial view that the Japanese economy by now had joined the ranks of advanced industrial states, and that the traditional approach of government-supported industrial development could be discarded in order to send the world's most competitive business into highly competitive free markets for maximum advantage, became widespread.

Outside Japan the free market had become the motto, as it had also in the USA, the UK and many other parts of the world. The Japanese wanted to see themselves as part of the trend that reflected their recently gained advanced status.

I have argued elsewhere that public initiative has been continuously promoted in an effort to maintain a stable economy.[13] Economic stability has been sought as the priority policy goal throughout the development of the country's economic strategy. In the time under discussion – from 1986 to 1992 – the concern to maintain economic stability slackened and the treasured 'will' was transformed to uncontrollable greed.

Many see the period from the end of 1992, the year when the bubble burst, to the present as the time when government lost touch and became incapable of contributing to the debates on economic development. It is true that the White Papers published during the period indicate what difficulties government planners experienced and how they failed to make progress in the traditional task of clarifying policy issues.

For six years from 1993 the White Papers' authors made an effort to understand what had happened during the boom, moving backwards and forwards (between Bi and Bii), asking what was the national aim and what economic objectives should be formulated without progressing beyond the first stage. The authors mistakenly assumed that the national aim was to restore Japan as a growth economy and hence the economic objective it assumed was the promotion of growth and business vitality.

The authors moved around these 'key' issues, asking in the eight White Papers from 1994, after the shock of the burst bubble had subsided, what investment opportunities there were that could be exploited at home and abroad and what new management approaches could be developed to increase Japan's international contribution (1994), how to revitalize the economy (1995), what could be expected from the proposed introduction of administrative reform (1996), the further promotion of administrative reform (1997), new trade rules and distribution framework to modernize the services industry (1998), how to revive economic dynamism (1999), and how to give birth to a new economic society (2000 and 2001) and once again reform and restructure of the economy for growth (2002–4).

I want to show that these assumptions were incorrect, that the authors failed to understand the state of Japan's economic development, that planning skills failed to encompass the true needs of Japanese society and, most of all, that they underestimated the real capacity of the people to build an 'ideal' economic society.

Some telling questions that can be summarized in this way: what conditions are needed for sustained economic growth?; how does the country progress into an open global economy?; and how should Japan aim to build trust and further opportunities for growth in the international community?

I want to make three observations about the writing of the White Papers – between the rising and falling of the bubble economy and the stagnant years – in relation to the effect on the economy of the EPA's inability to identify policy issues throughout the post-war years and the post-1992 'lost decade'.

The first relates to the guiding role that the White Paper provided to people in conducting economic activities. With the regular publication of the Paper, and its aim to give an accurate overall picture of the state of the economy, it would be expected that people would find it easier to plan for the future – whether business opportunities, choice of jobs, development of education and training, allocation of income and assets between consumption, saving and investment, structuring one's way of life, improving the well-being of family members, and so on. It is arguable that the publication of the Paper creates a planning environment in the economy.

The importance of this observation cannot be exaggerated given the fact that the official position of the White Paper is to present facts and figures on the national economy without making any proposals or policy suggestions.

The second observation relates to the specific characteristics that may be referred to as 'policy cycles', which have been at work through the five decades of the writing of the White Paper. The cycles occur because policy making in Japan involves problem-solving exercise and process, as discussed earlier. The time required for policy writers to complete the whole process is the duration of one cycle. This is applicable, however, only up to the early 1990s, the end of the bubble economy.

A third observation emerges as rather negative. As noted above, since 1992 the White Papers have only served to track government discoveries made each year that tell us that 'things are no longer the same as before'.

An obvious question is what should have been done to secure the economic welfare of the population in the changed economy – issues for policy making, business strategy, and people's individual activities. The White Papers have, however, failed to clarify the exact nature of the change and are thus unable to perform their role in promoting people's well-being.

Why? Was it because the Japanese were progressing with deregulation and withdrawing from public activities? Had they decided to withdraw from the traditional task of the Paper, which was to present the facts and figures?

Move to smaller government

At the beginning of the 1980s the Prime Minister, Nakasone Yasusuke, officially announced his ambition to present Japan to the world as a leading nation. He proposed to achieve this by demonstrating that in economic, political and social spheres the country had grown to join the ranks of such world powers as America and Britain. He argued for the importance of Japan in demonstrating to the world its liberal democratic way of conducting national and international affairs to the USA and the UK. The task would begin, so he argued, with a national effort to reduce the risk of being seen as a country practising various specific rules to protect industry from import and business from direct investment from overseas multinationals.

To start with, he proposed that the country should discard those images of 'Japan Inc.' that suggest that the country creates economic success through autocratic government intervention, the traditional approach of backward countries attempting to catch up with advanced nations in business and community affairs. He argued that protective approaches to economic management should be replaced by free-market principles, however effective the previous government-led approach might have been in bringing economic progress to the country. He believed that Japan's style of government control had been necessary during post-war reconstruction, but that, in the 1980s, the economy had established a new basis for progress without government intervention. Great progress and development since the end of the war had seen wealth accumulation as high as, if not higher than, that observed in the advanced West. So the time had come to free the system – and national thinking – from the orientation towards an artificial and interventionist mode.

The real message that he aimed to convey was that Japan had become a strong nation, and that it would no longer tolerate being under US domination. In order for outsiders to accept and respect Japan's new status, he argued that the country must first show that Japan followed an open, universal rule without the need for gimmicks, such as Japan Inc., to maintain its high standards.

The time was right for such a proposition to be supported by the Japanese people. Rising self-confidence after the successful weathering of the economic difficulties of the oil crises in 1973 and 1978 was followed by rising export performance. The accumulation of national wealth was illustrated at home by the rising standard of living, and abroad by rapid expansion and ownership of foreign production facilities.

Though this political message was taken as 'making sense', and some supported the initiative as a principle, there were still many who were busy enjoying the buoyant economic activities that had returned after the panic-driven years of the oil crises. They saw their salary and wages rising annually by as much as 15–20 per cent in real terms; business saw their efforts at rationalization in the factory office as bringing results through the reduction of costs and the rise in quality competitiveness. Many thought it unnecessary to introduce any reforms. Praise for Japanese management, culminating in that epithet, 'Japan as No. 1', led people to overlook emerging problems that were beginning to undermine the basis of the apparent success of the economy.

Nakasone's proposition, however, was doomed. By 1997, the Japanese economy had lost a considerable amount of its dynamism. The rise of the yen had been sharp and continuous throughout the 1980s. Despite stringent managerial efforts to introduce technical progress to cut production costs, Japan's export industries could not prevent a loss of international competitiveness. The development of industrial capacities in neighbouring Asian countries increasingly challenged Japan's dominance in the world export market and at home. The rapidly ageing population, the result of a marked fall in the birth rate and the blessing of longevity of Japan's people, drove up public expenses for health care, pensions and old-age payouts as high as the country had ever experienced. To make matters worse, this rise in public expenses could not be met adequately by tax revenues when the economy ceased to grow. Government could not balance the public budget. This was a new experience for Japan after decades of high economic growth when an annual expansion of public revenue was a matter of course.

Rising public deficits came to the USA and the UK governments during the 1980s, much earlier than in Japan. The Reagan and Thatcher administrations promoted reductions in the size of government to counter the problem. The Japanese encountered the problem a decade later, and their response was to take the same direction at the beginning of 1997.

This is how Hashimoto Ryutaro, in his second year as Prime Minister, took up Nakasone's reform proposal, which had been left idle since 1982.

By the time the economy had gone through the reckless speculation boom and its sudden collapse in 1990 and 1991, many corporations, banks and individuals had gone into massive debt, unable to recover investments made during the boom. People read the experience as an indication of the weakness of an economic system, the virtue and the strength of which they had been so convinced only a few years before. Hashimoto saw it as an opportune time to resurrect the reform proposal. In January 1997, he announced his decision to promote reforms in the public sector, with the aim of bringing corresponding reforms, if time allowed, into as many other areas as possible so as to introduce liberal democratic ways of conducting the nation's affairs.

The need for reform was related earlier, with Nakasone, to concerns about the country's international status and political position. But this time the motive for reform lay mainly at home, arising out of the change in relative power between government and business.

The essence of the change may be explained as follows. The Japanese economy had successfully weathered the problems it was feared would emerge during the oil crises in 1973 and 1978. It managed to turn anticipated economic difficulties into the basis for internationally competitive production. Business had developed new methods to build a production basis that many American and European management researchers and practising business managers came to admire.

Business claimed it had made a contribution and took great pride in rescuing the national economy from the crisis. But the government also wanted to claim its part in maintaining growth through its Keynesian counter-deflation policy. It claimed that, through skilful management of the economy, up to 1996 it maintained a growth rate of 2–3 per cent. And, as the growth rate had become steady, in 1996 the government discontinued the anti-recession policy and increased taxes as a natural way to balance the budget while giving people good health and social security services.

Business and the general population strongly opposed this move, differing in their views of who had contributed to making the economy more efficient and productive after the eruption of the oil crisis in the Middle East. People in the private sector thought it was their hard work that had rescued the country from the feared economic collapse in 1973 and 1977. They believed the public sector had lived through the troubled time with good revenue coming from the issue of bonds, which they spent on building many unnecessary public institutions and corporations, and in expanding and financing their highly paid bureaucratic staff members. They argued that if the nation needed to balance the budget, it was time for the government and public service to begin to think how to manage their activities economically, cutting waste and luxury spending instead of raising taxes.

The timing of the criticism could not have been worse for the government. In the late 1980s various scandals involving the misuse of public funds in government offices and public corporations were reported. The population supported the view held by industry and working people that it was their hard work that had resulted in international competitiveness in industry, while the government had been self-indulgent, spending money in a wasteful manner under the pretence of enacting a Keynesian anti-recession policy.

A national preference to move to smaller government and deregulation of economic activities at the beginning of the 1990s emerged as a result of this change in the balance of power between the public and industry. The country was in turmoil after the mismanagement of the economy and there was a general mood for change. Hashimoto took the opportunity and, in January 1997, announced his decision to reform Japan's economy.

The proposal was termed *gyosei-kaikaku*, or reform of administration. Reform was to take place in six areas, much expanded beyond the economic sphere, although its core was focused on economic management.[14] Reform was to take place through the introduction of free-market principles, which would replace traditional ways of doing things.

Officially, six areas were nominated for reform, including the public administration systems in the central government ministries. The aim was to transfer more of their power and influence to local government offices and their planning function to politicians; to reduce the amount of public spending across all areas; to reorganize the social security system by reducing government support to encourage people to support themselves; to revitalize the economic and business system by encouraging growth and expansion by removing public regulations and encourage free-market and entrepreneurial activities; to organize for a 'big bang' in the financial system and banking market; and to reform the education system to encourage an entrepreneurial and individualistic way of thinking among the young. Proposals were made to reduce the influence and authority of the Ministry of Education over the activities of schools, colleges and universities, with the aim of encouraging creativity and in the hope of building a new Japan with entrepreneurial spirit and innovative drive.

I will leave a detailed explanation of these reforms to other authors, but I cannot help noting that in these proposals there was a desire to adopt the American way of doing things in Japan. This involved privatizing public corporations and institutions, deregulating the market, and increasing ideas of self-help in welfare.[15]

At the time of writing, at the beginning of 2004, not much had been done to bring about the reform, except that the central government ministries had reduced their number and size through mergers, and several public corporations, such as the Japan National Railways, were privatized.

Observations and lessons

Three White Papers

Of 56 issues of the White Paper, four are memorable: those published in 1947, 1956, 1970 and 1980. They are important Papers that helped change people's thinking about the economy and had considerable influence among business and working people.

The 1947 Paper – the inaugural White Paper – gave readers a clear understanding of the economic condition, its capacity and limitations, through facts and figures, and a strong message for those in negative mood about how to rebuild the economy. The White Paper concluded by saying: 'With the combined efforts of government, business and working people, the country will once again restore activity in production and build a new prosperity.' The passage may sound overly romantic today but we understand the power it had to restore people's motivation to work and inspire confidence in the economy.

In June 1950 a war broke out in Korea. A procurement demand arrived in Japan from the US army. The war-damaged economy found a windfall opportunity to renovate and expand its production facilities. Within one year the production facilities regained their pre-war levels. By the mid-1950s the task of reconstruction of the war-damaged economy was completed. The 1956 White Paper did not waste the opportunity to make clear to its readers that the recovery and rebuilding of the national economy had been carried out both with special help from the US army and as a result of the need to rebuild war-destroyed production facilities. But the authors also warned that the magical work of the special demand force was exhausted and a new effort had to be made to develop the economy. The warning was articulated by these words: 'The post-war period is over. There are no more special conditions to assist economic growth.' As I mentioned earlier, the White Paper argued that businesses must modernize. They had fallen behind the standards practised in the West during the war years when technological progress had been ignored.

The 1970 White Paper pointed to the need to build a welfare economy in Japan to provide 'quality of life' for its people and the need to conserve the natural environment. The argument went on to show how, in order to achieve the proposed objectives, the economy itself must be reformed so that it followed a slow and steady growth path. The oil crises in the following years prevented the White Paper's suggestions from being adopted. But in 1971 the EPA was established, and many public reforms involving health schemes, old-age pensions and social security schemes were developed – to the credit of the White Papers' authors.

Two White Papers – written in 1980 and 1981 – were prepared by bureaucrats in the EPA. The authors noted that the Japanese economy had reached an advanced industrial stage, with a high production capacity and standard of living, equal to many advanced countries in Europe and America. The purposes of those Papers, with the titles 'The issues that challenge Japan as an advanced country' and 'Towards creative dynamism in the economy' were not to restate what had been well publicized, but to warn the population of the challenges – alien to a developing economy but pressing to a developed and advanced country – that lay ahead.

Writing a memoir ten years later, the author of the White Papers explains how he conceived the central argument through the study of the economic activities of Japan in the light of the world economy.[14] He regretted that the Papers did not arouse much interest, receiving neither strong support nor criticism. As a result, he called his White Paper *Itan*, 'heterodox'. But all was not lost. The 1986 publication of the Maekawa Report that raised again the need to build a welfare economy could not have been written without the 1980 and 1981 Papers.

It has been my argument that in writing these Papers the author followed four steps in developing the argument for his proposal. The Papers studied the economy through research and survey activities. With an understanding of the nature of economic activity and its structure, the Papers looked for a way to improve the working of the economy.

In following the development of the White Paper we can gain insights into Japan's approach to planning. It is an approach which some refer to as 'indicative planning' to differentiate it from the planning approach promoted in centrally controlled economies such as the (former) USSR and China. As a product of government, the White Paper has always taken an approving view of the present economic management, especially when considering proposing policies such as tax increases, wage control, or reductions in public spending, which may not be welcomed by everyone.

The White Paper has a tradition of putting its case in a positive and approving manner and, very often, without any critical evaluation of the economy. Whatever we think of that, we should not discount the importance of its contribution to people's determination to think positively and work for a better quality of life.

Failure in the Papers since 1992

In contrast to these observations, however, the Papers since 1992, after the collapse of the speculation boom, have lost their traditional approach.[16] They show how the authors have abandoned their traditional positive approach in their thinking, turning themselves into technical observers and economic analysts. Why the Japanese economy has lost its dynamism and is unable to generate growth is a question that must be asked, and the state, nature and extent of the ailing system must be explained.

Column Bii of Table 2.1 is headed 'Economic objectives', and these must be inferred by asking what new image the economy needs for its own improvement. The question should not be about how to bring growth to the economy because no one is sure that restoration of growth will bring an improved future.

Since 1993 the White Paper has moved away from its traditional plan approach. It has decided not to ask any more questions about the extent and nature of the economy in bringing about the national aim. Instead it assumes that the economy holds a vital role in achieving this aim once the national aim is understood as the restoration of growth and vitality into the stagnant mode of society. Instead of identifying the national aim in stage one of the policy, it began its planning activities at the second stage of promoting economic objectives, assuming the aim was the growth of the economy.

I argue that the Japanese government since 1999 has abandoned its traditional planning approach to economic management. The change has led governments to abandon traditional approaches and efforts to estimate the economy's potential. Governments have decided to pass this task on to business, and to give up their aspiration to make a contribution to the betterment of the country. They have given in to the view that the free-enterprise spirit will be more effective than their public planning efforts. This is how the economic objective has been sought in deregulation of the economy (as shown in Bii) and through dismantling of the public-sector economy (observed in Biii). The result is that government is denied all effective devices and means in public institutions and organizations that have been used previously in their effort to promote plans. Governments now understand that the economy had grown and industry had reached a high stage of development by the middle of the 1980s, whence progress will take place without guidance and encouragement from outside. And thus they see it is time to withdraw from making an effort to understand and be excited about future potential. If this is the case, there is no longer a need for large government, and deregulation makes sense.

Table 2.1 Economic White Papers, 1947–2004

| | A | | B, Structure | | |
| | Title | i | ii | iii | iv |
Year		General aim	Economic objectives	Economic instruments	Economic measures
1947	A report on actual conditions in the economy	Return to normal peace-time living			
1948	A Report on the economy – in retrospect and prospect		Resume peacetime economic activity that provides daily necessities to the population		Economic rehabilitation plan
1949	Economic analysis of the current problems in the economy			Government conveys its economic policy messages to the population	
1950	The economy under a policy of stabilization				Balancing the public budget, reduction and elimination of subsidies, a fixed exchange rate
1951	Annual report of economic conditions under a policy of stabilization			Plan to bringing economic stabilization through the control of government-selected key industries	

Table 2.1 Economic White Papers, 1947–2004 *continued*

	A		B, Structure			
			i	*ii*	*iii*	*iv*
Year	*Title*		*General aim*	*Economic objectives*	*Economic instruments*	*Economic measures*
1952	Growth capacity of the economy in the immediate post-war period		Resume normal peacetime production activities			Enactment of enterprise rationalization law
1953	Economic policy to restore economic independence			Create employment		
1954	Time for consolidation of economic independence				Create employment through public investment	
1955	Road to progress					
1956	Understand the relation between economic expansion and economic transformation of the economy growth and modernization of industries and production facilities		Modernize society through democratic ways of doing things in society and economy			Modernization of industry through imported technology

Table 2.1 Economic White Papers, 1947–2004 *continued*

| | A | | B, Structure | | |
| | Title | i
General aim | ii
Economic objectives | iii
Economic instruments | iv
Economic measures |
Year					
1957	Excessive speed of economic expansion problems		Modernization and democratization through economic equity and stability		
1958	Revival of business cycle			Control of public spending to secure economic stability	
1959	Speedy economic recovery and the problems projected in the future				Introduction of a mixed economic model for economic recovery
1960	Growth capacity and competitiveness in the economy		Build modern efficient economy through scientific management		The national income-doubling plan
1961	Results and future problems of a fast-growing economy				
1962	Changes in the pattern of business cycle			Formulate industrial policy to build competitive export industry	

Table 2.1 Economic White Papers, 1947–2004 *continued*

	A		B, Structure			
Year	Title	i General aim	ii Economic objectives	iii Economic instruments	iv Economic measures	
1963	Road to an advanced industrial nation				Government assistance to build social overhead capital
1964	Japanese economy under an open-door system				Trade and capital liberalization
1965	Stability of national living standards				Formulate financial and monetary policy to build a competitive strong economy
1966	Road to steady growth		Economic growth with economic equity and stability		
1967	Promotion of efficiency and welfare	To build welfare economy			
1968	The Japanese economy admidst internationlization		Economic welfare to people through production efficiency		
1969	Challenge from affluence			Building of social and production infrastructure facilities	

Table 2.1 Economic White Papers, 1947–2004 *continued*

Year	A Title	B, Structure			
		i General aim	ii Economic objectives	iii Economic instruments	iv Economic measures
1970	New dimensions of the Japanese economy				Anti-inflationary policy and introduction of environment protection law
1971	Internal and external equilibrium				The Environment Agency is established
1972	Building of a new welfare state			Expansion of the public-sector economy	
1973	Welfare without inflation				Promotion of public transfer for welfare and social security purposes
1974	Beyond economic growth – towards a new course of economic stability	In search of Japan's own welfare economy			
1975	Towards a new course of economic stability prosperity		Maintain stable economic growth		
1976	Laying groundwork for new economic prosperity			Control of public through monetary policy	

Table 2.1 Economic White Papers, 1947–2004 *continued*

A		B, Structure			
		i	*ii*	*iii*	*iv*
Year	Title	General aim	Economic objectives	Economic instruments	Economic measures
1977	The Japanese economy in the midst of structural change				Writing of policies to maintain high savings and their effective utilization in active investment
1978	The economy with high adaptability to changes	Economy in transition – expansion of service industry			
1979	Japan's trials and tasks as advanced nation		Government wishes to renovate the economy for further competitive and growth direction		
1980	New problems in economic development: the development of the Japanese economy, its environmental changes, oil supply restrictions, international economic friction, utilization of private initiative and socio-economic changes				Expansion policy in order to take advantage of strong investment activities in business

Table 2.1 Economic White Papers, 1947–2004 *continued*

	A	B, Structure			
Year	Title	i General aim	ii Economic objectives	iii Economic instruments	iv Economic measures
1981	Creative vitality of the Japanese economy	Build creative and innovative society			
1982	The way to give full play to economic efficiency			Need to reduce government role and its size	
1983	Preparing for continuous economic growth		Build strong free-enterprise economy		
1984	The Japanese economy coping with new internationalization				Structural adjustment and internationalization of finance
1985	The new economic growth and its issues	Build dynamic society against ageing of the population			
1986	The economy seeking international harmony		Meet competition from Asian economies		
1987	Progressing structural changes and future problems of the economy			Writing industry restructuring plan – reform of public-sector economy	

Table 2.1 Economic White Papers, 1947–2004 *continued*

| | A | | B, Structure | | |
| | | i | ii | iii | iv |
Year	Title	General aim	Economic objectives	Economic instruments	Economic measures
1988	Sustained growth		Expand domestic demand and make a large contribution to the international community		
1989	Embarking on the Heisei economy and its new trends				Policy for import promotion
1990	Towards sustained economic growth		Maintain economic growth and stability to bring quality of life to population		
1991	Conditions for long-term economic expansion and Japan's contribution to the world economy		Control business cycles and encourage economic dynamism		
1992	Seeking for a new prosperity beyond the adjustment process	Build a progressive Japan			
1993	Lessons from the 'bubble economy' – issues for discussion for the new stage of economic advancement		Restore growth in the economy		

Table 2.1 Economic White Papers, 1947–2004   *continued*

| | A | B, Structure | | | |
| | | | | | |
Year	Title	i General aim	ii Economic objectives	iii Economic instruments	iv Economic measures
1994	A challenge to new frontiers beyond the severe adjustment process		As above		
1995	Towards the revival of a dynamic economy		As above		
1996	Reforms usher in perspective			Review and restructure public-sector economy	
1997	Japanese economy in thorough reform			As above	
1998	Preparing for creative development			As above	
1999	Challenges for economic revival			As above	
2000	Enter into a new economic society				In search of better monetary policy, restructure institutions and network for technology and innovation activities

Table 2.1 Economic White Papers, 1947–2004   *continued*

		B, Structure		
	A	*ii*	*iii*	*iv*
Year	*Title*	*Economic objectives*	*Economic instruments*	*Economic measures*
		i *General aim*		
2001	No economic reform, no economic growth	Restore vitality to society through economic reform		
2002	No economic growth without restructure of the economy, I	Same as above		
2003	No economic growth without restructure of the economy, II	Same as above		
2004	No economic growth without restructure of the economy, III	Same as above		

3
Plans to Improve Living Standards

Capital-scarce labour-surplus economy

Industrialization

The Japanese economy grew at high speed throughout its period of industrialization. The growth rate accelerated as the economy developed to produce an annual GNP growth of 3–4 per cent in the early industrialization period of 1870–1913. It rose to 4–5 per cent in the pre-war years of 1913–38, and further increased in the post-1945 years to the phenomenal level of 9–10 per cent. In some years, rates as high as 13–14 per cent were reached, leading some to call this the 'miracle' period. There was continuous growth throughout the century and the rate of growth was twice as fast as the average achieved in advanced economies in the West.[1]

Despite such an achievement, the popular notion of the Japanese economy as simply growth-oriented needs to be corrected. In this view, Japan's policy progress can be summed up superficially as being all about the national well-being, leaving no room for the welfare of individuals. This is not correct.

Along with continuous high growth and the rapid development of the economy, proposals for further progress and ideas for economic reform have been generated regularly, with the aim of using economic resources to improve people's lives. Not only in Japan but also in many other economies, planners had to decide how to allocate economic resources and use them in such a way as to generate economic growth that would make the greatest improvement in people's lives. Conscious of the country's lack of economic resources, planners in Japan thought it necessary to make a further effort. As I argued in Chapter 1, they thought they had to create economic resources to supplement the lack of capital and the backward industrial technology, and to counter the hostile international political environment – at least as they saw it – by converting labour to human resources and in that way initiate the process of industrialization. The planners developed public programmes and policy measures, building a rich body of knowledge as Japan's own economic plans and policy writing. The task required social reform by raising people's aspirations and encouraging workers to find cooperative solutions in their workplaces.

The high growth in the economy in the post-war years came about as a result of these continued attempts to plan for growth as well as the accumulation of production and economic resources – natural resources, capital and modern technology and most notably the use of human capital – which became a characteristic of the Japanese economy. The economic 'miracle' did not emerge all of a sudden.

I argued in Chapter 1 that the Japanese people have traditionally thought that the function of a better-structured economy was to give people not only satisfactory economic conditions but also opportunities to develop themselves as fully human. Economic progress has been regularly monitored to see how good economic provisions have improved people's lives and responded to people's individual desires to develop themselves.[2] In the West, the approach has been to rely on technical progress to bring about economic growth. The benefits are distributed equally among people. In Japan, however, economic productivity is encouraged by setting up various economic and social institutions, developing innovative ways to organize and administer production facilities, stimulating intellectual activities and appealing to a hard-working spirit and industrious mind – an approach heavily dependent on human effort. The Japanese expected that the benefits would be shared while they were working. In other words, the Japanese wanted to build an economic system that generated satisfaction for people through its very operation. They hoped to draw satisfaction through their employment and not, as in the West, by working to earn income through which to buy satisfaction. To build such an economy, critical thinking was called for.

Intellectuals monitored economic development to see if it had brought the desired improvement in people's lives and asked if economic progress had brought *true* welfare to people.

Argument

In this book I want to examine how this monitoring was carried out and how it contributed to economic planning. This chapter will examine how those efforts increased people's living standards, but alas still fell short of providing people with opportunities to seek betterment in life and to develop themselves. They had to wait for several generations until the end of World War II to see this higher objective was to come within their reach.

Kenneth Boulding, an economist and social reformer, viewed economic planning in a positive light. In 1959 he argued that through active engagement in economic planning people accumulate knowledge about society and social processes and thus are better equipped to counter economic problems.[3] He sought evidence for his argument in the reconstruction of the war-destroyed German economy, observing that it recovered more speedily and smoothly in the years after World War II compared to those after World War I. He argued that the improvement could be attributed to the German planners' accumulated wisdom of war reconstruction in the 1920s.[4]

Although his argument is still only hypothetical, I wish to take up the hypothesis and see to what extent the Japanese were able to improve their performance by examining their trials and experiences. The studies will be done in the light of Japan's attempt to industrialize the economy, modernize society and build a modern affluent industrial state and a society concerned with people's well-being.

Many attempts have been made to improve the living standards of people in Japan through growth in the national economy and industrial development. Various studies have tried to construct welfare and social indicators to estimate how economic progress has brought improvements to people's lives. But if you want to consider the whole picture of people's welfare, it is very difficult to calculate the improvement, as people's living environments and patterns of life changed drastically as the country industrialized and modernized.

I will extend my analysis in an attempt to estimate the true extent of improvement in people's welfare that economic growth was expected to bring and in the process make my own observations of the efforts made by people in Japan to secure better living conditions.

Figure 3.1 shows the rise in real wages and net personal consumption as a result of Japan's economic growth. By examining the rise in personal consumption, I will endeavour to explain how the improvement in people's living standards in Japan has come about.[5]

An increase in the amount of money that people spend is a rough indicator of how their standard of living has improved, although material welfare should not be taken as the only indicator; other matters beyond an increase in disposable income affect people's welfare. This

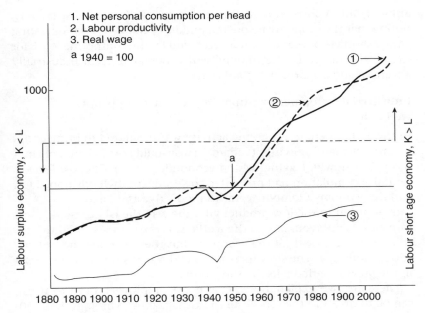

1. Net personal consumption per head
2. Labour productivity
3. Real wage

a 1940 = 100

Figure 3.1 Economic development, 1880–2004

should be noted, especially when studying the improvement in welfare over a long period when personal values and preferences might change, as the Japanese have experienced in the period studied.[6]

The figure shows that there are clear differences in the economic performance between the period before the middle of the 1960s and the one after. There are differences both in the extent of economic performance and the form of the economy.

The economy, estimated by the annual average rate of GNP, had grown regularly and continuously in both periods. The performance in the first half of the period (from the 1880s to the middle of the 1960s) was twice as high in the latter half of the period studied (from 1965 to 2004).

The economic form altered between the two periods. In the earlier years the economy was operating in an unfavourable environment, with a shortage of economic resources. It was a backward, developing, low-income economy with surplus labour. With economic growth, the environment improved: capital had accumulated, technology for production and management had been developed, and productivity rose. The economy was transformed into an advanced industrialized and affluent one. I show this in Figure 3.1 by K < L (capital < labour), noting that the economy before the middle of the 1960s was operating with a shortage of economic resources, and by the contrasting K > L for the newly transformed economy, which operated in an industrially advanced and resource-rich condition.

Industrial development without improvement in people's well-being

In the earlier period, economic activity was promoted to bring about an improvement in living standards. This would come about continuously, but slowly, lagging behind economic growth. The low level of capital accumulation had prevented the productivity levels hoped for, and the economy did not become as productive as desired.

In addition to the low productivity, the way the labour market was formed was unfavourable to the workers. People worked hard to contribute to the growth of the economy, but their incomes did not rise correspondingly. The slow increase in real wages shown in Figure 3.1 in the pre-war period tells the sorry story.

There are two explanations. One is the employers' need to retain capital to invest in the process of industrialization. Through the 1930s to the beginning of the war, employers retained a large share of the income by creating various managerial devices, such as a seniority promotion practice under which workers received less than their real contribution while they were young, known as 'deferred payment', and employment practices such as tax concessions and low-interest loans for business instead of sharing the benefits with the workers. In a disadvantaged surplus labour market, the workers had little bargaining power. Their disadvantaged position deteriorated further as economic growth and industrial development progressed. Growth and development were fast in coming but they were not fast enough to benefit the workers, whose numbers rose even faster as peasants living in poverty in villages went to factories in search of a better life. By increasing the amount of surplus labour, the workers weakened their bargaining position.

The fruit of economic growth became available at a much faster rate in the second half of the period, as if to show that people's hard effort in the first period was to be rewarded at long last. Economic growth had brought improvements, as expected, but, alas, it had not brought a better quality of life, at least not to any great extent.

In the first decades of industrialization (in the 1900s and 1910s), the Japanese economy established its industrial basis first in light industries such as textiles and clothing manufacturing, and subsequently in heavy industries such as railways and other transport industries.

As soon as jobs were created in the cities, there was a rapid movement of the population from the villages, which began in the middle of the 1920s and continued at an expanding rate through the 1930s. The wages of factory hands rose steadily but not as quickly as industry developed. To be more precise, the levels were estimated at barely above those observed in neighbouring poor Asian economies. The income of farmers was declining. But Japanese workers in factories and villages began to earn just more than they needed for the bare essentials of life. Life expectancy was below forty years of age, and there was a high death rate of mothers and babies at childbirth, and frequent outbreaks of infectious diseases such as dysentery and typhoid – revealing people's poverty and the country's poor public hygiene.

There are many studies that show the poor living and working conditions of the people at the time and how difficult it was to bring the benefits of industrial development to the people, especially at a time of overpopulation, a problem common to all economies in East Asia. What differentiated Japan from other Asian countries was that the people, despite living in poor conditions, saw that the national economy was progressing steadily and had potential for expansion and development. People read this as a sign of future improvement and it became an important force in driving economic and social progress.

Arthur Lewis, a development economist, made similar observations about Western economies, noting the importance of people's belief that economic growth is the result of human effort. He discussed the role of such a belief as a driving source of economic progress.[7]

If it is difficult to get an accurate picture of how the economy grew and to what extent industries had become modernized. But I can speculate that the steady rise in the level of real wages in the industrial sector had come about with the support of an equal, if not greater, rise in labour productivity. People's motivation to work was high because of the rise of their determination to participate in economic activities; it made up for the slow progress in mechanizing workplaces.

With the rise in labour productivity, investment to modernize production facilities soon began. The needs of capital rose faster than the accumulation of capital funds in enterprises themselves. The capacity to provide capital in banks, merchant houses and the households of landlords, wealthy families and individuals – the traditional source of capital funds in pre-industrial times – was found to be so inadequate that employers had to come up with various methods of forced savings.

The companies sought capital funds to manage this internally by accumulating profits and by delaying wage increases for workers' increased productivity, which resulted in the decline of labour's share in the total value added from 67.8 per cent in the 1900s to 57 per cent in subsequent years.

This level was not particularly low by international standards. The ratio in France and Germany, for example, was estimated as roughly the same as that of Japan during the period.[8] After the mid-1930s, however, the workers' share in the industrial sector began to decline rapidly as the process of industrialization accelerated. This skewed industrial development in the face of inadequate accumulation of capital was most undesirable and brought no corresponding improvement in people's welfare.

In industrial cities wages were depressed. But that was not all. The hours and the intensity of work were increased considerably, making working environments much poorer and ensuring that people lived at a much lower level than they had before industrialization. With the continuous increase in GNP, an improvement in the status of the nation internationally appeared to have been achieved. But the gap between the welfare of the nation and the well-being of individuals widened in this period.

Economic development evaluated

Kawakami Hajime (1879–1946)

Kawakami Hajime, an economic critic who later in his life became a Marxist, voiced concerns about this discrepancy. He was born in 1879, the eleventh year after the Meiji Restoration, the eldest son of a minor local administrator in Yamaguchi in western Japan, a place from which many political leaders emerged.

Perhaps reflecting the progressive thinking of the time, as a young man in high school Kawakami was already expressing his concern about the economic and social problems of Japanese society in a highly idealistic and moral way.

When he received a government scholarship that allowed him to make a study visit to Britain, France and Germany in 1913, he decided to observe the social conditions in those countries instead of taking part in formal university studies.

In the UK he saw poverty in the slums of London and in the backwater villages in England that was almost as bad as the poverty in Japan. To the Japanese, Britain at that time was seen as the richest, most powerful and most technologically advanced nation in the world. On this understanding, it was England that government and business in Japan was taking as its model.

Kawakami's discovery of widespread poverty in England raised profound doubts in his mind about the capacity of economic development and industrialization to give people what they needed for their well-being. He asked himself why English workers who lived in a society that was the richest in the world and who worked in some of the most advanced industries still led a life as deprived as the Japanese, and why poverty persisted in the midst of growing prosperity and the accumulation of wealth.

After examining many works of Western social research, including those of Charles Booth and Seebohm Rowntree, he came to see that, in the capitalist system, production is designed not to fulfil human need but to meet demand.

Business enterprises produced a mass of unnecessary luxuries to serve the idle desires and wasteful needs of the rich, he said, because the rich could support their desires and needs with real purchasing power. But the same business enterprises ignored the basic needs of the poor because the poor could not afford to pay for them. On this understanding he proposed that the rich be restrained and lead a frugal life. He came to view the economic system operating at the time as having an inbuilt deficiency that could only be countered by changing the thinking and behaviour of the people who lived and worked in it.

On his return home, he pursued his argument in a series of newspaper articles, which he later compiled into a book and published in 1917 under the title *Binbo Monogatari (A Tale of Poverty)*.[9] Despite its lack of stringent economic analysis the book became an instant bestseller. His observations and proposals found support and ready acceptance among many in the country.

Kawakami viewed poverty as an evil because it reduced the poor to a sub-human level and denied them their chance to live in a fully human way. His thinking may be summarized in three arguments, namely, that human beings will only act morally when their material needs are satisfied; that wealth alone will not bring happiness – indeed, excessive wealth may be as much a source of misery as excessive poverty; and that people should study economics in the context of taking part in economic activities, and not just in terms of the production and distribution of wealth.

Some people have criticized Kawakami on the grounds that his arguments are simplistic and his policy proposals too idealistic to be effective in the real world. Despite the criticism, Kawakami's ideas have had a long-lasting and popular appeal for people in Japan, and his contribution has never failed to be noted in the writings by all thinkers who have discussed the way in which Japan's economy should be managed for the good of the Japanese people. Kawakami has reminded people about seeking economic solutions in a moral and philosophical context. The planners and social and economic critics who were closely involved in the rebuilding of the economy after World War II were no exceptions.[10]

Fukuda Tokuzo (1874–1930)

At about the time Kawakami was conducting his study of poverty, Fukuda Tokuzo, an academic economist, was working on how to construct an effective and workable state-run welfare scheme in Japan. He studied in Germany under the guidance of academics in the German historical school and was introduced to various works of German social policy as well as Pigou's works on welfare economics in England. Early in his career, he directed his attention to the theoretical underpinning of welfare economics that had been developed in England and Germany. He came to believe that in those countries it was the introduction of welfare economic thinking, and not so much the advancement in industrial activities, that brought a higher degree of independence for people. Increasing welfare would not come through economic growth alone, he said.

His later interest – professional and personal – was focused on Japan's economic organization. He asked whether there was any way in which Japan, as a newly developing and industrializing economy, could be organized so that it could make people's welfare its greatest focus. He was acutely concerned about the way people in Japan ignored this aim in their enthusiasm for promoting national welfare ahead of people's welfare under the *fukoku kyohei* (strong industry independent nation), slogan, which was adopted as the national objective. He was anxious to correct this bias at an early stage in the nation's economic development.

At university he lectured on welfare economics, taking Pigou's *Welfare Economics* (1919) as a standard text, although most of the lecturing time was said to have been allocated to discussing the gap between Pigou's world and the actual social and economic conditions in Japan towards the end of the 1920s.

Fukuda appreciated the humane spirit of Pigou's teaching. Yet he could not accept the teaching in its original form in his own country.

He saw a wide difference in the economic and social environment between Pigou's England and his Japan.

Following Pigou, he was convinced that there was an urgent need for Japan, if it were to promote industrial development, to build a welfare system. He supported Pigou's argument that the growth of the national economy and the development of industries alone would not make people happy, and he questioned what structure the system should have and how it should be implemented in Japan, given the country's social conditions at the time. Fukuda saw the importance of building a workable system and structuring the welfare system as a means to modernize society and bring with it a democratic mindset. Fukuda was especially concerned about the unequal relationship between people in different social classes, which Japan had inherited from its feudal past. By establishing a welfare economy, he wished to dissolve those inequalities.

True to Japan's traditional *keisei saimin* (political economy) approach to economic studies, he saw the purpose of economic planning to be to build 'quality' in people, to encourage them to be better people by living in a well-provided economic society.

Fukuda published volumes of research and public speeches and participated in public debates and discussions with Kawakami to clarify just what kind of welfare system should be built in Japan. From the debates he developed the following proposals.

Japan needed to formulate a welfare economic system in close conjunction with a national economic strategy for rapid industrialization, he said. The system must be structured in a form that was different from that proposed by Pigou. Given the social make-up in Japan in the 1920s – meaning the unequal relations between employer and employees, the patriarchal role of fathers in families, and the hierarchy between males and females, and seniors and juniors – he did not think Pigou's formula of government grants to needy people was adequate. He understood that, as a result of the heritage of Confucian teaching and Japan's feudal background, this way of relating was still followed closely. What was more, in his opinion, the unequal relationship between employers and employees increased in the labour surplus economy of the 1920s.

Fukuda was convinced of the undesirable nature of such a relationship, not only on humanitarian grounds but also for the development of an economic society that was to produce wealth for individuals and the country. He went on to argue that the unequal human relationships dominant in Japan would hinder the development of the Japanese economy.

He believed that, at its core, a productive economy needs independently thinking people. Workers with free minds would make effective
demands and would support the development of productive industries.
He believed that the capacity of workers to make independent decisions on what to buy, and how much to save and invest, would allow
them to become efficient producers who would contribute to the
development of the economy in the form that served them best.

The welfare economic system in Japan, he said, should be structured
and managed in a way that would provide for people's basic needs, and
be adequate to allow people to live free from concerns about how to
provide for their daily needs. And people must be free to think and
behave in their own way, free from the impositions of employers.

In arguing this, Fukuda once again spoke of the unfortunate
condition of Japan's labour surplus economy in the 1920s, during
which workers lived continuously with a lack of bargaining power
against employers. Fukuda believed that people should be helped
to understand their right to live in a just society. He wanted people
to understand their need to be self-respecting and independent-
minded, to aspire to a good quality of life and in the process to
contribute to the building of a better economy.

The study of economics in Japan has been conducted with a close
understanding of how the behaviour of individuals changes as the
economy changes, and how the change, in turn, affects the economic
system. The Japanese may support this approach more than others
because of their decision to build 'efficiency through people'. It is thus
natural for Fukuda to understand economics in the context of human
behaviour and by questioning how to conduct economic activities
with the aim of helping people to become better and to live fuller lives.

In short, Kawakami studied economics to estimate the capacity of
the economy to help people improve themselves, while Fukuda
sought ways to build a better-structured economy in which people
lived to improve themselves. The two helped many people in Japan
to view the capitalist approach practised in Western economies
with strong reservations. They brought a critical view of free-market
capitalism.

The transformation of the economy

Observation during World War II

Improving people's standard of living was not on the national agenda
during World War II. People with critical minds who were looking to

improve social welfare, reform ideas for building a better society, and nurture 'quality' men and women were quiescent.

Despite that, the period left a legacy on which the post-war economy was able to build its welfare programmes.

I have noted already that Kawakami's and Fukuda's critical view of capitalism influenced many in Japan and diffused a widely anti-*laissez-faire* sentiment in pre-war Japan. As early as in the middle of the 1930s, many leaders and decision makers in government, politics, business, universities and the media had taken a critical view of free-enterprise economic management. Strictly speaking, the support for economic planning had come from the national need to restructure the economy and industry so as to increase production capacity as fast as possible. Government control of heavy industries was also sought as the only effective way to mobilize production bases for war. The whole economy was quickly transformed into one that was under total government control.

There was a rapid separation between ownership and management in business in wartime. I have noted already that from the early 1920s business corporations in Japan had faced the need to secure capital funds for investment as industrial development proceeded, and that accumulation of capital inside the corporation had never been adequate so that employers, in order to save and make a profit, began to delay giving a fair share of payment to employees. As the war effort progressed and business had to expand production capacity more rapidly than previously to meet the demand from military authorities, the need arose more sharply and such stop-gap methods as delaying payments to employees ceased to be effective. Corporations of all sizes had to invest fast and, in the process, many had to seek large sums of capital funds in the share market. Traditional wealthy people and family groups, such as the *Zaibatsu* family members, turned into minority holders of their companies, leaving the managerial control to employed executives.[11] At workplaces and in businesses in general, the separation of ownership and control quickly brought equity, although not because of any new benevolence from company owners. And this separation of ownership and control was further promoted by the Allied Authorities, who led managers to develop various management systems in the post-war years designed to bring benefits to employees rather than owners.

I have commented earlier on how many social policy measures and systems were established during wartime.[12] These were introduced to take care of soldiers and their families, but the benefits were not extended to the general population. They were introduced to maintain people's health and to ensure that they were fit and strong to fight the war. Many post-war welfare systems and policy measures such as the national health system and some basic social security measures and schemes for the sick, the elderly and widows were made on a basis established during the war.

The general repression and actual persecution of the political left had begun as early as 1923 when the Peace Police Law was enacted. Some academics and social critics continued their work and converted to nationalism, some engaged in various wartime economic planning activities to gain first-hand experience that would be used for the reconstruction of the post-war economy. Others chose to exclude themselves from active research and teaching so as not to provoke the military government, but continued to read, trying to refine the theoretical bases of their understanding of economics or simply to fill in their time translating and writing introductions for ideologically neutral works developed in the West.[13]

The economy grew by nearly 5 per cent annually through the 1930s, but the record turned negative in the 1941–44 war years. Throughout the period people's material living standards fell considerably, as seen, for example, in the sharp rise of Engel's coefficient, which rose from 40 per cent to as high as 60 per cent during the period, indicating that people spent most of their disposable income obtaining basic needs, such as food, clothing and housing, leaving little for education, travelling, or hobbies. As for the quality of life, living under the absence of freedom of speech must have reduced it considerably. At the same time, a great deal of the national wealth was dissipated and many human lives were destroyed.[14]

The war-damaged economy recovered to its pre-war level stage by 1953 (helped by the special procurement demand from the US army in Korea). Subsequently, the economy managed to begin its 'miracle' period of high growth.

Trapped in generations of cycles of poverty: Fujibayashi Keizo

Towards the end of the 1950s, the late Professor Fujibayashi Keizo of Keio University and chairman of *Churo-i,* the Central Labour Arbitration Council, told students that his lifelong hope was to see the Japanese economy grow out of its backward industrial state and spoke of how distressed he was to see conditions that were not much better than those in his childhood days in the early Meiji period.

He explained that with Japan's lack of natural resources, and the backward state of industrial technology, the productivity of most Japanese businesses and industries remained low. People working in those backward corporations and industries had lower earnings than they needed to live independently.

As a way to economize on expenditure and manage within their available income, they structured their way of life so that they worked in their prime (say from 14 or 15 until retirement at 50 or 55, as practised in those days). In this way they supported themselves as well as their family, including their parents and often their spouse's parents.

The result was that their earnings during the prime years were not adequate to allow them to save for their own old age. The workers found themselves in a dismal life cycle of supporting a large family while in their prime and, later, becoming dependent on the younger generation and having to live without freedom. He argued that living in a multi-generation large family was not a cultural or social tradition but most frequently an economic necessity.

Under these conditions people were destined to have a lifelong obligation to support others in their youth, and later in their old age to suffer feelings of obligation and that they were a financial and social burden to others in the family. These social arrangements not only deprived people of enjoyment but also deterred them from exploring new career opportunities and developing their own talents, leading them to a meek and makeshift life.

Fujibayashi's distressing scenario was shared by many before the beginning of the 1960s who did not realize that the 'miracle' high economic growth was only a couple of years away. So it is understandable that people reacted to the announcement of the National Income-doubling Plan in 1960 first with suspicion, doubting the nation's capability to make the projected target and, only later, on seeing the prediction of good economic results, drifted into the euphoria of growth and expansion of the economy.[15]

The continuous high-speed economic growth that went on for nearly two decades until 1972 brought many wonderful economic results to Japan that people had longed for from the beginning of industrialization.

Many fields of employment were created. In the five years between 1955 and 1960 alone, 5.4 million new jobs were created, with better pay than those available previously. The labour market expanded by 4.0 per cent annually. Statistically the ratio between the employment offered to job seekers rose continuously from its low level of 0.22 (i.e. 22 jobs were available in the labour market to meet 100 job seekers) in 1955, to 0.54 in 1960, and to 1.00 (full-employment condition) in 1967, resulting in the elimination of a labour-surplus condition with the ratio to rising to 1.41 (labour-scarce condition) in 1970.

Arrival of a capital-abundant economy

Figure 3.1 shows this transformation in the economy from capital-poor, labour-surplus economy by denoting K < L, and capital-rich, labour-scarce economy by K > L respectively, and that the transformation took place around the middle of the 1960s with virtually full employment across all industries.

With a continuous rise in real wages, the miserable time when people worked from a weak bargaining position and struggled at a subsistence level finally came to an end. Through growth and expansion, Japan rid itself of its distressing multi-generation family living arrangements and its reputation as a semi-developed, third-rate, country. People now saw their economy as modern, industrial and affluent.

The Japanese were proud of the fact that they were the first to achieve industrial development and eliminate poverty outside the Western world while maintaining their original culture and valuing their ideals and philosophy. This high economic performance, however, was subject to serious evaluation at the beginning of the 1970s with rising problems of environmental deterioration and again two decades later, at the beginning of the 1990s, when the speculation boom suddenly burst and a long period of recession began.

Looking at the subsequent period with the wisdom of hindsight, it is easy to see how carelessly and easily people, including those intellectuals with supposedly critical minds, forgot to monitor the progress of economic and social development. We saw in Chapter 2 that the economy through the 1970s and the 1980s was still unable to liberate itself from an excessive orientation towards planning for growth. Yet it is my argument that the Japanese are learning from the mistakes made during that period. In the next chapter I observe new efforts for planning of the economy that are emerging not only in government but also in labour unions and business. The rest of the book makes those new efforts the starting point for a discussion of how the Japanese will search to build a better economic system in the future.

4
Planning for Improved Living Standards

In Chapter 3 I drew a picture of economic thinking in Japan. In this chapter I want to look at the economic policies written in the years after World War II based on observations made during interviews with the bureaucrats involved in their development and administration.

In these years the economy was transformed from a low-income economy to an industrially advanced and affluent one. But for all the wealth, the Japanese have not discovered how to use it wisely. So far they have wasted a considerable part of their accumulated assets and built general dissatisfaction in people's minds. In this chapter I want to look at the fundamental thinking behind the writing of economic policies in the period, how the policies were constructed, how people responded, and what commitment they made to the spirit of the economic planning behind them.

Introduction

I will examine the economic objectives of the Japanese government by looking at three different aspects: economic planning, economic policy writing, and public administrative services. Each aims to solve problems in, and increase the well-being of, the economy. The approaches differ in the nature of the means used to attain the end.[1]

The economic objectives and the means of government planning

Economic planning is an activity that aims to reform the foundation of the economy. It is the most ambitious and far-reaching of the three. It examines the making of the economic system and identifies the features of social organization, the patterns of relations between people – as employer–employee, citizen–government official, or parent–child – to see how well they function. It addresses issues of long-term economic development and the selection of appropriate policies. It emphasizes not only the efficiency and growth of the economy, but also people's quality of life and their opportunities for development. The planning period usually extends over six to ten years. In specific terms economic planning is concerned with social security schemes, minimum incomes and guarantees for minimum employment, equal employment opportunities for people through education and training schemes, family planning, industrial democracy, and so on.

If the economic system is found to be short of the ideal, planning takes place to revise and reform it. This element of reform addresses the foundations of the economic system under which the economic activities of the nation and its people are conducted.

Economic policy writing assumes an existing economic system and is concerned with changing the less fundamental elements of social and economic organization. It does not aim to alter people's values and preferences, which are the foundation of the economy. Its main concern is the structure of the national economy and industry, the cost structure of products and services, the pattern of work, the shape of corporate organizations and their administrative styles, and the ways in which the market operates as a mediator of economic activities. Put differently, it asks if the nation's production resources are allocated and used efficiently. Policy may be designed qualitatively to change economic variables such as the level of imports and exports, the growth rate of the GNP, and the rates of unemployment and inflation.

Public administrative services involve the bureaucrats who work in the public service to supplement the working of the market. In Japan, free competition has been encouraged to achieve economic efficiency and industrial growth. The cost of free competition, however, has never been underestimated. When discussing Japan's rapid economic growth and industrial development, many economic researchers and political scientists have looked to the contribution of individual economic bureaucrats for the cause and explanation. Generally speaking, public administrators address people's general economic concerns. The nature of their activity is *ad hoc* and short term, aiming to mitigate problems as soon as possible. Few records of their work have been kept, making examination difficult. To overcome this difficulty I conducted four case studies of selected officers (see Chapters 6–9).

In a real situation there are many examples that would not fall neatly into one single group or another, and there are some that may find themselves in the margins between the three.

In his *Principles of Economic Policy*, published in 1959, Kenneth Boulding wrote that the task of economic planning is to search for the 'ideal' economic society, to cultivate 'social agriculture' in which planners deliberately distort the natural organizational structure in order to reform the management system. The strength of the conceived 'ideal' society lies in its capacity to give people the means by which to lead contented and happy lives. He argues that the essential provisions are economic progress (growth), economic stability, economic justice (equity), and economic freedom.[2]

These four will serve as a convenient device to help us to follow the development of ideas in government about building better and more workable economic plans and policies in Japan. How have policy writers in Japan sought these objectives? What order of priority have they placed them in?

Because of the record of high economic growth and industrial development in the middle of the 1980s, many observers have viewed the Japanese economy as growth-oriented. Accordingly, the aspirations and behaviour observed are understood as part of the nation's effort to expand the country's economic activities and modernize itself. This view is misleading and stereotyped. In Chapter 3 I warned readers of the danger of seeing the history of Japan's experience of economic development before the World War II years in the simple light of the national effort to expand the size of the economy. The same warning should be repeated in examining the more recent experience after 1945 although the period saw an extremely high growth performance that had not been observed elsewhere before.

In examining the thinking behind Japan's economic policies, I was immediately struck by how people, not only in government but also in business and unions, made efforts to draw up strategic plans and select economic objectives by carefully locating their priorities. As we will see, growth has never been the unchallenged priority. One objective may be selected to play a strategic position in the making of a plan, while others are viewed as important and desirable, but not vital for achieving the overall aim.

The 1950s and 1960s were the time when economic growth was pursued by almost every economic planner around the world. Japan is not the only example. But it would be wrong to understand public planning only in terms of growth. Other economies in Europe, the USA and some parts of Asia also experimented with planning in this period. For some time during the post-war reconstruction years the Japanese government, given the limited available economic resources, viewed economic planning as the vehicle for generating more goods and services, seeking ways to raise efficiency in resource use and increased productivity by increasing the scale of operations. But the overall aim was to raise the standard of living by securing economic provision and employment. After experiencing expansion in the economy, and seeing how growth satisfies other economic objectives at the same time, planners began to direct their efforts at driving the economy into fast growth. In this way, many economists and administrators continued to believe that a high rate of growth is the result of good planning and failed to see that it is not the end in itself.

People in Japan have always been very concerned about economic stability, particularly stability in employment markets, as a result of the difficulties experienced by many of them in depressed economic times – they lost jobs and faced insecurity in employment and an inability to maintain their standard of living. In the absence of adequate social security measures, it is natural that working people in Japan greatly fear the loss of employment.[3]

It is my observation that stability of prices, however, has not been adequately promoted in Japan. In the mistaken belief that it would encourage economic growth, many leaders in government saw an inflationary trend in the market as something to be tolerated, if it is kept within control.

As for economic justice, the maintenance of fair working environments generally across economic society has been regarded as very important for Japanese public planners and business leaders. Leaders in government and business promoted economic justice not so much out of benevolence but as an effective device to promote economic growth. These leaders thought the work ethic of the general population would be high when they saw they were getting a fair distibution of income which would lead to growth in the economy.

At workplaces, a particular Japanese style of management that aimed to provide employees with a long-term employment arrangement and the practice of career development according to seniority developed to give workers security and thus actively motivate them. It was my argument earlier in Chapter 1 that the efficient use of capital and resources by transforming labour into human resources had been relied on in the drive for industrial development. Nationally, economic equity, as observed in society in general, has been viewed as essential in order to encourage individuals to try hard to become human resources in response to the national strategy for industrialization.

Many authors have noted that the Japanese economy in the years after World War II was managed under a relatively high equity structure with a fair and just spirit among employers.

The economist Iida Tsuneo, for one, argued that the most important reason for Japan's successful economic achievements, at least until the middle of the 1980s, should be seen in the specific corporate management provisions that gave workers security and the prospect of regular promotion. This, he argued, made them feel valued and respected as members of the workforce. They believed that they had equal opportunities for material success and as a result showed a high level of what Lewis's 'will to economize', that is, willingness to participate in economic matters, which acts as a driving force for economic growth and development.[4] In this way economic justice has been used in Japan as a means of bringing economic growth.

Economic freedom is another economic objective for economic growth and industrial development. Boulding notes that it is difficult to capture the concept in a balanced way.[5] Difficulties lie in the fact that it not only means different things to different people but differs between people and different cultures. The experience in the West may not be applicable to Japan or to other economies in Asia.

All four objectives are desirable, but there are often trade-offs between their maximization, given the economic resources. In an effort to increase each, a conflicting relationship may develop between them so that, for example, an increase in the rate of economic growth may bring instability to the economy and create inequity in the distribution of income. Planners must decide how to rank the four at a particular time and at different stages of economic development, and thereby structure the economic system for the future.

I would like to note at this stage of our discussion of those four objectives that Japan's experience has, so far, followed a very skewed approach that aims to promote economic growth and efficiency first, an approach to which the other two, economic stability and justice, are left to serve as a device. However, a new development has emerged in more recent years, people have come to see the importance of the fourth, economic freedom, as the economy developed and general affluence came to their lives. It is an important development that challenges the preceding thinking and approach of economic planning. I will discuss this in Chapters 10 and 11 below.

The overall picture of the economy in the post-World War II years

It is commonly acknowledged that the high achievement of Japan's economy in the post-war years resulted from the development of an 'indicative planning' system, in which people from government, business, households and individuals all made contributions through work. The system has developed as Japan's own. It has, however, seen changes, and many experiments have been tried. I want to follow those experiments in search of the basic principles and mechanics of economic planning. The future development of the economy will be made on the basis of the learning from those past experiments.

I divide the post-war years from 1945 to 2003 into four periods – 1945–55, 1956–72, 1973–85, 1986–2003. In each period we can trace how government organized its 'indicative' planning approach and select policy initiatives (from the selection of economic objectives, economic institutions to formulate policy tools as discussed in Chapter 2 above in order to raise the work contribution from business and households for the continuous development of industry). Before beginning a detailed discussion of each period, I will give a brief outline of the activities at the time and put them in the context of economic development in the post-war years.

Reconstruction, 1945–55: the time when government planning aimed to reconstruct the war-destroyed economy so as to give it back its basis in production, and especially to restore the level of people's income to pre-war (1934–36) standards, which would secure their standard of living and provide a market for business. The government began by giving people carefully prepared information on its understanding of the condition of the economy, with the aim of informing them of what was left, after the destruction of the war, what was needed to begin production, and what efforts they would need to make to rebuild the economy. The government encouraged people to begin work again as soon as possible in the manner needed for the rapid recovery of the economy. In this way, the government began to develop its programme of indicative planning.

To resume production, the economy could use many of the facilities that had survived the heavy raids.[6] Economic systems and management approaches developed pre-war, however, were to be overhauled and renewed.

Economic growth, 1956–72: a period extending over almost three decades in which people across different generations took an active part in the economy. A new set of economic management approaches emerged. Some called it 'the *1955 taisei*, or socio-political system' to acknowledge its influence on the remaking of the economy in the subsequent post-war years. Some argue that its influence remains today, showing how difficult it has been for the economy to grow out of its post-war strictures, despite its move into a new stage of post-industrial affluence.[7]

It could be said that the whole nation's national energy was dedicated to the economy, including work in political, cultural and scientific fields, with the singular aim of building a modern industrial state and catching up with the advanced West.

During this period, the level of personal consumption is estimated to have risen almost 16 times, allowing almost everyone to enjoy material wealth and to see economic growth in a positive light. Apart from economic management, however, a single aim and unified approach was not achieved in government, business, the workplace or the family. The planners explored numbers of alternatives and invited the population to do the same. This, I argue, saved the Japanese from mistakenly falling into building a culturally barren country in these dynamic years.

A strategy of growth and expansion dominated this period. The economy pushed its frontier far and wide, aiming to take full advantage of the potential at home and abroad. The combination of an entrepreneurial spirit in business and a strong aspiration in the minds of people to improve their living standards built a modern industrial state.

Move to steady growth economy, 1973–85: the third stage of economic development, when leaders examined the preceding growth-oriented approach to see if it would continue to work in the future. The assessment was to be conducted on a national and individual basis. Out of it arose the need to search for a new direction for the economy and a new goal for society.

The state of affluence, 1986–2004: the first time in Japanese economic development in which a surplus accumulation of capital occurred in business and among affluent groups of people. Many looked for a quick and easy return from their over-abundant capital. Speculation in property and stock markets attracted this idle money. In a buoyant economic climate, people were misled to believe that the national economy was quickly and continuously accumulating wealth. Careless economic management, both in many business corporations and government sectors, continued through this booming time until towards the end of 1990.

In society, many lucky people made fortunes, but when the boom burst suddenly in late 1991 most were left with loans and debt. The national struggle to restore normal economic activities began in 1992, leading people to understand that the extent of the damage to the economy was much larger than originally estimated. Many rescue measures were applied by government and business, but there were few successful outcomes from their strategy to restore normal production. And so the lost decade continued throughout the 1990s and on into the present.

Planning experience

A new start – search for the promotion of economic freedom

It is said that the planning for the post-war Japanese economy began as early as 1943, albeit unofficially. That is, without waiting for the war to end, planning for the reconstruction of the economy began more than two years before Japan's defeat. This was on the initiative of a group of academic economists, economic administrators, sociologists, educators and journalists, almost all of whom were eminent intellectuals. They organized a study group and, despite being monitored by the military authorities, met regularly to discuss how to go about the task of post-war reconstruction, collecting data and collating the information necessary for the proposed programme of economic reconstruction.[8]

The war ended on 15 August 1945. On the next day, official planning began with the establishment of what was called the 'Special Survey Committee', this time as an official entity, to formulate ideas for post-war reform. The committee members began their work, closely following the economic thinking developed in the pre-war years. They wanted to build a Japan that reflected the ideals of the pre-war thinkers and a new economy that would provide satisfaction and a modern way of life for people. They did not aim simply to restore or reconstruct production facilities to replace what had been lost or destroyed.

Professor Tsuru Shigeto, himself a member, writes about the committee as an extension of the pre-war study group that had by then expanded to a thirty-member public planning body.[9] He recalls that the committee included presidents of six universities, the president of the Japan Science Council, a head of the Federation of Economic Associations, a Member of Parliament, an editorial writer of a national newspaper, and a member of cabinet.[10]

We read in daily newspapers, popular journals, academic papers and books that what the country lost as a result of defeat in the war was not only its production capacity but also people's fundamental confidence in almost everything about Japan.[11] The need for a large-scale reconstruction of the social structure as well as the economic system was on everyone's mind.

The question was how to begin the task. Among the planners there was a strong push for democracy. They wanted to reconstruct the economy as a means to do this. The basis for militarism was destroyed, but there still remained an element in society, so the planners feared, that would rise again to lead people to a top–down authoritarian approach in social and personal life if surplus labour persisted in the labour market. They were most concerned when they detected that employees, in their anxious efforts to secure their jobs, still behaved in an obliging and deferential manner to employers (as noted by Fukuda, discussed in Chapter 3).

Not only the intelligentsia but also a large number of the general public shared this concern and feared that the Japanese economy, even after Japan's total defeat in the war, still retained those undesirable elements that might again turn the nation to militarism – unless it was completely reformed.[12]

Those who came to planning with the aim of building a new Japan held many discussions before they formulated measures to restructure the economy. They agreed that the immediate aim, in a time of confusion, must focus on giving people basic security.[13] Planners were not content with providing employment. Employment offers would be made with the purpose of introducing democratic working environments to the country. This, the planners believed, could be done through job security for workers with a fair and equal employer–employee relationship, which would allow workers to think and behave as free people.

It was the understanding of the planners that under the obligatory pressure to secure employment employees took instructions and accepted unfair dealings from employers. This pressure had been created at a time when people had to work in a surplus labour market. The planners knew that they could not alter the structure of the labour market, but that they could alter employer–employment practices through regulatory mechanisms.

This was a socio-economic plan, with a much more ambitious aim than post-war economic reconstruction. Its aim was to build a better society. The planners sought to achieve social objectives through economic means.

At its first meeting, the planning committee, despite the members' varied backgrounds, expertise, interests and ideology, reached the unanimous agreement that they should conduct this large-scale reconstruction by economic means. They decided to address the socio-political issues of the war-ruined country only in the process of, and not at the same time as, the recovery of production and distribution of essential goods and services. In that way, the construction of economic policy was made the absolute priority task of government.

Economists and economic bureaucrats in the group were excited by the scope of their task and the potential for making a contribution. They were challenged to see how they might successfully transform their society into a democratic entity through drawing clear reconstruction plans for the economy, industry and the workplace. Other members, whose expertise lay outside economics, shared the excitement and supported the plan. Most members were oriented generally towards Marxist thinking acquired in their student days in the 1920s. In addition, the traditional approach in Japan that saw the *keisei saimin* (political economy) practised throughout history contributed to the group's selection of a combination of social and economic approaches.[14]

Professor Nakayama Ichiro, an academic economist and one of the leading members of the group, wrote about his understanding of the importance of studying the economic system as a social regime. He saw the economic system not simply as a collection of production facilities, but as the fundamental construction in which people make their contribution to the increase in material welfare of the society and, at the same time, gain living and working conditions in which they have the opportunity to construct a meaningful life.[15]

He came to believe that the time had come for Japan to begin comprehensive planning of the economy. By 'comprehensive' he meant planning of every aspect of society with a long-run and interdisciplinary approach. He believed that efforts before 1945 followed an *ad hoc* and industry-specific approach, so that planning and policy making took place only when problems arose. Nakayama wanted to see attempts made to evaluate the working of the economic system as a regular part of the management of the economy and to monitor it regularly to ascertain if any areas in the system could be revised and improved.

Nakayama's view received unanimous support from the members of the planning committee.[16] To begin their task the committee made a careful survey of the number of days of employment required for the subsistence of workers and their families. This was estimated to be at least twenty-two to twenty-three days each month. In the light of this estimate, the committee members were appalled to find that workers in Japan were struggling to find employment of any sort for only sixteen to seventeen days per month. The message was clear to the committee: they had to create jobs before anything else. They recommended to government that absolute priority in the allocation of capital and other production resources should be directed to a plan to achieve employment levels that would give workers the essential minimum number of days' work each month.

Numerous economic plans and administrative devices were formulated, evaluated and implemented to build the proposed employment plans. From these efforts the Priority Production Plan of 1947 was developed to ensure a return to industrial activity by allocating labour and resources on an exclusive basis to the coal and steel industries.[17] The Emergency Economic Policy of 1947 followed.[18] Its implementation was supported by the establishment of Keizai Antei Honbu, the Economic Stabilization Board, which was set up with a line-up of qualified officials drawn from government bureaucracy, private industry and academia. The board drew up many new policy proposals, such as those to provide social insurance, unemployment insurance and employment guarantees to employees, including casual day workers, to improve their working conditions and facilities, expanding housing construction for workers and increasing employment opportunities.

In the seven years of the Occupation period from 1945 to 1952 more than 4.5 million new jobs were created. The actual services realized under the proposal were not considerable viewed by today's standards and given the still underdeveloped stage of the economy of the country at the time. But the progressive thinking of the planners, as articulated in their intention to provide job security and a stable and better life, worked to build positive attitudes towards life at a most difficult time for the nation and its workers.

People began to speak about their aspirations for building a new Japan. It was in such an economic and social environment that the first Economic White Paper was published (see Chapter 2). People had ready ears for its analysis of the economic situation and its presentation of the theoretical basis for its policies, and believed that a new start should be made and that progress was possible. The writing of an 'indicative' plan began. It was a time when employment was scarce and living was hard and unstable. The principal purpose of the publication, to begin with, was to provide people with a positive view of society and with hope to improve their future life.

Even after several years of hard work, as late as 1952 the planners' objective of rebuilding the employment structure remained unfulfilled. For a start, not enough jobs were created and the GNP was lower as a result of fewer people employed. At the beginning of 1953, there were still 5.3 million unemployed workers with eight million more underemployed.[19]

Skewed industrial structure in a labour surplus, capital-poor society

In the process of attempts to create employment, some additional problems arose that could be described under the rubric of 'excessive competition' and the 'differential' or 'double (or dual) structure' of industry. Various kinds of forces operate in the economy. Some are disadvantaged workers without adequate training and experience, and some are marginal and small operators without adequate capital funds, equipment and technical and managerial knowledge. Yet they attempt to operate in competition with better-equipped contenders in the industry. In their efforts to secure jobs, disadvantaged workers accepted low wages and poor working conditions while marginal operators undercut profit margins and accepted undesirable trading terms, leading them, in turn, to become providers, offering poor wages and substandard working conditions.

These factors worked to increase the differential in income, work conditions and productivity between marginal and disadvantaged and well-provided sectors and industries, between villages and cities, farming and industrial sectors and smaller and larger enterprises.

Many economists and social researchers studied this 'excess *kato-kyoso* competition' and '*niju-kozo* differential industrial and employment structure'.[20] The planners felt they were a double failure – they saw themselves as failing to bring economic stability to people's lives and also as creating inequity in society in general. The supply of workers seeking employment rose and entrepreneurial efforts to create business opportunities grew but, with the economy's shortage of capital and the lack of purchasing power in the market, this dynamic power not only failed to bring economic growth but also created more unemployment or underemployment and an excessive capacity in production facilities. Although planners created strong participation among people in economic matters, this was not matched by employment opportunities. In short, there was a strong desire to develop economic activities, but this was not matched by capital accumulation and development of markets in the economy.

In such an unbalanced economic environment, people, managers and investors in businesses of all sizes sought opportunities for employment and investment in the hope of engaging in economic activities to the greatest extent. Businesses competed for market share, and workers competed for employment. Continuous new entrants flowed into markets, resulting in their operating below an optimal level. A high turnover of businesses, as a result of frequent new entries, business failures and withdrawals from the market, brought instability into the economy in general.

It is true that the differential structure and dual nature of the economy had existed in the pre-war years. But it had widened in this period despite, some argue, economic growth and the consequent advances in the capital and market development of the economy. This seems to suggest that economic growth and an increase in industrial activities will not only be ineffective in mitigating the extent of the differential structure but will work to destroy it.

Thus the problems came to be viewed as inherent to the economic and social structure of the country that had developed in the accelerated industrialization process that Japan had undergone.

To see the peculiarity of Japan's socio-economic system as the most important cause of the 'skewed structure' and to believe that it drove the economy into excessive competition became the standard view of economic researchers of the time. Many argued that the elimination of excessive competition would only be possible through modernizing the socio-economic system itself and not through expansion and growth of the economy.

The disappointing experience of the planners' growth efforts (for economic stability and equity) was seen as an illustration of how accelerating growth without appropriate policy supplements would bring more entrants into business and trade and make already excessive competition even more damaging. A policy of growth that aimed to create employment without an increase in productivity drove the economy into rapid inflation. Production facilities were overused without making due investment for depreciation. Some expressed concern about a quickly expanding economy that would help larger and better-equipped firms to grow faster than smaller and disadvantaged ones, leading the former to develop monopoly power. This would squeeze their smaller counterparts and enhance the differential structure even further. According to this train of thought, towards the end of the 1950s, the overall approach among the planners was to recommend that Japan's economic problems would be better dealt with under a reduced rate of growth.

Road to high economic growth

At the beginning of 1959 there was an opportunity to challenge the existing dominating negative view of the economy. Shimomura Osamu, a bureaucrat in the Ministry of Finance, presented a thought-provoking way of looking at the potential of the Japanese economy. He argued that looking at how the post-war reconstruction had progressed, businesses and corporations were expected to have accumulated enough capital to allow the strong entrepreneurial spirit to be realized through new investments. At the same time, people appeared to have accumulated substantial amounts of money to support the industrial expansion. He called this a time of upheaval in the economy. He estimated that the economy had developed the potential to grow very fast – at an annual rate of 10 per cent – and that its capacity to increase the rate every year would produce rapid social development in the country. By upheaval he was suggesting that the economy's high accumulation of resources would allow it to expand its production frontier and enlarge the scale of the national economy.

At first, most people thought Shimomura's prediction of 10 per cent growth highly optimistic but, as growth data for 1959 and 1960 became available, and showed that the economy was in fact continuing to grow fast, many began to see substance in his forecast.[21]

Nakayama Ichiro, a professor of economics, took up Shimomura's argument and drafted an economic plan to realize the projected growth potential in the economy. This is how the National Income-doubling Plan of 1960 came to be written.[22]

Shimomura is said to have believed that it was the duty of economists to present a picture of a better economic system to people outside the profession and to show them how it might be achieved. With this belief, he explained the growth potential of the economy. Nakayama also held a positive view of pursuing economic growth arguing that, to the extent that there is growth in the national economy, there is a corresponding potential in the economy to provide job security.

A plan was formulated to see economic growth leading to full employment with the effect of giving workers a better bargaining position so as to spread democratic ways in society in general.[23]

The political atmosphere under Prime Minister Ikeda encouraged policy makers to take maximum advantage of this predicted growth potential in the economy. There was also a pressing need to address the heated labour disputes and public protests of the time.[24] Nakayama understood this political atmosphere and saw that the economic recovery in Japan had reached a point at which it would be possible bring a rapid and widespread increase in personal incomes for people in general.

Shimomura's intuition proved to be correct. And it was fortunate for the Japanese economy that it had, at an opportune time, an economist such as Nakayama who could provide the theoretical underpinning to allow Shimomura's intuitive reading of the economy to be turned into relevant economic policy.

It was not formulated as a comprehensive plan for creating high-speed economic growth, but written to let people understand, as Shimomura wished, the high growth potential of the Japanese economy and to give governments a blueprint for an 'ideal' economic system. What the planners and policy writers formulated as a result of their experience of developing free enterprise with government help could be called 'Japan's mixed economy system'.

The motive for planning for the reconstruction of the war-destroyed economy in 1945–52 was the planners' determination to democratize the nation, yet pragmatically they used their wartime experiences to build a public-controlled economy inside Japan as well as building Manchuria in China.[25] Shimomura's argument and Nakayama's policy proposals led many in academia and government to speculate whether they would be able to use the planning know-how accumulated from the war years to build a planned market economy as part of the effort to catch up with advanced economies in the West.

In the six decades from the end of World War II to the present, successive governments have adopted many comprehensive national economic plans and industrial policies. Some have been forgotten because they did not provoke much public response; others are remembered because of the impact they made. But all are viewed as having contributed to building Japan's advanced and affluent economy.

Of all those national economic plans drawn up throughout the years since the first plan in 1947, the National Income-doubling Plan of

1960 is said to have been the most influential public plan written in post-war Japan and is remembered as marking the beginning of Japan's economic 'miracle', its period of high-speed growth in the 1960s. In terms of scope, its influence on the economy and the improvement that it brought to people's lives, it cannot be compared with any other plan.

Despite this, the plan was misinterpreted and the objective distorted and not followed correctly. Let me explain.

The aim of the plan was to bring an improvement in people's living standards as quickly as possible by building full employment rather than simply looking for rapid economic growth. To achieve this, five interrelated objectives were projected: to build adequate social and economic infrastructure facilities in industry and the economy; as a result, to build a high value-added production structure in industry; to promote export and other international economic activities; to promote human resources and research and development; and to reduce the dual production structure in industry and prices throughout the economy.

Of those five, the first was viewed as the most important for realizing the plan. It was at the heart of the economic development strategy. The plan saw securing adequate infrastructure facilities as bringing economic growth and industrial development and, as a consequence, better living standards for people. To achieve this, the government projected an active public investment of 60 per cent of the total capital investment during the planning period (to build infrastructure facilities), leaving private investment from the business sector to meet the remaining 40 per cent of new investments in the economy. In this way, the plan aimed to generate economic growth through public investment initiatives, thereby achieving a high, but controlled and stable, economic growth during 1961–70, the period under projection.

The economy, drawing on great enthusiasm for investment from business, grew much faster. The government was unable to keep pace with private capital formation, and an acute shortage of and deterioration in infrastructure facilities was created as the planning period advanced. Price rises were also rapid so that the projected stability in the economy was not realized. What was achieved in the planned period was a sudden rise in people's incomes and an equally fast improvement in the labour market, where jobs were secured by the arrival of virtual full employment. But the mode of the economy became highly erratic, eroding infrastructure facilities in the workplace so that the quality of people's life deteriorated rapidly.

It was certainly true that, by an improvement in people's living standards, the planners were looking at more than rising incomes and job security. They had higher aspirations than that. But as high economic growth emerged, failure to achieve the plan's objective was excused. Most people thought economic growth justified every shortfall in the economy and that the loss of economic stability and quality of life, and the deterioration of the natural environment, would be dealt with later.

The error has had a lasting adverse influence on the economic system. The achievement of high growth through the enthusiastic responses of entrepreneurial spirits in business and the population generally was exactly what the Japanese had hoped to bring about through its 'indicative plan'. A result had come, but not in a controlled or projected way.

Policy for economic adjustment, 1973–85

A turning point in the development of the Japanese planning mind came at the beginning of the 1970s, separating sharply the periods 1945–55, 1956–72 and 1973–85 from the periods 1986–92 and 1993–2003. It came suddenly and coincided with the arrival of the first oil crisis. It shook the very roots of the economy and became an evaluation point at which decision makers in government and business as well as the general public reflected on the country's economy, which had gone through such drastic changes in the preceding period of high growth and rapid industrialization. They began to ask what high economic growth had brought them.

The economy had to reallocate its workforce and production facilities to ensure that the national economy maintained high productivity and avoided creating unemployment. Skills in public administration were needed to carry out this task without raising unnecessary anxiety and causing confusion in the process. People began to see the administrators' task in government as adjusting conflicts of interest rather than planning for a better-performing economy.

Initially many officers enjoyed being called to the busy frontier of adjustment policy. Before long, however, their enthusiasm subsided, as they became physically exhausted as a result of long hours of work. They began to find that the adjustment policies were not giving them enough job satisfaction or fulfilling their work aspirations.[26] Japan's public administrators in economic ministry offices are elite appointments for which many able graduates keenly compete. They are trained to perform tasks to guide the economy, through planning and

policy writing, leaving such tasks as adjusting interests among industries and business to less qualified practitioners. A fall in work morale
in economic ministries such as MITI was to be expected as adjustment
policy continued to demand their time and effort because the officers
were recruited from the wrong group and had different motivations
and expectations.

Three forces emerged to fill in the vacuum left by the traditional economic bureaucrats. They arose in: (a) labour's initiative to control wage
rises; (b) labour unions' decision to work with government so as to take
part in public economic policy-writing activities; and (c) government's
(MITI's) new initiative to formulate relevant policy in its need to
respond to people's demand for improvement in quality of life.

First, workers won wage increases through the traditional efforts of
labour unions, particularly of Nikkeiren, All Japan Trade Unions. In the
decelerated economy, their concern was to seek the optimal wage
increase. It would be modest enough to be acceptable to employers,
given the deterioration in business conditions, but adequate to allow
workers to maintain their living standards in a time of severe price
rises.

During the high-speed economic growth in 1955–73, industrial
workers had received a high rate of real wage increase, which was
possible because the rise was supported by an equally high growth in
productivity.

The economic growth before the crisis in 1973 was certainly worthy
of the term 'miracle'. Both real GDP and labour productivity rose
rapidly between 1955 and 1965 (the real annual average growth rate of
GDP is estimated at over 10.0 per cent, while the rate of increase in
labour productivity is estimated at something between 8.0 and 9.0 per
cent during the period).[27] Labour unions demanded and successfully
gained high wage increases that exceeded 20 per cent every year during
the period. Such a high performance continued until it reached its
peak in 1973, when the unions demanded phenomenal wage rises of
39.9 per cent and succeeded in receiving 32.9 per cent. But even in the
industrial sector, where technical and technological improvements
have been actively introduced, the productivity increase was lower. In
other sectors, such as agricultural and services industries, for example,
the modernization of production and management fell behind,
causing price rises for products and services. The relative poor performance in those sectors brought unbalanced results, which influenced
the overall economic performance. This brought a rapid rise in consumer prices by nearly 20 per cent annually during the boom years.
Such inflationary trends, however sharp and continuous, had been

tolerated when the economy enjoyed boom conditions, when people made some gains one way or another. So it was not until the end of 1973 that academics, bureaucrats and business leaders began to express their alarm over the expected effect of the loss of international competitiveness of Japan's exports.

When consumer and wholesale prices rose sharply from 1973 into 1974 and 1975, many people began to discuss a causal connection between large-scale wage rises and inflation.[28] The need to understand the extent and the nature of the link between the two emerged as an important issue.

The government, through the EPA, organized a study committee in May 1974 before the annual regular *shunto*, spring offence.[29] It conducted a large-scale econometric study. The committee eventually published its findings just in time for the nation's wide wage bargaining campaign, so that the possible problems of a wage–price spiral could be discussed widely across industries.[30]

The study confirmed the causal relation between wage increases and rising prices, particularly consumer prices. Consequently, the government recommended that, in order to keep inflation between 6 and 8 per cent (so that Japan's export industries maintain their international competitiveness), the annual wage rises should be kept between 15 and 20 per cent.

Observing the results of the government survey, Nikkeiren made an independent study of the relationship between wage increases and inflation. It organized a study group with twenty members drawn from the ranks of executives in industries and corporations and seven from the academy. The study findings were in line with those of the government. The study group saw the need to keep the demand for wage increases sufficiently low so as not to lose real income increases through the wage–price spiral. In 1975 the Nikkeiren's voluntary wage rise ceiling was 15 per cent. It was reduced to 8.8 per cent in the next year to match a corresponding rise in the consumer price of 10.4 per cent in 1975 to 9.5 per cent in 1976 and further to 3.8 per cent by the end of 1978.

Throughout the second half of the 1970s and the 1980s, industrial firms in Japan faced severe competition in the world export market. As a result, workers decided to cooperate with employers in their attempt to reduce production costs by restructuring their production and workplace arrangements.

Workers agreed to work, for example, long hours into the evenings and during weekends and to take up different jobs on production lines. At the beginning they began to cooperate merely for the purpose of securing employment in difficult times, but gradually employees began to take on new roles to find ways to reduce costs on the shop floor and to take the initiative in restructuring work schedules. They began to see the benefits from actively participating in employers' decisions about investment and general corporate management practices. A specific form of employee participation in management tasks developed.

Workers also decided to develop themselves as a human resource, selecting a non-conflict, non-militaristic style that they believed would bring them better conditions and well-being. In other words, they chose to look for an improvement in living standards through national prosperity. As part of their strategy for wage increases, but later as a result of their own actions, workers showed a growing interest in the nation's economic planning.

Following Nikkeiren's initiative, other trade unions began to be politically active, seeking partnerships with policy-making offices in the government. They decided to push their influence in national economic management so that their 'ideal' would be reflected in the public policy programme.

Workers had begun to see that the time had come for them to take the initiative in making economic policy. In particular larger labour unions – those industry-based ones and some enterprise-based trade unions in large established corporations – began to work closely with government in writing economic policies for the country. They began to study macroeconomics to gain skills to enable them to make proposals for tax reform, employment and income policy formulas and social security structures. Those proposals addressed the need to secure the minimum welfare conditions for workers and protect their living standards. They believed that union leaders should take the initiative in planning and policy writing now that the economic bureaucrats were preoccupied with day-to-day administrative tasks and formulating adjustment policies.[31]

Despite concerns by union leaders, it would not be entirely correct to argue that the government had lost its planning mind. The Ministry, for example, had developed an industry structure policy in writing the 'Vision Policy for the 1970s', published in May 1971.[32] In this policy, the Ministry announced its decision to direct the public effort towards the improvement of people's living standards from the previous target of growth of the national economy. They had come to see that the Japanese economy and industry had reached a high enough standard of development with adequate capital accumulation and industrial and managerial technologies which would allow the country to plan for a high stage of social development. The Ministry called for an active contribution from government, both in the allocation of public funds and in the initiation of public programmes to build an economy whose purpose was to improve people's living standards and provide them with opportunities. The Ministry officially endorsed the proposition of promoting social progress – made earlier by Shimomura and Nakayama as the principal logic for the National Income-doubling Plan – by installing infrastructure facilities across the country. It is progress towards building a welfare society. Yet as we will argue later, the thinking of the Ministry was still constrained because of its orientation towards economic growth. Its aim of improving people's living standards without any discussion of the quality of their lives reveals its limitation as planning for the true welfare of people.

Unfortunately, this idea of building a welfare economy was put to rest as soon as the economy met the oil crisis in 1973 and in this way adjustment policy developed throughout the 1970s, and the leading minds in government, including those in MITI itself, were occupied on day-to-day administrative work. It was only in 1980 that the Ministry eventually came to regain its planning approach and published its 'Vision Policy for the 1980s'.[33]

This policy was to resume the traditional approach that had brought a successful result in 1948. The planners once again appealed to the population for their understanding of the difficulties that the economy was experiencing difficulties and called for their cooperation in order to overcome the problems.

Instead of proposing any economic policy to solve the problems, this time the planners asked the population what the role and function of government should be. In this way, the Ministry let people know that this time government was unable to plan the shape of the desired new economic society and was thus unable to guide them except to say that they realized that Japan had reached a stage where they had to revise their approach towards economic, social and educational activities. The Ministry was clear in its understanding of the scale of the task, noting in its vision policy that it was as large as, if not larger than, the task that challenged the Meiji people at the time of the Restoration. By making clear that the task was large and fundamental, the Ministry hoped that people would understand that the task would involve rebuilding the country's economic structures and was beyond piecemeal devices that had been used until that time. To clarify the position of government, in 1981 the Ministry published its vision policy under the title, 'Japan is in search of new national goal'.[34]

The Ministry, then, moved away from its traditional leadership position and began its new approach. It called for ideas from industry and households, urging people to come up with proposals and to articulate ideas about the direction the nation should take. In this way, the government withdrew from initiating plans and writing policy and began to consult people generally on the policies they wanted.

At the beginning of the 1980s foreign observers began to praise Japan as the economy made a swift recovery from the oil crisis, reading in it a sign of the superior quality of Japanese economic management and corporate strategy. The view of 'Japan as No. 1' arose.[35] Soon economists and sociologists reported examples of the effectiveness of Japan's approach. It was a quite change because, until then, the Japanese had always been sceptical about the worth of their corporate management skills and practice.

As the high economic performance continued, many in Japan began to see their approach as superior to that practised in the West. The lifetime employment system, the practice of seniority-based promotion, enterprise-based labour unions, and the national economic management observed in macroeconomic and industrial policy received the most positive evaluation. In this reverential mood, people in business and government forgot the Ministry's plea in its 1980s vision policy to initiate their own thoughts about Japan's future direction.

The move towards smaller government

The publication of the Maekawa Report in 1986 eventually provoked the minds of the self-satisfied people of Japan. The report was commissioned by the then Prime Minister, Nakasone Yasuhiro, in response to his concern about how to mitigate the pressure arising from demand in overseas economies. He feared that the criticism, if not countered adequately, would cause Japan to lose its international market.

This is how the pressure developed and forced Nakasone to act as he did. Throughout the 1970s, with the aim of solving difficulties caused by oil crises, industrial firms in Japan made considerable efforts to revise and reform their production structure. Various new managerial approaches were tried to reduce costs and improve the quality of products so as to secure export markets. The effort brought results in the high praise of Japanese management systems from corporations abroad, as I have noted earlier. Exports from Japan rose, but imports into Japan did not increase. This drove trading economies abroad into an accumulated trade deficit against Japan.

Suffering from problems of trade imbalance, they began to criticize Japan, seeing it as highly selfish in driving exports without allowing a free inflow of imports. Japan's behaviour was branded as against the spirit of international cooperation for world peace and prosperity. Government initiatives thus far promoted in Japan were taken to remove almost all import restrictions, encourage imports and refrain from exporting. Yet nothing brought the desired results.

The criticism alarmed Nakasone so much that he believed Japan's actions would isolate it from the international economy. He commissioned a survey to examine the problems and the Maekawa Report was compiled in 1986 in response.[36] It concluded that Japan's imports would not increase, despite the growth of the economy and the rise in people's incomes, given the way industrial activities were conducted in business in the country.[37] It said that the increase in people's disposable income would only result in a rise in their savings because most workers, having been driven to work hard and for long hours in the employer's effort to reduce costs, could not find the time to spend their disposable income.

Entrepreneurial efforts in business brought an increase in exports but not in imports. What, then, should be done to counter the criticism from abroad? The report prescribed the reduction of work hours. It recommended that people be given free time for leisure activities with a view to spending more on goods and services and this, as a result, would produce an increase in imports. This was a simple piece of economic logic. The importance of this argument, however, lay in its suggestion that the Japanese economy would have no future unless the Japanese changed their attitude to work by reducing the pressure of intensive matters of life and long working hours, without free time for leisure activities – in other words to improve the quality of life for its workers.

The writing of the report was induced by political concerns of international diplomacy. But when it was published it immediately provoked people's discontent about their poor quality of life, which did not match their industrious efforts. The search for a better-structured society began.

Yet so far no clear ideas have been formulated about how that society might be designed or structured. The persistent demise of the economy since the middle of the 1990s speaks of this failure, and there was an urgent need to pull the economy out of what appeared to have been an economic stalemate.

5
The Spirit of Japan's Political Economy[1]

Study through interviews conducted in 1994–2005

In this chapter I examine the professional and personal profiles of several public administrative officers working in the Ministry (formerly MITI and since 2002 METI) between 1994 and 2005. I examine their professional work in promoting economic welfare and their individual attempts to solve problems, and the difficulties they encountered while doing so.

Because I believe economic planning and policy writing reflect the quality of the people involved, I examine closely the officers' personalities and backgrounds, and how they uphold their values and preferences. To explain why economic policy has been written in the form in which it appears, I need to know what economic understanding the economic policy writers have, how they perceive the economy's problems and potential and, most of all, what they regard as the ideal economic society. In any job people project their own image through their work. This is especially true of economic planners.

The public administrative officers I study in this chapter are grouped into three generations. The first group consists of those senior officers who were born before the end of World War II and whose formative years were in the 1930s. The second group includes the generation born towards the end of the 1930s who have seen the effort the country made to restructure the war-damaged economy. The third group consists of those who were brought up in the 1950s and 1960s in a period of high economic growth and without much memory of Japan as a low-income economy. In addition I have some preliminary findings on of younger officers who were born at the beginning of the 1970s.

National economic planners draw an overall picture of economic activities to demonstrate that the government believes it is bringing about the ideal form of economy, and that public help of various kinds will be available to business so that it can contribute to building that ideal. Part of such help is provided by the public administrative officers who write economic policy, regulations, and rules to guide business and households in following a productive path in a controlled and proper manner, and to make the proposed ideals become the reality.

I asked the bureaucrats a series of questions, such as what was their style in conducting their public duty; what motivated them to become public servants, and in particular to work at the Ministry; how they see themselves as public servants; what qualities and abilities they wanted to develop in their public service career, what they understood as their duties and obligations, and their satisfaction in working as public servants compared to employment in private business, or as academics, artists, or self-employed consultants; how they adapted professionally and personally to become the best person for their work; and what kind of society they wanted to contribute to building in Japan.

Through interviews I studied the development in personalities and professional attitudes of the bureaucrats so that I could determine if any changes took place between my initial interviews in 1994 and 1995 and those of 2003. Since the initial interview meeting I have continued to meet some of them to follow up our previous discussions as opportunities arose.[2] Those follow-up interview meetings were conducted on a more informal basis than before. This allowed me to study how their professional approach had developed, their views on the Japanese economy and the country in general, along with the industrial and economic development that has led the Japanese people to make different demands on the government and its planners and policy writers.[3] I hoped to see what kinds of people were suited to the job, and what education and career development they needed in order to make a useful contribution in the newly emerging developed and affluent Japan.

I also wished to follow the change and development in their own personality as they accumulated experience and progressed in their careers.

In Chapter 4 above I discussed how the national economy has begun in recent years to replace 'growth and efficiency' with 'quality of life'. At such a time of change, it was to be expected that the Ministry would also change its administrative style and would attract different people with various talents to respond to the new tasks entrusted to them.

The interviews gave me a rich opportunity to observe the diversity in work styles that reflected the personalities of the officers and the range of assumptions they held about the economy and society on which they assessed policy issues. In general my interviewees were ordinary public administrators without exceptional political or economic power. Despite this, I viewed their role in making Japan's economic society as significant because, when people with different personalities, backgrounds and aspirations are attracted to jobs in government offices still with the expectation of lifelong employment, they can be expected to alter the direction of that society.

Interview surveys

Samples and meetings

I conducted three different forms of interview at different times. As noted above, the first were conducted in 1994 and 1995 with a relatively large number of officers. (There were 71 in total; Appendix Table 5.1 shows their personal details in the year when they joined the Ministry and their age and rank held at the time of my initial interview meetings.) In the process of the interview meetings I decided to select four officers for an in-depth study of their experience. I held many regular meetings and discussions with them up to the present (2004). I report the study results in Chapters 6–9 below as case studies.

The first interviews took place during 1994, when 71 'career' civil service (class I) officers at the Tokyo Home Office were selected for my study.[4] They were responsible for policy writing and high-level administrative tasks. They were the staff members who were expected to rise to the most senior positions in the Ministry during what would be lifelong service (generally spanning 20 to 35 years).

My interviewees were selected by a group of officers in the Ministry who agreed to help me.[5] The 71 officers were selected as representative of the staff of the Ministry in terms of personality, attitudes to work, observed political orientation and career paths. Except for the group of very senior officers at or above the rank of bureau head (generally in their early to middle fifties), at least two were selected from each year's intake in the years 1958–91. (The number of career officers the Ministry appointed each year ranged from 15 to 26 or 27, depending on the budget allocation and the availability of quality candidates.) There were few very senior officers in active service at the office.[6] I got the impression that in the years of my study the Ministry had been very pleased with their success in attracting high-quality candidates.

Procedure

I took special care in designing the questions and style of interview to encourage the officers to discuss freely their motivations and ways of decision making. The central questions were about their understanding of their work, what contribution they hoped and felt confident to make, what policy and administrative devices they selected – and how they assessed them against other alternatives, and how they evaluated past achievements of officers in the Ministry.

Before each interview, I gave my interviewees a two-page explanatory summary (in Japanese) of the purpose of the study and my academic and personal background. The interviews were conducted as free discussions so that we – the interviewer and the respondents – would come together as equals to exchange views on matters of mutual interest, in this case their work at the Ministry.

I chose this approach to help me explore their views, ideals and motives. The interview was relaxed, and conducted without time constraints to enable the interviewees to expand on the topics and give the interview as much depth as possible.

In almost all cases I had given the interviewees time to study my questions and research proposal before meeting them to discuss their thoughts. All but a few very senior officers met me without setting any time limits on the interview. Most of the conversations were not taped, but I took notes during the meetings, frequently pausing and interrupting the flow of the discussion to encourage the interviewees to think aloud, debate and confirm what they had said. Each interview usually lasted one and a half hours. Of the 71 initial interviewees, 26 agreed to see me once or twice more.

Officers in the Ministry

It is estimated that in 1994 there were 638 administrative Class I officers working at the Tokyo Home Office who had been recruited over almost four decades. During that time considerable changes had taken place in Japan's economy and society. We expect that those 638 officers brought a rich variety of personalities and talents into the Ministry with their diverse social, educational and personal backgrounds and their distinct ways of thinking and personal values, all of which I hoped to identify during the course of the discussions.

I was interested to find out 1) what sort of people were recruited to the Ministry throughout the period between 1958 (when my most senior interviewee joined the Ministry) and 1994–95 at the time when our initial interview meetings took place, and 2) whether any differences appeared in their personalities and abilities as bureaucrats. Besides individual differences, I expected to see differences in policy writing and administrative styles, and the development of new ideas among each generation of officers. This would be possible despite the Ministry's distinct administrative style and mode of conducting economic and business matters by providing 'on-the-job' training to new recruits.[7]

Preliminary findings, 1994 and 1995

Self-assessment

It is well documented that popular ministries in the central government, such as this Ministry and the Ministry of Finance (now called Zaimu-sho), have been staffed heavily (more than 80 per cent, often approaching 90 per cent) by graduates from a limited group of universities. The most notable is Tokyo University, with its Law School the most important training-ground for would-be public servants in the popular ministries. This came about because Tokyo University was established in 1886 with the aim of creating administrative officers to build a modern industrial Japan following the Meiji Restoration in the same year. Since then, the University and, in particular, the Law School, has attracted young students wishing to seek a career in public service and has continued to provide what was regarded as the required training.

Given the traditional importance of government, particularly central government, in promoting industrial development as the national aim, many talented young people sought public administrative careers. The university was open to anyone, regardless of social standing or family background, who passed the standard public entrance examination. Many young people were encouraged to study hard from their early schooldays so that they would succeed in entering the University and finding a position in the Law School in preparation for being recruited into those ministries that would give them good careers, a stable income and high status in society. The tradition is still practised to a large extent today although a gradual change has taken place, as discussed at the end of this chapter. It is therefore generally correct to state that people who are recruited to the Ministry are those who came with a fine academic record from school and university and, understandably, had good self-esteem, confidence in themselves, and a belief in their ability to achieve whatever they wished. People around them acknowledged their worth and approved of their self-esteem.

As a result, a sense of élitism grew among the group. I will argue later that this appears to have introduced a style of working in which officers relied on their intellectual judgement and the group's accumulated knowledge and experience as the basis for administrative and policy decisions.

To get a basic understanding of what kind of people they really were when they entered the Ministry, I put a question to my interviewees about their personal views on and attitudes towards serving as public administrators in government offices. Specifically, I asked if they could recall and illustrate the original reason that led them to seek a position in the Ministry in preference to work in private enterprise, succeeding in their family business, or becoming a professional such as an academic, lawyer, journalist or critic, what they expected to achieve, and the nature of the satisfaction they were looking for in such a job.

What I received were simple and clear answers from the majority of the interviewees. They said that they selected a public service vocation because, in their words, they wanted to serve the community and society and people in Japan. In other words, they wanted to work to serve the public and for 'larger ideas' than 'private interest and profit'. When asked to clarify that phrase, they used the word *koeki* (in the public interest) for their preference for seeking employment in the public sector. Such an answer may sound too simplistic and idealistic to be credible. What I want to see is what it actually means.

For almost all of the interviewees, the Ministry, MITI, was the first department they chose. (There were only three exceptions – people who said that, at the time, a judicial administrative position appeared to give them more opportunities to serve society.) Behind this choice was their decision to select a public service vocation in preference to the available alternatives. Such a decision was made in most cases during, if not before, their final year of university.

How did my interviewees obtain their position in their Ministry? To be selected for a public service vocation as a Class I career officer in one of the popular ministries such as MITI, one must first pass the senior civil service examination held each year in July. A graduation record from a prestigious university in Japan within the top 10 to 15 per cent academic record is also required.[8] In addition, I observed that the successful candidates had to demonstrate that they had the 'right' personality for the Ministry, that is, someone with an open and friendly manner who is ready to take on challenges rather than an earnest and hard-working but inflexible person, regardless of high intelligence. All the interviewees recalled their strong preference for a 'public' service vocation, particularly one in the Ministry, with its specific work style and officers' profile. Other ministries, such as Construction or

Transport, were the second choice, with their work closely connected to the building of a modern industrial basis for national economic expansion.

Up to the middle of the 1980s we may understand that by 'private' interests they meant working for private corporations. However, to some senior (by age) officers certain private companies like Nippon Steel and Industrial Bank (now Mizuho Financial Group after it merged with Fuji and Dai-ichi Kangyo Banks) were excluded from this 'private' category. They viewed Nippon Steel and Industrial Bank as equal to government ministries, appreciating the important role they played in promoting industrial development in the country, and acknowledging that steel making in Japan had been traditionally positioned as central to building the country's industrial basis before and after the war. As for the Industrial Bank of Japan, throughout the 1950s and 1960s it worked very closely with the Ministry, and by providing cheap finance it assisted the development of industries designated by the Ministry for rapid establishment of heavy and chemical industries. These two companies appear to have made their way into the semi-public category because of their close working relationship with the Ministry.

In a similar vein, some officers in the 'core' group recalled that they contemplated joining trading companies as their second or third choices after MITI. This reflected their appreciation, at the time of their entry in the 1970s and the early 1980s, of the importance of exports to the promotion of industries in Japan. In essence, these interviewees sought a lifetime commitment to making a contribution to the industrial development of the country and found the Ministry the most appropriate place to do it.

Public servants, as the term implies, must have as their basic work motivation desire to serve for the public good. For all that, I find it striking that there seem to have been virtually no changes in these students' aspirations to 'serve for the public good' or more specifically 'serve the industrial development of the nation' across the overall generations to which my interviewees belong. Are we to understand that all these prized students had sought and gained a position in the Ministry with a motivation that has remained virtually unaltered from 1958 (the year when my oldest interviewee entred the Ministry) until 1994–95 when I met them to conduct my initial interview meetings, despite the fact that the Japanese had begun to question the importance of economic growth? The motivation that led these young people to seek a position in the Ministry is not much more than a general desire to be associated with a 'large and public task'. They discounted the importance of 'activities of private companies'. I presumed that they had developed this respect for government and private business without being clear about how they would engage in these public works, how they might contribute, and why and in what ways work in the private sector would prevent them from making such a contribution. Their ideas could only be articulated clearly after they had observed how the people in the Ministry worked, receiving on-the-job training and working in a team environment.

The making of public administrators is the issue. Through discussions with my interviewees I tried to understand how the new recruits had been trained and to identify the characteristic features that make them different from their counterparts in business, academia and other work places. I soon saw that all of my interviewees had the same aim. It was their view of how best to achieve it that differed. That arose from the differences in their personalities and from their understanding of the needs of the economy as much as from their own assessment of their own talent and lack of experience and training.

Koeki (in the public interest)

Concept

Japan is not the only place where working for the public good has been practised as the work principle. Many attempts have been made to clarify the concept, but to evaluate the quality of public service it is important to see how administrative staff apply this concept in making decisions and carrying out their responsibilities.

In 1987 Glendon Schubert set out to define the concept of public interest in administrative decision making as taking three distinct forms. He named them 'administrative rationalism', 'administrative Platonism' and 'administrative realities'.[9]

In essence he argues that advocates of 'administrative rationalism' accept the goals as given to them (by politicians, for example). He thinks the decision-making process in administrative and policy writing is value-neutral. The bureaucrats are a group of experts who carry out a technical process and therefore public interest, or *koeki*, will be at its best in rationalizing the decision-making process. According to this view, elected politicians choose the direction and values of public policy. Public servants, on the other hand, remain neutral.

The advocates of 'administrative Platonism', however, hope to build an idealistic state. Public servants in this category may be persuaded to make the best of the scope of their administrative autonomy when they view the available legislature as an inadequate source for public policy. They prefer to replace these shortfalls with their own judgements, imagination, expertise and dedication in working towards the good of society – as they define it.

The advocates of 'administrative realities' are sceptics who do not find any substantive value in the concepts of 'the public interest' or 'the public good', however they may be defined. Instead, they see administrators as mere catalysts who balance special interests in society and translate the outcome into the public interest.

Public administrative responsibility lies in the skilful running of procedures to realize peaceful adjustments between conflicting interests. In Chapter 4 I have shown how bureaucrats in this mould worked in the period of 'adjustment policy' in the 1970s in Japan.

To begin with, I introduced a discussion about their interpretations of *koeki* at our early stage of meeting. This was done to gain a clear understanding of the types of personalities to be found among my interviewees, the kinds of value judgements they rely on when writing policy, and the administrative styles they prefer to follow.

I asked two questions: how different is the work of bureaucrats from that of business executives, managers and academics, for example? and what conditions are needed to initiate 'good' programmes and write effective policies?

Many older groups said that good conditions would be found where there is a clear national aim driving the public will in a politically autonomous direction. Under these conditions, economic bureaucrats can concentrate on developing effective economic objectives and identifying adequate economic and administrative instruments. But if there is no clear aim, what do they do? Do they integrate politics and administration for the sake of speedy delivery of policy results? Or will this allow bureaucrats too wide a scope for discretionary decision making?[10]

The problem is that it became more difficult to secure those 'good conditions' as Japan moved in a post-industrial affluent direction with 'public will' expressed in increasingly diverse ways.

As a part of its programme of administrative reform, the Koizumi government is evaluating discretionary decision making and the bureaucrats will be asked to establish clear guidelines for their work approach so as to bring transparency to public administrative and policy-writing work. Not much progress appears to have yet been made.

Characteristics of officers

I soon found a discrepancy between the work pursued by public administrative officers in Schubert's world and that by my interviewees. Schubert argues that (1) his officers seek to maximize the welfare of the population, (2) their work is carried out on a value-free basis without their own contribution to shaping this public purpose, and (3) they experience dilemma and difficulty when they find that there is no clearly drawn public purpose. To counter the problems and difficulties, they seek better administrative skills. They strive to be good and responsible public administrators.

The counterparts in Japan behave differently. My understanding of the role of public administrative officers through the discussions with my interviewees can be outlined as follows: (a) it is also true that the Japanese counterparts seek the improvement of the welfare of the population as our discussion above on *koeki* showed, but differences emerge when we see that (b) the officers in Japan do not see and treat the public purpose as value-free. They work to draw their own picture of the public purpose. To achieve this, (c) they rely on their own judgement and intellectual capacity. This is a difficult task and it is where individual officers develop their own approach and devices. They strive to be good and responsible public planners and policy writers. On this understanding I expand and incorporate the three characteristics suggested by Schubert into my own.

The characteristic features of the Japanese officers are shown in Figure 5.1, with a general observations of each of my types. An in-depth examination of the observation will follow in the specific experience of the four selected individual officers in Chapters 6–9 below.

Characteristics of Japanese public administrative officers through my interviews

In Figure 5.1 four bureaucratic types are separated based on their preferred approach to their professional work. The matrix measures 'intellectually directing' against 'society consulting' along the vertical axis, and 'planning' against 'administrative technique' along the horizontal axis.

In comparing the 'planner' (right hand of the diagram) with the administrator (left hand of the diagram), I explore the difference between reliance on intellectual competence in the former and reliance on the messages

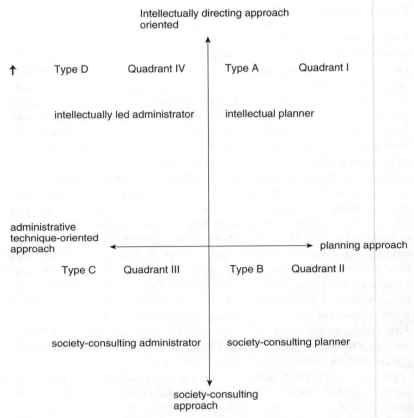

Figure 5.1   Administrative profile (as observed in 1994–96)

coming from and/or sought in society in the latter. The officers who choose to rely more on 'planning and directing' approaches (positioned in the upper part of the figure) are those who believe there are people in society wise and informed enough to understand the problems and thus able to guide social changes (they see themselves as such). The officers positioned on the opposite pole (on the right axis of the figure) believe that no one individual or group in society can achieve a high degree of competence in the organization of social change for a better end.

Since my first interview meetings in 1994 I noted an increase in personal differences in the professional approaches among my interviewees. The different styles that had begun to develop reflect the difference in their evaluation of the importance of 'uncertainty' in the economy after the period of growth was over and the transition made to Japan's affluent stage. This was a time when government planners no longer felt confident that they could interpret people's needs or their concept of welfare, and feared that they had lost the basis on which to write policy with confidence. This fear was felt as a common concern, but the extent differed between those who were older and had work experience at a time when steady and stable economic growth was promoted as a national aim, and the younger ones who came into the Ministry after the growth period and were looking to find a new direction for the economy.

Let me show how the difference emerged. Through my observations I constructed four types, A, B, C and D, into which our interviewees are grouped. Figure 5.1 shows the relative position of the four images in the light of the degree of importance of 'intellectual' as against 'society consulting' approaches and reliance on 'planning' as against 'administrative' techniques.

In grouping individual officers into each quadrant, I took account of the differences in the worth of the administrative contributions, as against planning efforts, that is, between technical and administrative skills, on the one hand, and the quality and content of public programmes, on the other. Officers who try to maximize *koeki* through the promotion of skilful and often innovative administrative procedures (like those in Schubert's argument) are thus located on the left axis. Those who believe that the value of public programmes and the contribution of bureaucrats to society are based on the quality of good public programmes are on the right axis.

Now, to explain the four types of public administrators, let us move horizontally, west to east, measuring bureaucrats' preference for conducting their work through public administrative means over the planning and policy writing method. Thus Types C and D represent public administrators. Moving vertically from north to south, I explore the difference between reliance on intellectual competence in the former as against reliance on the message coming from and/or sought in society in the latter. Types A and D represent intellectual director types. To repeat, D and C in the left quadrants of the figure represent administrative types, distinct from A and B in the right quadrants who represent planner types; and A and D in the upper part of the figure represent director types while B and C in the lower part of the figure represent the liberal society-consulting type.

We find C and D officers in older (by age and seniority) groups of officers. They entered the Ministry in the 'golden age' of industrial policy in the 1960s when the national aim was clear, allowing them to operate as 'neutral' administrative promoters of public programmes until the confusion brought about by the oil crises in the 1970s and the transformation in the economy. They have lived and worked in the Ministry where the notion of the public purpose they were serving was closely aligned with industrial development and economic growth. The change in the economy was too sudden for them to react other than in a stopgap way by writing policies for 'adjustment'.

Most of them indicated at the interviews that they felt uncomfortable in stepping outside the 'neutral' boundary of the 'classic public adminis-trator' when confronted with the need to make their own decisions about policy issues and make priority rankings. They were likely to continue to rely on their already-formed beliefs and the comfort of the familiar administrative approach in the face of changes in the country's economy.

I locate them in the third quadrant in Figure 5.1 and call them Type C bureaucrats, a 'society-consulting administrators', with their orientation towards the administrative approach by expecting guidance from outside to them to tell what they should aim to maximize through their public service work. Let us draw further the professional profiles of each type.

Type C

Type C, society-consulting administrator, is the most traditional type we come across in the Ministry. When formulating this type I had in mind one specific interviewee. At our first interview he told me that he remembered his tasks in the second half of the 1960s, when heading various fields in the industry policy bureau and the industrial structure bureau, as comparable with those of a chairman of a committee. Subsequently, while holding a senior position, he spent much of his time organizing meetings with industry interest groups, bringing them together for discussions to find out their concerns and thus select the Ministry's policy issues. He then came back to his office in the Ministry and organized a task force by allocating his staff in the department to assess the writing of policy within the immediate needs and demands of these interest groups.

He stressed that he saw the basic nature of the working norm in the Ministry as approximating, contrary to the popular 'revisionist' observation made among economic and business researchers and polit-ical scientists in the USA, to the 'chairman' of industry and business gatherings. Should we call this approach one of public leadership? he asked himself. He finds that the approach that the Ministry followed, and which in fact he himself practised as a very senior public servant in the 1970s, was to make efforts to build consensus support for what the government wanted to see among a group of interested business representatives.

There was another officer who appeared to share the approach of the officer discussed above. This officer pointed out the 'generalist' nature of the skills of the bureaucrat in the Ministry. As I discuss in one of the case studies in Chapter 6, the customary appointment procedure in the Ministry is for career officers to move regularly every two to three years between bureau and departments. It is true that their administrative and technical skills may develop, leading officers to be good at accessing administrative and policy matters on an overall economic and social basis to provide general welfare improvement to the nation and people. But when the maintenance of this economic and social basis itself meets a challenge, their 'generalist' skill will not work effectively. When fundamentally new reform is required, bureaucrats with generalist skills and training appear to make only limited contributions. They could be called 'regulatory agents', who make the utmost effort to fulfil the public will in the most cost-efficient manner by wielding the administrative skills, information and personal and professional contacts available to them through public and industry personnel links and organizational networks. They are the masters of 'administrative manipulation'. The most distinct contribution they try to make is to crystallize common and popular purposes in the society of the time so as to articulate the purposes (public aim) as economic objectives. Without their initiative the purposes of society may otherwise be left standing in the market, aimlessly waiting for articulation. This is where their public contribution comes in.

Type D

Type D can be called 'intellectual administrators', who share the appreciation of administrative skills with their seniors in Type C, but differ from those seniors on the basis of their approach towards the market mechanism. They do not see the market as given and allowed to guide their administrative responsibilities and the implementation of public programmes. They study the market so as to predict the equilibrium solution; that is, they try to predict the equilibrium point the market will eventually find. They try to predict it one step ahead, in order to save time. They believe it is important to foresee the equilibrium solution. They are proud of their craft of locating and identifying what the general public wants – which has not yet been expressed in a clear form by people in the market. According to them, the responsibility of administrators is not to alter that equilibrium solution but to help society to find it and save industry and the workers from experiencing the meddling process of the market. 'Soft landing' is the expression that has often been used to describe the administrative skill of smoothly and swiftly guiding the competition process to the eventual market equilibrium foreseen by government.

The role of public administrators is seen in this case as their ability to guide the economy to avoid the misallocation and thus the misuse of resources in the trial-and-error process of the market. Type D bureaucrats fear the misallocation and misuse of resources not only because they bring inefficiency into the economy, but also because they introduce unemployment, bankruptcies, and other economic and social problems associated with economic uncertainties, and reduce the general welfare of the people. They believe good public administrators should minimize the casualties and accidents in society, which emerge in the dynamic process of economic growth and industrial development, as much as promoting the process of growth and development.[11]

What differentiates Type D from Type C is the former's wish to use more of their intellectual judgement than the latter.

Type A

Officers in Type A are busy because they follow, so they say, the old Confucian norm of *senyu-koraku* (prepare for the problems and difficulties ahead to enjoy peace) as their fundamental 'mission'. They wish to promote such a norm with their faith in the support available in their own intellectual capacity *supplemented by* available public information and experience accumulated in the Ministry. Their concept of 'public will', however, is not the same as that described by Schubert as 'administrative Platonism'. They have to find it through their work and articulate it by the full use of their intellectual capacity, public information and experiences gained through working in the Ministry. They are ready to have a debate for a better understanding of the 'public will' and the shape of an ideal society in which the officers seek to incorporate the 'public will' as much as possible.

Further, they are ready to direct their administrative skills to manipulate the expressed form of public will in order to write plans and policy that should be workable with public support.

Those in Type A are aggressive in their personal behaviour, speaking more loudly than others at various occasions as if to make up for their lack of numbers in order to present themselves as representatives of the Ministry.

Type B

The staff in this group are by no means the forgotten minority but comprise officers who are in one way or another slightly to one side of the traditional officers in the Ministry. Based on my interview enquiries conducted in 2003, I formed an expectation that this group would become the majority in coming years. Their somewhat odd-man-out postures are reflected in their personal characteristics, mannerisms and educational background. Their educational backgrounds are mostly outside the mainstream; they have reached the Ministry through the traditional avenue of degrees from Tokyo University and other prestigious universities, but their qualifications (in economics, sociology, history and general culture) may be seen by some as 'soft' options as against the 'hard' and 'main' subjects in the law degree. Their personal manners are more reserved and quiet. In comparison, they do not project themselves, as some of their seniors do, as 'shining bright champions' in the public service profession. During the course of the interviews I occasionally sensed their detached feelings towards their colleagues in Types A and D who, in their own words, appear to behave as 'patriots', carrying all the problems and burdens of the national economy on their shoulders.

Fundamentally the Type B officers are hesitant to believe in society's ability to produce comprehensive theories of social change that serve to guide society's improvement. Equally they are sceptical about any 'super' personalities who are expected to guide others either through personal intellectual power or administrative skills and political manoeuvre. They are inclined to think that society can, at best, produce only scattered partial theories – about selected industries and markets or the national economy. They think that society, even with the successful collection of individual theories and relevant observations, is unable to build that understanding into a comprehensive set of guidelines. Despite having such doubts, the officers see that it is important for bureaucrats to make positive efforts to seek ways to increase the well-being of the nation and the people and hope to write public plans and programmes towards this end.

To sum up, the officers I met are, in general, optimistic about Japan's future despite observing the long-recessed economy. They appreciate the economic achievements that work towards providing people with an improvement in their lifestyle and the opportunity for further education and self-development throughout both buoyant and depressed economic conditions. For instance, they spoke of the choice of remaining traditional hard-working members of Japan's competitive economic society and seeking high income and social status. Alternatively, people can make more individual choices of career and lifestyle, which may be at the personal cost of accepting a lower income and a relatively lower social standing in comparison to the first option. A 'good' public programme must be written in order to provide a workable mix of the two options for industry and the national economy to remain viable and productive. In this context, officers of Type B talked about new concepts and innovative ways of building a 'social infrastructure' in cooperation with traditional 'economic and industrial infrastructure' facilities. They are positioned in Figure 5.1 in relationship to their preference to remain distant from 'plan and directing approaches' and their strong desire to formulate good public plans and programmes to build a 'good economic society'.

In search of an effective 'economic objective'

Tetsuo Najita, a *nisei* (second-generation Japanese American) historian at Princeton, spoke of the importance of the effective working of collective bureaucratic expertise in Japan's government institutions, which contributes to the efficiency of public work via the maintenance of national integrity.[12]

It is true that one of the main concerns of the top leaders in the Ministry has been to articulate the role and mission of the Ministry clearly and powerfully to gain support and moral commitment from every office member. We read in various reports how the Ministry often promoted its selected targets and policy objectives more effectively than other ministries, often in the face of opposition from other offices in government, business and the community. Yet it is important to study how diverse views are developed when there emerges in society a demand for changes in planning directions, and the preceding approach to policy writing and administrative work is questioned by many. The reaction differs according to the nature and the extent of that change of direction.

The change of direction suggested in 1986 was large and significant enough to drive all the officers in the Ministry to evaluate their accustomed approach to their work and, most of all, their understanding of their 'mission'.

As I mentioned in Chapter 4, 1986 was the time when the Maekawa Report argued for the pressing need to restructure the country's economic activities. It aimed to introduce a new economic paradigm that would directly address the workability and adequacy of the national economy in terms of its achievement up to that time. There were tough discussions about macroeconomic issues which are outside the traditional field of work of the Ministry, but the Ministry took up the challenge and made an effort to evaluate the message in terms of business and industrial activities. The publication of the vision policy for the 1990s followed, in which the Ministry presented its views on the desirable form of activities in industries and business, as well as in the wider and more general areas of people's work and living patterns that the Japanese economy ought to aim to achieve.[13] It attempted to articulate the proposed national aim in its focus on improvement in people's quality of life through better management of industry and business. In the following decade the Ministry attempted to formulate various policy devices to achieve this objective. As noted earlier, in 2002 the official title of the Ministry was altered to the Ministry of Economy and Trade and Industry (METI). It is possible to read into the addition of the term 'economy' and the dropping of the phrase 'international trade' that there was a determination to conduct matters in industry and business for a larger purpose in the national economy.[14]

The Maekawa Report has been interpreted in different ways by many readers and critics.[15] Apart from the evaluation of the quality of the document as a policy paper based on accurate data and information, people interpreted its basic message of a changing paradigm in varied ways. Equally, the concern for the improvement in quality of life in the vision policy met with varied reactions from the officers in the Ministry itself. The diversity of the understanding of the paradigm change was considerable among individual officers. It led me to question if bureaucrats were beginning to have difficulty in maintaining the national integrity that Najita observed before the early 1970s and the arrival of industrial development in Japan. And if it had, in what ways and to what extent?

More importantly, I was led to ask if new types of bureaucrats were emerging when the country faced a new challenge in which the economic and social paradigm was due for change. Was the changing paradigm so powerful that it would create new types of bureaucrats to rebuild the economy?

Alternatively, has economic development and industrial progress in Japan encouraged the development of wide diversity in the minds of planners in the same Ministry?

What exactly are the new types of bureaucrats that are appearing in post-industrial Japan? To secure the building of a commendable post-industrial society, what types of bureaucrats should be encouraged? To achieve this, who – and with what personality, education and other personal attributes – should be selected to enter public service offices and be promoted? What training should they be given so as to promote improvement, progress and reform of society that will bring regular and continuous improvement in individual well-being and national welfare?

If a new type or types of bureaucrats are emerging in the Ministry, it is important to understand the nature of their personalities and the behaviour expected of them in the new form of industrial policy and business–government relations in Japan. Thus there is an urgent need to find out exactly what types of bureaucrat will more effectively respond to the challenge of the emerging changes of paradigm in society, so as to guide economic and social development in a better direction.

As the first approach to the questions raised I will draw some general observations from my interviewees on how differently officers classified as different types responded to quality-of-life questions – a new national aim – as opposed to questions about economic growth and production efficiency – an old one – of the task of the Ministry.

One officer recalled in 1996 how puzzled he had been on reading the report and the policy published by his own Ministry as 'Vision Policy for the 1980s'. He took the message recommended in the report as suggesting that workers should not work too hard, even become lazy. He was concerned that, if the tradition of hard work was eased, this would quickly lead to a fall in productivity. His concern, however, was soon allayed in the second half of the 1980s when the economy experienced a downturn and the Vision Policy for the 1990s came out. His colleagues, including those senior staff holding directorships in various departments and bureaux, were asked to encourage their younger staff to produce practical policy guidelines for business and workers to make efforts to achieve some progress towards the proposed new direction. The efforts were directed towards a common end, but the understanding and the reasoning to make the efforts varied widely among the groups.

Let us see how officers using different approaches and holding different views put forward their ideas on how to transfer a newly conceived quality-of-life orientation into the economy.

Once again I will begin with public administrators, Types C and D. Discussion of the planners, Types A and B, follows.

Type C officers attempt to purchase quality of life through economic growth. They recommend that the Japanese economy and industry pursue economic growth as much as international trading conditions allow. They believe it is most essential that the economy and industry restructure and build a high productive and a high value-added production structure if the country is ever to raise the living standards of the population. For this, they estimate the increase in the annual growth rate of the national economy needs to be 2 to 3 per cent per annum, that is, a rate that is nearly 1 per cent higher than that proposed in the national economic plans for the period between 1996 and 2003. This figure also exceeds the estimated recommended economic growth rate for preserving the country's environment.[16]

The officers believe that a large part of environmental problems will be dealt with through the accelerated development of anti-pollution techniques that the Ministry is devising: the installation of anti-pollution devices in factories and cities, possible only with heavy public subsidies, and the building of a modern, environment-friendly infrastructure. The 2 to 3 per cent growth in the national economy is expected to generate enough funds to achieve the public programme they want.

Type D officers aim to gain opportunities and entrepreneurial enthusiasm for the growth of the national economy and for the further development of many modern industries. They believe that such opportunities and enthusiasms will be generated through national efforts to promote people's quality of life itself. To illustrate the value of such beliefs, the Ministry produced its working report, *Sozoteki Kakushin no Jidai*, or 'Time for Innovative Creation', and nominated numbers of business opportunities that would emerge in the transition of Japan's economy and society into a post-industrial and affluent one.[17] Many new markets are expected to emerge in the fields of general health, care for the aged and leisure activities, as well as high value-added products and service industries. They believe that if and when economic activities are maintained through the process of economic transition from growth-oriented to quality-of-life promotion, various economic problems such as the relocation of the workforce and production facilities could be managed through public administrative devices. They expect that, with their effort, economic stability and equity will be maintained, avoiding many of problems of unemployment and business bankruptcies. Against such optimistic views held by public administrative Types C and D, public planners Types A and B have more concerns about the future of the economy.

Officers of Type A ask if national efforts to promote quality of life will produce a better economic system. They see the need to carefully assess the exact nature and extent of the transition of the economy. They said at the beginning of 2004 that they wanted to spend more time and collect further information in order to correctly assess what problems could be expected to emerge in the process. What's more, they asked what potential and opportunities would be opened up for them to build a timely policy to guide the economy into its next stage. Specifically, they see it as necessary to clarify concerns about Japan's management systems that have been closely followed.

These officers think it necessary to begin with a quantitative estimate of the level and the standard of Japan's national economy and industrial production capacity as compared with its major competitors in the international economy. They want to see whether, to what extent, and how well the economy and industry are managing to introduce reduced working hours without risking loss of productivity. In addition, they want to see if there is still a need to sustain lifetime employment practice in industries. They ask this question in order to challenge the view maintained among part of the government that sees the desirability of the practice being maintained across as many sectors of industries as possible. The government's concern lies in how to sustain economic stability and provide employment and thus security to the working population. This proposal is expressed to counter ever-increasing business decisions which began to promote restructuring and reduce the size of management and production activities inside Japan and to relocate production overseas to reduce costs.

Type A officers ask if such a proposal, which aims to reverse/reduce business activities, will ever be possible, because they see an increasing proportion of workers wishing to develop their work career by exploring various career paths. They see that this traditional practice, though it has served the nation well in the past, has rapidly lost its effectiveness and relevance in the Japanese economy, with its accumulation of affluence and with its wish to promote issues of quality of life. They seek a new direction for the economy with revision and reform of management practice.

It could be said that those Type A officers, together with Type B, are more professional in their approach and focus their effort on assessing how quality-of-life issues challenge the foundation of the employment and payment systems of the economy. They take the view that Japan's high productivity in industry is based on the country's traditional approach to work. They understand that hard-working attitudes among workers seeking promotion, and the tradition of lifetime employment, have been the source of high productivity. They expect that the promotion of quality of life will directly destroy this source. In other words, younger workers have, so far, traditionally accepted pay lower than their real labour contribution on the understanding that they will be rewarded later though lifetime employment with the company they are employed by. This traditional work norm has been challenged through the demand for quality of life from the same group of people. With quality-of-life priorities, employers are facing larger wage and salary payments as young employees demand payment equal to their labour productivity contribution. This is resulting in a wide difference of income among workers, reflecting their abilities and work effort and forcing the economy to not only lose some of its productivity, but also to face the consequence of the end of the 'equal' society.

They expect new forms of management styles, work norms and ways of living to emerge in Japan's affluent society, demanding a rapid revision in those areas. They see the need for a rapid revision of public economic policies. Privately, they express dissatisfaction and distrust towards their seniors for their inability to see how and where new needs for public efforts are emerging.

Type B officers are not sure at this stage whether both managers and employers understand the consequences of implementing quality-of-life preferences. The officers themselves want to have more time to examine the developments in the Japanese economy to see if the accumulation of wealth and the technical advancement of society is adequate. They ask if various serious problems will arise in industries, and society in general in the transformation of the management of the economy. They are concerned if many problems will occur in the transformation of the management of the economy. If they feel that the problems will have a negative effect, despite their support for the improvement of quality of life as the national target, they would prefer to postpone (as their discretion) their public commitment to the issue until they can work out how the reformation of the employment system will provide a better quality of life to the population, while causing reduced productivity.

On the other hand, those classified as Type B feel ambivalent towards the concept of a national aim. They think that national aims are neither available nor easily created by administrative manipulation under present structures. Consequently, they are inclined to think that discussions about quality of life in the Vision Policy for the 1990s are without substance. They believe a new planning approach should be developed to deal with quality-of-life issues. They wish to initiate a new planning mind set for an affluent society with the clear understanding that it should be distinct from the previous one that was developed to serve economic growth and industrialization of the country.

Emerging types among the 'young recruits'

Serving the public

In February 2003 I met 11 young recruits to the Ministry, already selected to start work in April of that year. I had discussions with them individually and with others as a group. I wished to review their profile and speculate on what public administrative service and economic policy they wish to provide in the future. Who are they? From where have they come?

I give below some of the observations I made through meeting them. It should be noted, however, that those I met on this occasion were not representative of all the new recruits. I met them because they were available at the time I happened to be in Tokyo in 2003 and thus the study result should be read on a preliminary basis.

First, I understood that their social, family and educational background was surprisingly similar to those of my 71 interviewees. Most are male, with one or two females joining the two dozen others, born and brought up in the Tokyo metropolitan area and other large cities (nearly half of the total are from Tokyo, Yokohama and Osaka), with degrees from the Law School, Tokyo University and graduating from, if traced back further, the same set of prestigious private and leading prefectural high schools.

Second, they are from quite well-to-do upper-middle-class families with either the father or both parents executives in large established firms, professors in universities, solicitors and doctors, or bureaucrats in the Ministry or in other government offices. I observed, though I could not find adequate statistical support, that many were in fact second-generation bureaucrats (sons of those serving or old boys of the Ministry). It could be said that they come from a group of families consisting of well-informed people in society.

Third, a high proportion of them have overseas pre-university education or living experiences. Because their parents hold professional appointments and work as expatriates, they have had the opportunity to live overseas for a couple of years. Otherwise it is now the Ministry's practice to send many of them to overseas universities for one to two years.[18] Most destinations under this scheme are to North American universities, the most popular of which are the Harvard Law and Business Schools and, influenced by their free market ideology, many come to view the Ministry, with its traditional planning and regulatory approach, as archaic. At least, that is what I sensed in their talks during the interview meetings.

Fourth, these officers have gone through times when they were tempted to leave the Ministry. This experience has hardly existed for the seniors, but with young bureaucrats who joined the Ministry after 1995 it is not rare to see some colleagues leave the Ministry after a couple of years, going, most frequently, to foreign financial corporations for better money, and, according to them, with opportunities to engage in more exciting, responsible jobs than those provided by the step-by-step, on-the-job training and seniority-based promotion that is still largely practised in the Ministry. To be specific, this group of younger officers are the 70 per cent (11 out of the total 16 new recruits to the Ministry in 2003) survivors of the original intake into the Ministry.

Their responses to my question about why they had entered the Ministry were expressed in the same manner as those of the seniors. They said they sought a position in the Ministry because they wished to work for others' welfare and build a better society. Once again I noted that they hold as high a view of their intellectual abilities (although not yet knowing in which direction they should develop their talents) as their seniors. They wished to make full use of their capacity, not only for their immediate benefit but also for making a substantial income and acquiring fame.

When asked in what way they wished to serve others in society – that is, for *koeki* – this is how they differentiated themselves from the seniors. I found that some showed some embarrassment in speaking of their *koeki* motives in working in the Ministry. When pressed, some actually spoke of their feeling of embarrassment, finding it 'out of fashion' and not 'cool' to speak of 'the public purpose and national aims'. Yet privately, I observed, they still hold traditional feelings of pride in reflecting that they are among the selected few who can be trusted to think on behalf of the general public. Being young, they are anxious to make full use of their ability, which they estimate highly.

These young recruits chose to serve for *koeki* because such purposes are large. For them, after careful discussion, I found that works for *koeki* are 'large' in scale and 'grand in nature'. It is through their potential in scale and scope that they wish to be associated with *koeki*. It is not work for the nation/country and for one's fellow-Japanese, but the expectation that they would be engaged in world affairs, and contribute to the welfare of people in the world, that attracts them. They are very much in sympathy with the spirit and mode of 'globalization', with their hope to engage in the promotion of Japan's role and presence in the world economic activities and cultural development. Given this, they are at any moment prepared to *move out of* government offices to join in private business and other institutions in search of better opportunities and facilities that will meet their aspirations.[19]

Without actually having begun working in the Ministry, they find it difficult to discuss 'policy' and 'policy issues'. They talked of their concern about how to understand the notion of the 'public will' and 'the national aim' while working in the Ministry and away from people in society. I came to see that they are believers in human judgement and experience, like their seniors, and could, with care and effort, work for the advancement of the country and society rather than for mindless markets. I would like to record here that as far as my interviewees were concerned, the young can be said to hold similar, traditional views about planning as their seniors and wish to develop a good planning mind if the chance arises.

Appendix Table 5.1 Officers (senior 'career') at Tokyo Home Office, MITI – selected officers interviewed as at August 1994 – the ' initial interviewees'

1 Year entered into Ministry	2 Age*	3 Total no. in MITI in 1994	4 Position**	5 No. interviewed	6 Coverage 5/3 (%)
1958	58	1	Administrative Vice-Minister (Jim-iikan)	–	–
1959	57	1		–	–
1960	56	2	Chief of Minister's	–	–
1961	55	3	Secretariat and Head	1	33.3
1962	54	3	of Bureaux	–	–
1963	53	7	(Kyoku-cho)	1	14.3
1964	52	7		1	14.3
1965	51	12		2	16.7
1966	50	13		3	23.1
1967	49	17		2	11.8
1968	48	19		2	10.5
1969	47	19		1	5.3
1970	46	18		2	11.1
1971	45	18		3	16.7
1972	44	19		1	5.3
1973	43	20		3	15.0
1974	42	20	Chief of Department	5	25.0
1975	41	25	and Sections	2	8.0
1976	40	19	(Bucho and Kacho)	1	5.3
1977	39	23		3	13.0
1978	38	26		3	11.5
1979	37	25		3	12.0

Appendix Table 5.1   Officers (senior 'career') at Tokyo Home Office, MITI – selected officers interviewed as at August 1994 – the 'initial interviewees'   *continued*

1 Year entered into Ministry	2 Age*	3 Total no. in MITI in 1994	4 Position**	5 No. interviewed	6 Coverage 5/3 (%)
1980	36	25		1	4.0
1981	35	26		3	11.5
1982	34	27		4	14.8
1983	33	29		2	6.9
1984	32	23		1	4.4
1985	31	27		4	14.8
1986	30	29		4	13.8
1987	29	27	Deputy Section Chief (*Kachohosa*)	2	7.4
1988	28	26		3	11.5
1989	27	26		2	8.0
1990	26	28		4	10.7
1991	25	28		2	7.1
Average	(41.5)	(638)		(71)	(11.1)

Notes:

*   There are limited numbers of officers whose ages are older by one or two years, depending on their age of the entry into the Ministry, reflecting the variation of the entry into, and graduation from, universities.

**   Because the minister and parliamentary vice-minister (*seimu-jikan*) are members of the Diet, they stay in the Ministry only for a brief period. In contrast, all career civil servants such as our interviewees are taken into the service on a traditional lifetime basis and the actual administrative work is usually left almost entirely in their hands. They are headed by the Administrative Vice-Minister (AVM: *Jim-jikan*). The AVM reaches this post after 30 to 35 years of service (aged from 32 to mid/late fifties) by passing a competitive scrutiny of their career records as is the case for permanent secretaries in the British civil service organizations. The AVM is supported by senior bureaucrats such as chiefs of the office of Minister's Secretariat (OMS), of Bureaux (CB: *Kyoku-cho*) and Departments (*Bucho*). They reach their senior ranks through parallel procedures to AVM. The AVM, OMS and CBs together form the echelon of the administrative networks of the Ministry. The bureaux are further divided into sections (*Ka*). Sections are led by their chiefs (*Kacho*, mostly in their forties), assisted by a few young deputy section chiefs (*Kach-hosa*, in their late twenties and mid/late thirties with an average of six to thirteen years' service in the Ministry). The size of *Ka* differs depending on the function. These *Kacho* and *Kacho-hosa* are, perhaps, the most important officials in the entire structure actually engaged in the initiation and writing policies of the Ministry. They are the vital link between the senior administrative (AVM, OMS and CBs) and the career and non-career officers in the Ministry. For further general information concerning the appointment and personnel management of public administrators, see Nishio and Muramatsu (1995).

Note that given the seniority promotion system practised in the Ministry in the period, age and rank are shown to be closely connected.

Part II

Case Studies of Economic Bureaucrats

6
The Society-consulting Public Administrator: Mr M., Type C Officer

The experience of Mr M. could be seen as one of the classic cases observed among bureaucrats, particularly in the central government offices not only of this but also of many other ministries in the post-World War II years up to the mid-1970s.

His case is classic in the sense that to many in business and the Ministry his approach and behaviour have been seen as good. I will follow his work experience and report his explanations of why he chose to do what he did, not so much to evaluate what he *actually* achieved as to follow his work spirit – the personal and professional aim that inspired him. Through this I want to show the 'classic' and 'ideal' work norm of his time in Japan for public administrators.

Family, schooling and university days (1938–60)

Mr M. was born in a suburban town outside Fukuoka city in Kyushu, one of the important industrial bases of the country with its production of coal, steel and ship-building. His father worked in a bank and his paternal grandfather in local government, making them exceptions to most of their relatives and neighbours, who made their living from farming. His father's position gave the family a secure and relatively comfortable life until his death from illness. Mr M. was then 15 and in his final (third) year at a junior high school. He was the eldest of the family and had a sister and brother. His mother remained single from choice and brought up her children with the life insurance payout of Mr M.'s father, plus some small but regular contributions from grandparents on both the paternal and maternal sides. He recalls that the financial state of the family was relatively comfortable though by no means affluent.

Mr M. remembers his childhood and youth as being stable and peaceful, with the death of his father bringing the family even closer together than previously. He made every effort to behave as a dutiful and thoughtful son to his mother, and to be a kind big brother to his sister and brother.

For Mr M., the 'duty and thoughtfulness' were manifested in the traditional ways of life still persisting in Fukuoka. It is also the case that he could not escape completely from the obligatory pressure to behave to win the approval of his grandparents. The fact that his family received financial support from them, although it came in a most benevolent manner, acted as a constant reminder that he was being assessed by the seniors. He felt he must grow up behaving as a model son, admired by relatives and neighbours. From the day of his father's funeral, he felt obliged to behave in a more grown-up manner than many of his counterparts, and represented the family in all the traditional memorial services at the family temple.

He was successful at school. Mr M. was a prefect praised by the headmaster, and his academic achievements were praised by teachers in all subjects, including non-academic subjects such as music and technical studies. He was an all-round honours student from his primary school days and went to the top prefectural high school. This school was the one at which all the bright students in the prefecture and the surrounding districts aimed to get a place as it was the stepping stone to the prestigious universities in Tokyo. He was also good at sport. He remembered how grateful he often felt for the good fortune that gave him such high ability to manage at school. Already at that age he had begun to believe that he had to contribute to the welfare of others who were not so fortunate as himself so as to express his gratefulness, otherwise, so he feared, a jealous god might punish him in some way.

In his final year at the school, his classmates selected him to be captain of the school's basketball team, which won the prefectural championship in the final school year. He remembers that as the most memorable occasion in his life. Local newspapers reported the match, and he was the centre of attention for some time in his school and his neighbourhood. After finishing school, Mr M. left Fukuoka and went to Tokyo to study at the Tokyo University Law School, a choice that his class teacher strongly recommended. He was invited as a free lodger to the house of one of his distant relatives in Tokyo. He stayed there happily, being treated as one of their family. To return the favour, he gave regular tuition to the three primary school age youngsters in the household and tried to make himself useful to the mother around the house and garden, and took their dog for regular walks.

Being in the limelight when young had helped his confidence grow, as is often the case with people from villages and less populated places. In his time, Fukuoka was still a provincial place where various events could get public attention. For example, besides his success in the basketball competition, his acceptance into the Law School in 1956 was reported on a local page in the national papers. In this way, he could be described as a big fish in a little pond. His confidence certainly contributed to his effort to develop a professional approach when working in the Ministry.

I will describe how he began his public service work in the spring of 1961 when the Ministry was at the forefront in constructing industrial policy.

Career path

Entry into the Ministry

Mr M. joined MITI in April 1961 with 19 others who had just graduated from university. Sixteen of them were from the Law School of Tokyo University, one came from the University of Kyoto and one from Okayama University, both are national universities like Tokyo University, with good academic reputations. All the students assumed that they were among the brightest of their generation, graduating from prestigious universities which had long been regarded as the training places for top public servants.

Their entry into the Ministry in 1961 also marked the entry of the national economy into the 'miracle' high-speed economic growth era with Prime Minister Ikeda Hayato publicly launching the national economic plan, 'The National Income-doubling Plan' (sometimes referred as *Shotoku Baizo*, the 'double national income within ten years' economic plan),[1] published in December in the previous year, with his official promise that 'economic progress will provide effective solutions to all social and political problems'.

While studying at the university, Mr M. took part in several political protests and demonstrations, as many did at the time. He remembered that it was fashionable for students to be 'political' in one way or another. 'But in reality,' he said, 'it did not prevent me allocating more of my time and interest to writing good essays by assigned dates for better marks, taking up sporting activities and having fun with girls if possible.'

Most students around him who wished to get a public service job and were seen by others as 'serious, straight and nationalistic' must have thought the same. So it seemed natural for Mr M. to seek a position in government where he could work for economic success, a newly emerged aim of the nation in place of 'political independence'.

Every summer before graduation students begin active job hunting, and employers begin their careful search for the best graduates. Given the lifetime employment principle, which was still highly valued at the time, particularly among top graduates such as Mr M., and given that the practice was closely followed in government and large and established corporations, it is an important occasion for all new graduates. A popular joke went that *shu'shoku* (selecting where to be employed) is a 'more important matter in life – certainly more important than marriage', for it was believed that one may divorce one's wife but not change one's job.

The expectation of those top graduates was particularly high, with their careful evaluation of how to make the most of their lifetime career perspective by selecting industries and companies in which they expected to work for the next 30-plus years until retirement. Equally carefully, large established companies and government would evaluate new recruits as if launching large investment projects, commencing R&D activities or selecting business partners. Encouraged by 'the Double-national income within ten years' economic plan, summer 1961 saw the national economy grow by an annual average of 11.3 per cent over 1966–70.

The search by newly graduating students and employers eager for growth and expansion for a better place in the job market in that year was, if anything, particularly active and as buoyant as the economy itself.

Mr M. began his enquiries about his future employment opportunities as soon as the customary time for such activities began. He soon learned that there were many good jobs on offer from the nation's top-ranking industrial companies, as well as banking, trading and distribution firms.

He wanted a public service job from the outset. If possible, he wished to get into a prestigious ministry in the central government like the Ministry. With his academic record only just in the upper range, he was not sure if he could hope to achieve this. He wrote his name down for Fuji Steel (the second largest steel maker before its merger with Yawata Steel to form Nippon Steel in 1970, allegedly under the guidance and assistance of the Ministry), the Industrial Bank of Japan, a private bank but established by government to serve public purposes, and the Tokyo Electric Corporation, a public corporation.[2]

Mr M. decided to try his fortune by sitting for the entrance examination at the Ministry while attempting the Transport Ministry as the second choice. He did not seek a position in the Ministry of Finance (MoF), as might be expected of a graduate who sought a position in the Ministry. He had, somehow, formed an impression of authoritarianism in MoF from his general observation of the university alumni who had chosen to join that Ministry and those of his classmates who were talking about joining them. MITI, the other top Ministry, appeared to be free from that image, yet had great prestige.

Why did he choose the Ministry, apart from its obvious prestige and its central position at the time of economic expansion and industrial development? Thinking back on how he made his decision, he admitted that he had no particular explanation for the decision other than that the selection was, in his own words, a natural choice for someone like him. That is, he simply followed the path laid down for graduates of his calibre.

It could be said that any graduate from the Law School of Tokyo University with the combination of a middle to top academic record and good public service entrance examination results would be expected to apply for a public administration position in the MoF or in the Ministry. He received job offers from all five of the authorities he applied to, and accepted the offer from the Ministry.

I want to examine what contributions he tried to make to the economy and, more generally, to the economic society of Japan; what, in fact, he has done in his own capacity and what he has aimed for but not achieved in his 30-year working life (from 1961 to 1991).

Mr M. spent his early days as a young bureaucrat (the 1960s to the 1970s), a hard-working middle manager (the late 1970s to the mid-1980s), and an experienced senior to top officer in the late 1980s to 1992.

Work mechanism of the Ministry

In 1995, after retirement from public office, Mr M. summarized his work experience as follows: He understands that the planning approach of the Ministry is not particularly different from that practised in other developed economies. What distinguishes MITI's approach is that the policy tools have been formulated and applied over a fairly long period of time, from the middle of the 1950s to the beginning of the 1990s, in a consistent manner. Industrial policies have been formulated to supplement the working of the market and to pick up signs of entrepreneurial initiatives and provide them with public administrative guidance and often also with subsidies.

Such a proactive and growth-oriented form of government has arisen because of the closed nature of the market, its backward features, and the fact that a large part of economic activities are conducted through customary and traditional arrangements without going through the appropriate market transactions. To avoid wasting entrepreneurial initiatives and making sure that resources are allocated in productive ways, the Ministry's policies are called in to supplement the working of those omitted transaction channels. The Ministry has always feared that, if it is not picked up and drawn into the appropriate market, entrepreneurial drive will be wasted.

For example, Mr M. divides the work of the Ministry into three different categories, each with different administrative and policy-writing approaches. There is one category that may be called 'regulative', with an approach that relies on making regulations and writing business and commercial rules so that business activities are conducted on a fair and competitive basis. The second category consists of 'promotional' activities. Their purpose is to provide encouragement to enterprising planners, with guidance and financial support at their early stage of development. Mr M. sees in the effective working of this method one of the most important reasons for the successful growth and development of the Japanese economy in his time – the 1960s and 1970s. He makes this remark based on his observation of the Indonesian and Australian economies while working at the Japanese Embassies in 1973 and 1981 respectively. Of Indonesia, he spoke of the still poorly developed markets in various sectors of the economy; of Australia he spoke of an over-reliance on the market mechanism, despite its limits, leading to the emergence of oligopolistic non-competitive markets, causing inefficient allocation and ineffective use of economic resources.

The third category is the 'forecasting and guiding' activity of the Ministry, by which the Ministry draws up a desirable image of future industrial activities and regularly writes 'vision' policy statements which had been tried at the beginning of the 1970s. Mr M. himself had been involved in the programme, yet he had become increasingly unsure about how capable the Ministry would be of achieving such a task. He noted that the economy was getting more complex, for example, with the advancement of technology and scientific and engineering knowledge, global economic and business activities and the requirement of people to become more varied with the affluence of society. He believes that discussion of the future, even if it is directed only to industry matters specifically, cannot be conducted by one ministry but requires evaluation by all ministries and government offices as well as business and the population as a whole.

Because of this, Mr M. hopes that in future all public servants will be appointed to one central office where young bureaucrats armed with a general liberal arts education will first be trained to acquire a general understanding of public service work and see how they will be able to contribute to the betterment of people's lives and social make-up before being located in individual ministries to engage in specialized work. The selection should be made carefully to attract all sorts of people with varying family and educational backgrounds. The office could be called 'the Ministry of Planning for Human Betterment', and each ministry, such as MITI, Ministry of Education, Environment, Labour, and so on, would go to this Ministry and request the second-ment of some of their officers for their work.

In 1999, at our meeting, Mr M. spoke of his idea with excitement but commented that the time was not yet ripe to discuss the matter widely in the Kasumigaseki government circle because bureaucrats are pre-occupied with how to maintain the authority of their own Ministry in view of the changing size and the role of government under the pro-gramme of public administrative reform promoted by all governments since the mid-1980s.

During his 31 years working at the Ministry Mr M. undertook 15 assignments. Most of his appointments have been concentrated in the second category: support and promotion of emerging signs of entrepre-neurial effort. Since his first appointment as *kacho*, section head, in 1976 until 1988 he held positions of secretary general of various departments with the entrusted duty of drawing up new policies every two years. Leading a team of 10 to 12 staff members in the case of smaller depart-ments, and between 30 and 35 in a larger ones, his main role has been to encourage younger staff to go out to workplaces in industry to establish what the policy issues are and then to draft policy proposals in the light of other policy proposals drafted in other departments. As a result, he has formulated many policies directly and indirectly for the Ministry.

Work experience

Rank-file-officer

In April 1963 Mr M. began his career as a bureaucrat in the Ministry at its Household and Miscellaneous Goods Division in the Small and

Medium Enterprise Office of Light Industries Bureau. Through the following three decades he rose slowly but steadily from this rookie beginning to Bureau Head up the traditional spiral staircase of career development set for bureaucrats by moving up a step and, then, by a side-step, to higher and more responsible positions, widening and enriching his experiences every two years.

Mr M. spent his first six months on preliminary training and was subsequently assigned to the quite responsible task of rewriting an existing trade law to promote some household supply industries, such as enamelled ironware, plastic and other synthetic resin products.

His task was to improve and strengthen the existing law into a slightly more up-to-date version to assist the industry to restructure its production efficiency. There were too many marginal procedures in the industry. Most firms were family owned and family run, with traditional labour-intensive production and business approaches. Little stability is found in the industry and employees have no job security – a typical problem that developed in Japan as *kato-kyoso* or excessive competition.[3] The Ministry wanted to reduce the problems by prompt introduction of regulatory measures with the support of administrative guidance. The Ministry took the view that the problems were specific to each individual enterprise and thus needed equally individual rescue approaches. It is a typically labour-intensive approach that imposes much work on young recruits like Mr M.

Under the supervision of his *kacho-hosa* (deputy head of the office, in his late twenties, with ten years' work experience in the Ministry), Mr M. organized numerous meetings with industry representatives. He chaired meetings, discussing business problems to find out what new policy measures were needed in order to rescue individual firms from falling continuously into hand-to-mouth operations. With as much information collected through interview meetings and discussions as possible, he was able to list a set of policy issues that his office considered necessary for constructing policy measures. His subsequent task was to study the present regulations, laws and acts, revise them and formulate a draft regulation for his office. Subsequently he drafted the proposal with the help of the same *kacho-hosa* and circulated it for discussion around his office for endorsement before taking to the head of the bureau. After numerous discussions and rewriting, the proposed revision of the law was in its final form and ready for the bureau's endorsement for a budget request (to be made by mid-December) in the new financial year.

This is how Mr M. received his first stage of on-the-job training. The eight months gave him a good knowledge about the industry and the ability to write regulations and acts and rules.

He gained two things. One was the obvious joy of working together with colleagues and supervisors with a feeling of pride and high expectation that says 'I am doing something very important and useful for society'. The other was related to his personal attitude towards his public work. He understood that the value of his effort was all in the value of the outcome, the relevance of the newly formed regulations and their effectiveness in achieving the policy aim. He had to write good regulations using personal sincerity and honesty, and his previous knowledge and skills. He was excited by the task as it gave him a strong sense of responsibility and personal satisfaction. What his seniors frequently talked about began making real sense to him. They often spent their after-office drinking sessions talking proudly about their achievements and experiences with comments such as, 'Such and such industry became an export success because he wrote this policy and gave that guidance, etc.'

To support his explanation, he added how important he found his traits of 'sincerity' and 'honesty' in conducting his assigned task throughout. He meant that he wanted to maintain through his whole working life that his work was as good as he could possibly make it so as to secure the quality of his policy measures and administrative services.

Mr M. was convinced that when public work was delivered to business and people in the community with *sincerity and honesty* on the bureaucrat's side, it would be received with equal sincerity and honesty by the beneficiaries. He believed that personal commitment with good intentions made in a kind spirit gets equal responses.

How far his belief reflects reality is difficult to evaluate. My purpose in writing this is to record the specific nature of the experience of an officer who, I am sure, is not an isolated example, at least among those in the Ministry up to the early 1970s. I have confirmed some of this understanding through subsequent interviews and in reading many memoirs, semi-autobiographical and biographical writings by journalists and critics of bureaucrats and the bureaucracy itself in Japan.[4]

Mr M. remembered how elated he felt that he was part of an 'élite' and that this influential group was promising a great future for him. It was the time that not only he but also many others in the office felt happy because they were able to see 'improvement' coming to the national economy and people's lives, with a 10 per cent rise in income every year. The progress outlined in the national economic plan seemed possible. What is more, he was happy, as he put it, that 'I could be in this current of "improvement" and "progress" and play my part in it'.

Kacho-hosa, deputy section head

After six years of apprenticeship, Mr M. was promoted to *kacho-hosa* at the beginning of the 1980s and was now able to initiate policy of his own choice.

His next job was highly pressured and he recalls it as the most 'demanding' in his career. Appointed to the Finance Division, Small and Medium Enterprise Agency, Mr M. spent many nights on a couch in a corner of his office trying to find time for meetings, writing reports and checking laws and acts of trade and banking networks so that he could think of ways to secure loans and subsidies for struggling businesses.

This division is assigned with facilitating the financing of smaller enterprises, and Mr M.'s job was to think of various ways to assist them, through liaising and negotiating for cheap bank loans from public banks, financial institutions and tax concessions and subsidies from the Ministry of Finance (MoF).

To secure the required endorsement he went out to see relevant officers in MoF whom he knew well as classmates at the university. Mr M. was pleased that he had, through careful and thorough work ever since joining the Ministry, built a 'good' reputation as a 'trustworthy' person among the government offices. He could count on his image as a 'reliable guy with good, balanced judgement' to assist in his professional negotiations. He was working at the time when professional work – the need to allocate budget – was often judged on an individual and personal basis. The worth of the programme was estimated on the basis of the personality of the officer who proposed the programme.

Kacho, section head

Mr M.'s three appointments so far had involved him in formulating policy devices to guide and assist industries with finance and in observing them behave in a responsible manner to secure good work practices and a natural environment. The Ministry began to work in close cooperation with the Environment Agency, which had been newly established in 1971.

With these three assignments he had completed his junior *kacho* appointments. He was expected to move up the promotion ladder in the Ministry, taking more senior *kacho* assignments in which he involved himself in close and frequent contact with equally senior counterparts in business.

Before moving to one of these senior positions, however, he was appointed to an overseas office, to the Embassy in Jakarta, Indonesia, as the Counsellor (Economics) in the Embassy to gain an understanding and make observations on the economic matters of the Asia Pacific region.

It was the time when the Indonesian government was organizing its ministry for international trade and industrial development matters along the lines of Mr M.'s Ministry. Mr M. was asked to give various practical advice to achieve this task. A public power plant was built outside Jakarta with the help of a long-term and cheap loan from Japan. The aim was to help establish and operate the affiliated Japanese plants, such as automobile and household electric appliance factories. Mr M.'s job was to collect and collate the information that was required for the Japanese public financial institutions to allocate the fund that they had set aside to develop industries in Asia, for the city banks to assist the finance of the project to establish plants in Indonesia with Japanese know-how, and for the general trading corporations in Japan to establish import and export networks for the expected output to Japan and neighbouring Asian countries.

After returning from Indonesia, Mr M. spent the following three years overseeing policy matters and staff personnel as the head of the general affairs divisions of two bureaux, the Industry Policy and the Consumer Goods Industries Bureaux.[5]

As his many appointments indicate, Mr M. had now, at the age of 47, with 24 years of work experience in the Ministry, established his position and reputation as an experienced and competent senior officer. He had also secured his good name as a trustworthy and honest bureaucrat in the Kasumigaseki head offices of leading ministries. He was comfortable with his knowledge of the Ministry's work mechanisms and his awareness of the capacities of many of the staff. His professional and personal networks were well established not only within both government circles but also in industries. For example, he now had the trust of other government officers in various ministries and agencies. He felt confident going into negotiations with other Ministries, particularly with the Ministry of Finance, to gain the vital budget allocations with which to implement his policies. Many leaders in business make it their custom to visit and consult him before they begin any of their important investment decisions.

Top bureaucrat

In 1988 Mr M. returned to Fukuoka, Kyushu, his native town, as the bureau head of the Kita-kyushu (Northern Kyushu) regional office.[6]

The bureau had grown considerably, reflecting the rapid development of industries in the area. With 'Return home in glory' pencilled in, the Minister handed him the official letter of appointment. By appointing the native-born Mr M., the Minister aimed to promote close and positive relationships between the policy makers in the home office and the regional business community so as to prepare for the time when the Ministry would find it necessary to control the export drive of the emerging business.

Mr M. energetically called on office and factory sites and workshops, small and large, in the district, studying the working conditions of the executives, owner-managers and employees. Many welcomed his visit, congratulating him on his success.[7] Those visits gave a strong message to local operators that the central government was closely following their efforts. They were encouraged, and their motivation was enhanced through this message and they came more frequently to Mr M. with their plans and proposals and requests for assistance and guidance. In the process, he cemented further the communication channels between industries in the district and the Tokyo head office as the Minister had planned.

In 1991 he was called back to the Tokyo head office to take up the position of Deputy Director-General, Machinery and Information Industries Bureau. Despite being well located on the path to *Jikan* Ministry Head, it was not a job he enjoyed. By now the competition and anxiety over the next appointment appeared to have increased – he was in the last stage of competition among the few remaining of his *doki* and the seniors. To his relief, he was sent to the Economic Planning Agency to work on the newly established inter-ministry advisory committee. Its purpose was to formulate national macroeconomic policy by coordinating the activities of the Bank of Japan (monetary policy) and the Ministry of Finance (fiscal and taxation policy) with the activities of MITI's industrial policy.

The committee used the experiences of a group of very senior officers with information networks across various ministries and agencies in government as well as business circles to draft national economic policy. He was now asked to act as an economic planner and social engineer for building Japan's economic society. The time was at the turning point of the economy, faced with a sudden burst of the boom. None at the time appeared to understand what was happening to the economy, except that they saw a sharp fall in the prices of land, buildings and other forms of property and stocks. The committee was no wiser than anyone else.

Despite his experience and knowledge, Mr M. found himself not quite up to the task of piecing together the situation from information that was coming to his desk every few minutes. He considered himself a total failure. Although he was provided with all core information on business and national economic activities before it was made public, and he had the support of statistical data, he felt highly frustrated with his inability to draw effective plan proposals and take actions in any effective way.

The final recommendation arrived at his office towards the end of 1994.[8]

Post-Ministry career in business (*amakudari* appointment)

In the summer of 1994 Mr M. began his post-Ministry *amakudari* appointment. He was transferred for two years into one of the associated financial organizations of the Minsistry, following the customary convention of serving a so-called cooling-off period in semi-public office before moving into private business employment. The Ministry has installed many of their retired officers in economic institutions and business organizations of national importance. In order to avoid any misconduct that might arise from this '*amakudari*' reemployment arrangement, the Ministry has placed the operation of these private-sector organizations within its close jurisdiction. The establishment of a 'Cooling-off' period is one such device that has been instituted to minimize the misuse of the pecial, advantageous position that these private-sector businesses might seek through the *amakudari* appointment.

Setting some cooling-off period, normally as long as two years, is regarded as minimizing any risk of developing a direct link between the Ministry and private business through the *amakudari* procedure. The particular organization in which Mr M. was allocated to serve his term was established by the Ministry in order to channel public funds, particularly that of FILP (the Fiscal Investment and Loan Programme) to smaller farmers and agricultural enterprises.

After two years with this financial corporation, by invitation Mr M. took up a senior executive position in an industrial company. The appointment was recommended and arranged by the Ministry itself. His case was a good example of the *amakudari* system as it followed closely the customary procedures and arrangements between public service and industry.[9]

Overview of Mr M.'s work experience

How do we review and evaluate the 31 years of Mr M's work in the Ministry and his efforts and experiences, and what concluding observations can we make?

Questions arise about why he decided to become a public servant, how he acquired his sense and understanding of *koeki*, how he developed the work principle which seemed so natural to him and how he eventually developed his own generalist approach.

Koeki revisited

I began Mr M.'s life story with an account of his successful schooldays when he felt that learning came easily. It seemed natural for him to become a conscientious and industrious student. He was comfortable in pursuing this role, and his family and others around him encouraged him and appreciated his efforts to develop himself further.

As a comparison with his own experiences, he made a few observations about the people in the Ministry. First, he noted that most of his colleagues and seniors who came to work in the Ministry had a similar background. Almost all came as honours students. Yet he also saw that none of them had a particular talent in arts, literature, the sciences, or other fields. They seemed to lack the strong personal drive required to focus on one specific personal interest. Instead, they used the school curriculum as their guide and were led to work hard to improve their classroom learning following instructions given by the teachers.

As prized students they attempted to reach a high standard in life and at the workplace, yet they found that for all their efforts they still remained within the confines of their teachers' guidelines. Their intelligence is good enough only for school-level learning. They do not possess any obvious great wisdom, a highly logical mind or a rich imagination. That was frustrating.

Thinking back to his last year at university, Mr M. reached the conclusion that it was not possible to develop his general academic ability in 'high' directions. He was already beginning to suspect that it was also the case with many of his friends of honours calibre. He wondered if serving others, whether for the reputation of the school, the good management of the class, or the welfare of the group, was compensation for their inability to attain high academic success.

That was his observation and the explanation of his experience. What follows is my speculation based on the various discussions we had during our formal and informal interview meetings. I have constructed this speculation in order to understand Mr M.'s personality and, to some extent, the personalities of the other three in my case studies, and to follow the development of their attitudes towards public duty.

When many of the interviewees talked about the reasoning behind their decision to select public service as their vocation, motivated by their own interpretation of *koeki*, I understood how important it appeared to them. But I was not quite clear what it meant exactly; how their interpretation came to serve as the basis for their standard of behaviour when working in the Ministry. I also wanted to know how their interpretations compare with those of other officers in the same Ministry, and other officers in government in general.

It is not only Mr M. and the other three in my case studies (Mr N., Mr K. and Mr O. in the following chapters) but also a few others among my interviewees who liked to talk about how, as youths, they saw the coming of economic times when the nation's energy and interest would be directed exclusively towards economic matters – the growth and expansion of the economy and industrial progress.

All held, in varied ways, the memory of how economic prosperity came to the country. All my interviewees had lived in the same 'economic time' and developed their approaches to life under the influence of the progress of the national economy. In the pursuit of material betterment, political concerns and the appreciation of life and nature, as promoted in the world of arts, literature and philosophy, were pushed into a secondary position. So the discussion of *koeki* has also been conducted within the confines of 'economic' concerns and for 'industrial development' purposes.

Let us imagine Mr M. as a teenager in the general context of Japanese society in the mid-1950s. With the successful accumulation of capital for investment and the introduction of modern technologies (most of them still imported from abroad), the economy began to become a labour-scarce one. As discussed in Chapter 3, the national economy was flexing its economic muscle to begin its new stage of industrial development. After the launch of the 'income-doubling' economic plan by government in 1961, the employment markets turned in favour of workers, particularly of young school leavers. Trainloads of school leavers (14 to 15 years old) began to arrive at large railway terminals from the less-developed farming areas from the northern part of the country. The young people from villages were to be employed in the factories and shops of the industrial towns in the central regions of Japan. They were to be absorbed in fast-expanding auto, auto-parts making and electric industries. The trains were called 'job trains', and the passengers on them were called 'golden eggs' – to be welcomed by the employers in the industrial towns who needed more workers to expand production to respond to the booming markets.

'Golden' or not, in reality they were only young people at a loss, making their way in a totally new environment in large industrial cities. They were a long way from their homes and families. A popular song was written to express their feeling. Its lyrics began, 'I went to the Ueno station to see trains arriving from the North carrying that dear sweet smell of home ... I cried, missing home and all that goes with it ...'[10]

Every week, on his way to and from school, Mr M. saw at Fukuoka railway terminal trains full of young boys and girls arriving from the 'farming north'. He also saw them in his neighbourhood in factories, working in car-part and machine-making shops. If not in factories, they were engaged in delivering takeaway noodle dishes, groceries, and in well-to-do households as housekeepers and garden hands. They were students who had left school after completing only the nine years of compulsory schooling.

Mr M.'s closest friend at school could run faster and hit balls higher and further into the outfield than he could. He could also write a better, more stylish and imaginative essay than Mr M., always getting better marks in chemistry, maths, Japanese and Japanese history despite having to allocate his weekend and after-school time to washing bottles with his father in a nearby *shoyu* soy-sauce manufacturing plant to earn some money for the former. When the time came for Mr M. to go to study at Tokyo University, the friend found a job at an electric manufacturing factory as an assembler of transistor radios.

Why was it this friend, and not he, who had to give up schooling, leave the world of learning that they both enjoyed so much? Mr M. lamented the misfortune of his friend. This question led him to recall a brief piece of traditional philosophy in one of the books he borrowed from his school library. It gave a short introductory explanation of several thinkers of old Japan that outlined their background, beliefs, and achievements. Yoshida Shooin (1830–59), who lived in pre-restoration Japan, was portrayed as a great personality who in his short life influenced many young people, among them several who became distinguished politicians and public administrators in the Meiji government.[11]

Under the influence of Confucius's teaching, Shooin thought about the ways of life of people in each part of feudal Japan, where everyone was, by birth, allocated to live in specific groups as a *samurasi*, down to the peasant farmer, artisan and merchant. He himself was born to the *samurai* class and to engage in public service. Given this arrangement he asked how he, a *samurai*, should live and follow the behaviour expected of his class. He questioned the justification that gave a *samurai* the right to rule people and live above others without engaging in any productive activities but only consuming what others made for him.

In the mid-nineteenth century *samurasi* were working as public administrators. It seemed to Shoin that the duties and responsibilities of a *samurai*'s life and behaviour were to be devoted to governing society for the well-being of the nation and the people. He thought it must be a God-given duty to study hard to find ways to govern people well and develop better public policy and administrative skills. Mr M. found Shoin's life, with such high standards of moral behaviour, worthy of being taken as a model for his own.

Such a way of thinking was not particularly popular among many young people in his time in the 1960s. But Shoin was a well-known writer who was respected and admired. His teachings appeared in many students' textbooks and historical works. Despite this Mr M. remembered that he felt embarrassed to find himself impressed by such old (perhaps archaic) moral teaching. So he decided to keep what he gained from the teaching but to hold the guiding message in his mind.

Mr M. cannot deny how this plain, perhaps too simple, moral force had guided him eventually to want to become a public servant. This came when he understood that he had no specific talent to create value of his own in the way that scientists, artists and sporting people could. It was a sad thing for a young man of high school age to accept. Eventually, however, he came to value his role in assisting others. It was time for the country to begin active economic growth. Many efforts were emerging before adequate funding and technical skills and managerial know-how had even been secured to establish work shops of all kinds and sizes in the steel making, textile, clothing, porcelain, furniture, and jewellery making fields in Fukuoka. Even to the inexperienced Mr M. such efforts appeared to be very high in risk. Nevertheless, a rising surge of entrepreneurial energy was evident. Mr M. was drawn to this energy and felt the need to find some way in which to help others. He thought his academic ability, albeit high school level, might be of some use.

Mr M. joined the Ministry. This appeared to him to be the right move. He remembers his time working at the Ministry as the best and most enjoyable time in his life. He felt confident that he was learning new things every day while, at the same time, working to help others.

He began to appreciate the value of public information. He decided to make full use of any available central public information and public networks. These gave him a perspective on ways in which to coordinate the otherwise scattered individual desires of managers and entrepreneurs, to establish new business ventures. He wished to organize as many cooperative works as possible, by bringing together business and enterprising activities for their mutual benefit. I call this approach 'matchmaking'. Mr M. cannot claim this approach as his alone. However, by promoting many new investment activities and business programmes through this approach, many in the Ministry began to see the effectiveness of this 'matchmaking' approach, leading to this practice becoming one of the most popular administrative approaches in the Ministry through the latter part of the 1960s. Mr M.'s first assignment at the Ministry was to find ways to rescue troubled smaller firms under excessive competition pressure. His subsequent experience fulfilling varied attending varied assignments through his biennial transfers between offices and departments led Mr M. to appreciate the value of the comprehensive nature of public information and administrative networks.

The time was favourable for this approach. He could gain and make full use of supports which Najita had earlier called Japan's 'bureaucratism' widely within the Ministry and across various offices in other ministries. Bureaucratism is the general attitude towards work and life of the top bureaucrats in Japan in Mr M.'s time. They share a high sense of 'mission' in maintaining the national well-being and the dignity of people in the country. Together they are highly conscious of their distinguished educational backgrounds. Mr M. could find ready support from colleagues for his programmes. His approach to serve others by assisting other people to create value could received a sympathetic hearing from his colleagues.

I locate Mr M. in the third quadrant in Figure 5.1 in Chapter 5. This is because I see him as an administrator and not a planner, on the basis that he does not hold his own views and make his own value judgements about how to build a better society through his public work. Growth maximization was the economic objective that Japan followed at the time, and Mr M. worked to bring this objective about. His knowledge of business and industrial activities is directed towards the interaction of individual activities that he makes an effort to assess in the general light of the economy. He does not enquire why and how each business and industrial activity is promoted, but he studies most carefully why and how each activity affects any other. He does this in order to locate any potential business partnerships and to find ways for productive cooperation. On this basis I have called him an 'intellectually led generalist' public administrator, acknowledging his intellectual effort to create partnerships between otherwise individual entrepreneurs and help them design cooperative work programmes.

What I now wish to discuss is the characteristic features of the generalist administrator as observed in Mr M.'s case, and examine whether this bureaucratic style will be useful in the post-industrial economy.

We saw how Mr M. found the strength to work in the central government office while building observations and experience through biennial *ido* appointments. The practice of *ido* is a specific employment/ promotion arrangement traditionally developed throughout all government ministries in Japan. Under this arrangement, officers are asked to move between offices and departments within their ministry, usually on a biannual basis. The officers experience new functions and work at each stage of this process, as they gradually 'spiral' upwards towards a position of greater responsibility. The Japanese bureaucracy developed this practice with the belief that it is more desirable for career officer to participate actively in the policy making process with a well balanced judgement and full understanding of both the economic and the non-economic aspects of a situation, rather than to come from a limited point of view derived from specialized experience in only a single legal, economic, social or political field. Mr M. was provided with 'central' economic information together with public authority to go out and acquire further information and data. He was pleased to find that he had the ability to see the big picture and make sense out of scattered pieces.

Mr M. enjoyed seeking ways to encourage economic growth and industrial efficiency from various angles as he travelled across different departments with different assignments in the Ministry. He attended different economic and business activities and worked in varied areas of economic management. It was a great pleasure and very exciting to see a sharp and rapid rise in the living standard of people (measured by a regular increase in per capita GNP comparable with that in the USA, the UK and Germany, for example) and the national status of the country in the world (measured by the expansion of total GNP). The high record appeared regularly in government economic statistics as if to confirm the importance and positive contribution of the work of the Ministry, which was conducted with the clear aim to increase economic growth and efficiency. He felt a great satisfaction professionally through his contribution to the growth of the economy and the expansion of industrial activities in the country.[12]

The approach was growth-oriented following the 'double national income' economic plan in 1960. Mr M. carried out his public mission by promoting the wealth accumulation of the economy. He promoted the objective by formulating various methods and arranging well-prepared meetings and business forums and investment missions so as to show business how to discover new investment opportunities, and encourage them to take these up by providing whatever assistance he could.

Because of his style of work, Mr M. could be likened to a 'match-maker'. He helped business by seeking and locating sources of public funding or making arrangements to generate funding through industry or tax concessions. He led enterprising businesses to become aware of how to use resources to their advantage.

It may be an exaggeration to give all the credit to Mr M. for the development of this approach, which has become popular in the Ministry.[13] He tried hard to locate active enterprises of various sizes in varied fields by regularly visiting work sites across many industries in the country, attending many business meetings and developing professional and personal relationship with managers. His open and friendly personality, with his trustworthy nature and his keenness to serve others have contributed to his success.

He added his comment about the development of this approach at one of our interview meetings. He said he was most appreciative of the confirmation that he was not alone in experiencing satisfaction in this way, and saw his work 'ethos' confirmed and shared by his old class-mates and colleagues. He found himself working in a select and privi-leged group that encouraged him in promoting what he did. He was content to mix with them and valued the opportunity to share experi-ences with them, since they had come to the University and conse-quently to the Ministry from a similar background and with similar ethical views.[14] The approach worked well with the support of like-minded colleagues in the Ministry at the time. He made an effort to locate that talent in others, and succeeded in this, but he was not sure whether it would work with bureaucrats of the coming generation in the reformed Ministry. He spoke of his concern at our meeting in early 2003 over the fast-declining capacity of the Ministry to develop a 'vision' of the future economy. He referred to the rapid development of R&D activities promoted at home and throughout the world as well as the expansion of global activities by individual firms and the national economy. He expressed his concern about the need for a clearly under-stood government role and an appropriate method for recruiting and educating bureaucrats for the future.

7
The Intellectual Public Administrator: Mr N., Type D Officer[1]

Mr N. is a Type D administrator whom we are able to locate in the third quadrant in Figure 5.1. His administrative approach is directed to effective gaining of cooperation from business.

Towards the end of 2003 he was a senior career public administrator at the Ministry with 24 years of work experience behind him (he was born in 1954 and entered the Ministry in 1978) and was looking to work in the Ministry for another 20 years, assuming that he remained until the official retirement age of 65.

In practice, given customary employment practice in the Ministry, he expects to be able to stay with them for a further five to six or eight years before he will be asked to move to a research organization associated with the Ministry or a public corporation or agency as a senior manager or an executive in private business.

Mr N. is not sure how far his work experience and practical understanding of the economic and industrial activities in Japan will enable him to take up an academic appointment. He does believe, however, that he would be able to write a record of the workings of the administrative offices. He believes it is important to keep such records, including those of aborted attempts and accidental results in a comprehensive and candid way so as to allow any interested researchers to examine them. It became his dream to compile, some day, a historical record of Japan's industrial policy that would give readers the facts and figures and inside information about the workings of the office and economic policy-writing efforts. In his view, this record would show how the policies were conceived, how they were formulated and implemented and how some were aborted.

A comprehensive record of the history of the Ministry was compiled and published in 17 volumes from 1992 to 1994 and Mr N. worked on

131

this publication as part of the editorial team. It was through this work that he began to cherish his dream. He viewed the official approach as inappropriate, believing that the Ministry had made it into a lifeless collection of figures and events.

Career path

Mr N. was born in 1954 in a little town on the outskirts of Nagoya, which was then the third largest city in Japan. Nagoya was at that time in the early stages of becoming part of the modern industrial base of Japan through the production of automobile, auto parts and machinery.

Mr N. had two sisters, but was the only son in the family. His father was an administrative officer in the district police office. In his native town, where the total population in those days was less than 300,000, his father's position gave him a more 'public' face than would be the case in larger or more industrialized places. So he was brought up with the self-imposed pressure to behave well and to attain good academic results at school – the same kind of pressure, perhaps, as felt by the sons and daughters of school principals and ministers of religion often observed in the West. Apart from this, he remembered his childhood as being materially comfortable (he classified his family as belonging to the middle class with a relatively stable income). He enjoyed a happy family atmosphere.

He studied well and excelled in each class through his primary and secondary school years. His high school is the top prefectural school, originally established for boys only, and it took pride in seeing its old boys reach top positions in government, business and other professional offices in Tokyo and Osaka. Post-war education reform turned his school into a coeducational one, but when he attended it it had a majority of male students who competed hard to get into the prestigious universities in Tokyo. In his year, there were 300 boys and fewer than 50 girls. He liked to study every subject carefully and thoroughly, and gained many distinctions. He did not, however, allocate much of his time to any extracurricular activities such as debating and essay contests, which some of his classmates pursued. He was simply not interested in taking up such activities. With his quiet manner and his somewhat 'introverted' personality, he was aware he risked being seen by casual observers as someone who would not quite fit the culture of the Ministry, which was perceived as dynamic and sometimes aggressive, its members always busy solving problems and dealing with policy issues, creating new projects with 'innovative' ideas and approaches.

At our early interview meetings in the mid-1990s Mr N. told me that he had decided, at the time of entering the Ministry, to see how far he could go in making a contribution to the Ministry's work without attempting to conform to the 'extrovert' culture of the Ministry. One aspect makes him an exception among his generation and those of his seniors in the Ministry. He did not come to the Ministry with the traditional background of a law degree from Tokyo University. He failed to get into the Law School there twice before he gave up and entered the Department of Politics and Economics in another university. On this account, he could certainly have been seen as not quite up to the standard of the others. He was 24 when he entered the Ministry, two years older than others who went to university straight from high school.

I recall how, after nearly an hour's discussion at out first meeting when we began to feel relaxed and comfortable with each other, he said proudly that he would pursue his own style in his office, allocating extra time and care compared to many of his colleagues, who might be quicker and smarter.

What led him to seek a position in the Ministry, and what made the Ministry accept him out of many keen candidates? When he sought a position in the Ministry in 1978, the rate of unemployment had reached a peak of 2.09 per cent, which was seen as extremely high in those days after virtual full employment throughout the preceding decade and a half. The economy was going through the post-1973 oil crisis.

Mr N. found the job market very tight. Many good graduates who might normally have made their careers in business chose the security of public service. As for the possibility of getting into the Ministry, it appeared almost impossible for him without the standard Tokyo University degree. Reflecting the general mode of the economy, where business spoke of the need for the Ministry to play an active role to counter the downturn in business growth, it was enjoying a high profile and thus attracting many candidates.[2]

Ministry staff were seen as trouble-shooters, flexing their muscles to challenge the emerging friction in international trade and structural unemployment in traditional industries as a result of the sudden decline in economic activities at home and abroad. Mr N. did very well in the civil service examination. He decided to try his luck. After the initial pre-entry interview examination at the Ministry, he was invited back as many as four times to meet senior as well as younger officers for further discussions. As the numbers of interviews accumulated, he became more eager to get into the Ministry. During these interviews, he was asked to explain his view of the duty of public administrators and his reasons for seeking a place in the Ministry. It was explained to him later that these general questions are asked with the purpose of understanding the candidate's personality. The interviewing officers looked for specific personal qualities in the candidates whom they hope will develop into trustworthy and cooperative work partners.

He was happy to have been invited back to interviews so many times. When asked why he was seeking a public service job, he talked about his childhood memory of Ise Typhoon in September 1959, which inflicted large-scale damage on the whole Nagoya region, destroying houses and buildings, ships docked in the Ise Bay and agricultural fields and forests. It also caused the death and injury of more than 40,000 people across the mainland of Japan. Mr N. was then five and a half years old. His father was busy taking charge of the safety of people in his town. What he remembered most vividly was how his father attended to his public duty without sparing any of his time for the safety of his family (his sisters were pre-school children) so that he, as the eldest son, felt it his duty to help his mother evacuate the children to higher land with bundles of daily necessities.

He told the interviewing officers how the incident made a strong impact upon him as a child, showing him what public duty meant to his father. He explained that he remembered how he looked up to his father's behaviour with admiration, making the incident one of the most memorable of his life. He was not sure what impressions this simple childhood memory gave the interviewing panels. Possibly, making a guess based on his later experience as a member of such a panel, the fact that he had thought about 'public duty' in his youth and had formed some idea of what it meant to him must have convinced the panel of his suitability for the Ministry.

At the beginning of his third year at university he began to search for a suitable topic for his honours thesis. He read a textbook on Keynesian economics and was introduced to the study of economic policy and welfare economics.[3] He wrote his thesis on the importance of planning in the economy, a topic slightly different from the popular ones of the time which were mainly in the fields of mathematical economics and econometrics.

By the mid-1950s, the national economy had achieved considerable expansion, of which statistical records were readily available in government publications. The computer had become easily accessible to university students, and mathematical economics and econometrics had become popular subjects among bright students, who found it intellectually exciting to experiment in building econometric models. Many of Mr N.'s classmates chose to write their theses on quantifying national and industrial economic performances and forecasting the future growth of the economy. Young lecturers returning from North American universities gave lectures to Mr N.'s class condemning Japan's traditional approaches to political economy.

In this climate, Mr N. wrote his thesis asking what the economic role of government was, and how to incorporate the concepts of justice and equality into economics and economic policy for growth. He got a high distinction as the best thesis in the year. He said, 'I think I got a good mark for my work not so much for its quality but by touching the lamenting heart of some of the old professors in the thesis examination board who appreciated my enthusiasm for a policy-oriented voice.'

Although this comment comes from his wish to show his modesty, there is, however, justification in noting the 'lamenting heart' of senior professors. It was a time when there was a growing gap in the understanding of the public role in economic activities between the old and young generations of researchers and students. This gap grew out of the different emphasis on the importance of economic growth and industrial efficiency as against quality of life, which emerged as the national concern in the 1970s. People were aware of the importance of the issue, but bureaucrats and academics were slow to understand its significance, let alone policy devices needed to respond to the emerging need.

Mr N. was among the 26 young men who were accepted into the Ministry in 1978. Sixteen were drawn from the Law School at Tokyo University. The remaining ten were from economics departments in various universities. Although not from a traditional pre-Ministry background, he found himself among the majority who had provincial backgrounds, with only five of that year's intake being born in Tokyo. The Ministry was beginning to seek officers from diverse social groups, but female recruits were rare.[4]

Entering the Ministry (1978–80)

Mr N.'s first appointment was a research-based one. Subsequently he followed the biannual rotation of offices across various bureaux so that in 23 years he rotated between offices with 13 different assignments in a manner similar to the generalist career path of Mr M.

His first job was to work on the compilation of an official history of post-war industrial policy (1945–71) and his responsibility was to research and organize research meetings and discussion sessions to coordinate the works of the contributors who were selected from universities.[5] Through this he learned much about the Ministry and its history.

He formed two impressions during this period. One was about the working style of individual officers around him and in the Ministry as a whole. The other concerned the nature of his contribution to the public task of the Ministry. He became conscious of himself as not quite the same as most of his colleagues.

Certainly, his failure to get into the Tokyo University Law School had, despite his later brilliant academic record, a negative effect on his confidence and self-esteem. He was forced to find a unique worth and special talent in himself that would allow him to make a unique contribution to the Ministry. He was to stay outside the circle of 'bureaucratism' that Najita observed in the working of public offices in the Japanese government.[6] He had to be himself and wanted to be better than those high-flyers.

The two years spent at the *yobi-ko*, preparatory school for university entrance examination, placed him two years older than most of his colleagues (he was turning 24 when he entered the Ministry). This enabled him to observe the behaviour of his colleagues with some advantages. They appeared anxious to be quick in thinking and sharp in responding to assignments, and could be said to be adopting work behaviour somewhat akin to that of firemen who were busy extinguishing a blaze, but not knowing why and where the fire had started. They seemed to take pride from their strength in these skills. Mr N. tried to distance himself from the motivations that were driving the anxious novice officers, who appeared to him keen to follow instructions given by supervising officers.

Some believe that the Ministry had enjoyed a good reputation for being strong in developing innovative ideas for industrial development, and it is said to have formulated various industrial policies, developed many new administrative devices, found solutions to economic and social problems – all resulting in high praise for the Ministry from observers inside and out. They viewed the Ministry as having been clever at selecting winning horses in infant industries and nurturing them to be internationally competitive enterprises, foreseeing the future pattern of the economic and social structure of the country and identifying new markets both at home and abroad.

I observed that, throughout the 1950s and 1960s, industrial expansion was pursued as a national objective and that people in Japan trusted the Ministry to undertake a leading role in formulating industrial policy measures beyond traditional tariff protection and public subsidy provisions.

Good administrative skills and many innovative policy measures were said to have been designed by the Ministry, resulting in its high reputation. The standard *ido* bi-annual promotion system was used to drive this dynamic policy making in the Ministry in which intellectually active public service administrators were trained as generalists.

The Ministry was quite small in comparison with other ministries in Japan's government, as well as equivalent bodies overseas.[7] Under the pressure of living up to its reputation with relatively small resources (funding and manpower), officers felt obliged to behave in a hyperactive way the whole year. In the Ministry it is not enough to be productive in designing policy devices; you must also secure a large budget allocation to be able to implement policy programmes.

As stated earlier, Mr N. observed that many Ministry policies were written by identifying problems in the economy long before they emerged as obvious difficulties. Yet the wisdom of predicting those emerging problems before the event was not adequately accompanied by attempts to find the causes and to examine the nature of the economy. He saw this as a grave shortfall in the Ministry. While following its history of industrial policy writing, he read of many incidents where the same economic problems frequently recurred, though taking on different forms in different contexts, so the old policy measures were proposed and formulated repeatedly, involving different officers across different generations.[8] It had become customary for the Ministry to organize the bi-annual promotion system to direct its officers to develop plans and policy proposals. The Ministry organized the bi-annual promotion system to direct its officers to develop plans and policy proposals as frequently and regularly as possible so as to present the image of the Ministry as highly pro-active.

Under this system, officers were expected to complete their assigned task within one to two, in some cases three, years depending on the nature of the tasks and the work arrangement of the host offices.[9] It could be said that he stayed in the administrative field rather than plan formulating and policy writing field to provide *gyosei shido*, administrative guidance, to industries and individual firms. The system operates rotating officers between departments and giving assignments that develop through four stages.[10]

First, in April each year new officers arrived from other departments and bureaux. Within the years of their appointment they have to familiarize themselves with and understand the business and industry concerned; second, identify the potential and problems for their development with the aim of articulating them in specific policy proposals;

third, write economic programmes and industrial policy before March in the second year; circulate the drafted ideas and programmes within the Ministry – starting with within the department, taking it up to the bureau head; and gain the endorsement of the vice-minister's office to make the proposal the official programme of the Ministry which, with the endorsement secured, the proposal will be circulated widely among government authorities. Fourth, this task takes place some time towards the end of the calendar year so as to gain a budget allocation from the Ministry of Finance in March of the next year.

Mr N.'s first two years provided him with ample opportunities to observe the work environment of his office, assess the style of his fellow officers and study the past work of the Ministry. He found himself more interested in observing and evaluating the policy-making process than in working on it himself.

By 1999 he had managed successfully twelve *ido*, transfer assignments, between offices, including three *shukko*, on loan appointments, to work at the Economic Planning Agency (now Naikaku-fu) and Ministry of Labour rather than plan formulation and policy writing to provide *gyosei shido*, administrative guidance, to industry and individual firms.

Administrative guidance is one of the most extensively used industrial policy techniques that the Ministry developed at the time when it promoted growth and modernization of industry from the second half of the 1950s through the early 1970s. It was also used when the growth period was over and many industry and business enterprises had to curtail production and refrain from further investment so as to adjust to the declining business climate. The Ministry decided to achieve this adjustment by promoting cooperative enterprises and by coordinating activities in industries and between firms – a preference for managing a 'soft landing' on the market equilibrium position as against a drastic 'hard landing' in order to avoid sending many firms into bankruptcy. We saw Mr M. adopted a matchmaking role in the growth period of the 1960s to encourage new investment programmes and trade activities. He used administrative guidance for growth and expansion. Mr N. used the same method for managing the adjustment to recessed growth.

Mr N. also used the same adjustment method but, this time, to mitigate difficulties of recessed industries and ailing firms.

Administrative guidance

The previous active growth industries were to experience difficulties in the period after the first oil crisis in 1973–75. The Japanese economy had to meet numerous challenges caused by the rising costs of raw materials and energy, a shortage of youth labour leading to a general rise in labour costs across industries and the appreciation of the value of the yen against the American dollar that began in 1971 and culminated in the 'Nixon shock'. To make matters worse, the export drive from newly emerged Asian economies resulted in a sharp fall of international competitiveness of Japan's exports in the world market. For the first time since the end of the World War II, the Japanese economy was thrown into serious and long-term economic depression. The Ministry had to rescue struggling businesses and industries by various policy means and administrative devices.

To begin with, the Ministry compiled a list of industries with difficulties and grouped them as under the heading 'structurally depressed industries'.[11] The Ministry understood that their problems arose from the general and total decline in demand and not because of inadequacy in their management. It came to believe that standard macroeconomic anti-recession policies would not solve many of industry's problems. It believed that special public measures should be formulated to address individually each of the problems specific to the industries and firms in difficulty. New laws and regulations were introduced as part of the Ministry's adjustment policy during those years.

Administrative guidance measures developed by the Ministry have attracted little criticism. But some economists have found no clear evidence that the measures ever brought any substantial results.[12] It is difficult to estimate the extent of their contribution given the fact that the policy instruments have most frequently helped firms in an informal way, so that there are few records available for researchers to see what measures were taken, how they were administered, and to quantify actual results or negative effects.

With the strengthening of the antitrust laws after the mid-1970s, the use of administrative guidance has become less frequent and it has been replaced by other newly developed policy approaches such as 'vision' policies. Despite this, I believe administrative guidance deserves careful examination and would expect to see in the development of the policy of administrative guidance a clue to understanding the making of Japan's economic society.

Mr N. has practised administrative guidance twice, first in the electric furnace steel-making industry in 1978–80 and, second, with an LPG (liquefied petroleum gas) industry in 1990–92.

Electric steel-making industry, 1980

After two years of introductory training at the International Trade Research Office, Mr N., by then 26, began his career as an economic bureaucrat in the electric furnace steel-making industry.

The steel industry in Japan consists of two industries, one with shaft furnaces and the other with open-hearth furnaces. The former is a modern, large-scale and capital-intensive industry, which produces steel sheets, tubes and rolled steel by smelting imported iron ore. The latter is one of smaller scale that makes steel rods and wires out of reconditioned scrap metal available from domestic sources. Mr N. was assigned to look after the welfare of the latter.

There were many small-scale operators in this industry. The market is segmented and competition is very strong in contrast to the former, where an 'oligopolistic' structure is observed. Because its production technique is relatively simple, requiring only very small initial investments to set up the operation, many new entries into the industry took place during the period of high economic growth. There were 74 operators in 1976, of which 39 were reported to have been very small, with only one or, at most, two furnaces and a total employment of ten or twenty people each. The manner of production was hardly modern with old equipment, some of it pre-war in origin. Its management was also pre-modern, relying on semi-trained employees consisting of family members and workers available in the neighbourhood. Managers and senior employers seemed to spend a great deal of time and energy doing on-the-job training of those less skilled and experienced staff members.Even after adjustments in production capacity were made during the depression years after the first oil crisis in 1973–75, the electric furnace steel-manufacturing industry found it extremely difficult to cope with the problems of under-utilization of production capacity and excessive employment. In May 1978, the Diet passed the Temporary Law for Stabilization of Specified Depressed Industries (the Depressed Industry Law). This law was designed to encourage and help firms operating in those structurally depressed industries, including the electric furnace steel industry. They were to receive government guidance and assistance to curtail their production activities and relocate them to other more profitable and expanding areas.[13]

Mr N. was thrown in at the deep end. Here he could observe at first hand how government and business made contacts and negotiated cooperative forms of working. The government attempts to bring its public view of the 'ideal' form of industry structure and business practice into the national economy, while business, on the other hand, tried to adhere to earlier ways of operating the activities.

The official purpose of the Ministry is to secure stable and internationally cost-competitive supplies of materials such as steel, non-ferrous metals and chemicals. The Ministry viewed it as unwise to increase reliance on the supply of those materials from imported sources. It wanted to secure continuous efficient operation of the industries for the growth and industrial development of the national economy as a whole.

The Ministry organized a survey of this particular industry before the formulation of policy measures and found that no firm had been making a normal profit during 1980 and 1981. It was feared that, without the prompt introduction of some public measure, the industry would plunge into cut-throat competition in an effort to secure a minimum operating scale for its survival.

The specific task of Mr N. was to help his *kacho* and his team to apply the proposed restructuring plan to this declining industry. In this job, he had frequent exposure to discussions that were conducted between his colleagues and industry representatives. The public aim was twofold: to reduce the scale of production as soon as possible, thereby maintaining the level of prices and bringing stability; and to provide each firm with an essential profit margin, thereby ensuring that workers in the industry secured a minimum standard of well-being. In this way the Ministry was acting as a provider of social security.

In 1980, when Mr N. was appointed, there were 60 firms operating in the industry. Each firm, on average, was estimated to be actually operating only at a third of capacity.[14] The Ministry forecast the demand for the type of steel for the coming few years and the total production capacity of the industry. The gap between demand and supply was calculated. With this information on the estimated size of overcapacity, staff in Mr N.'s office went out to visit each firm to ensure that each manager understood that the size of the future market would not support the present number of firms even if each made efforts to reduce its operations to the minimum.

As well as providing this general overview of the industry, Mr N.'s office began to introduce new administrative devices to encourage and assist the withdrawal and relocation of capital and labour into alternative fields and trades.

As a start, senior officers in the iron and steel division searched for capital funds, cheap loans, tax concessions, public provisions and subsidies, unemployment and job-retraining help and other measures in government and industry. Relocation of production abroad, particularly to the industrializing part of Asia, was also encouraged, and generous public funds were allocated. The government thought this would serve two purposes simultaneously – alleviate the problems of overcapacity in the industry and reduce Japan's large trade surplus.

The task required substantial bureaucratic knowledge about public acts and regulations in the public network and sources of finance in industry and the government sector. With only three years' work experience, what Mr N. could contribute was relatively limited.

During 1980 and 1981, through Mr N.'s office, the Ministry arranged six meetings to which representatives of each of the 60 operators were invited to hear the official views and to discuss how the industry might restructure in such a way as to mitigate overproduction. No representatives missed any of the meetings, with owners or the most senior managers attending to show how seriously they valued the meeting. During the meetings these representatives were encouraged to talk candidly about their problems and to evaluate their operations in relation to the whole industry. The Ministry believed that candid communication between the public service and business was essential to finding practical solutions.

Mr N. remembered how the spirit of the meetings was maintained, with many industry representatives even airing some highly private concerns about the welfare of employees and their family members and employees. He saw how closely business activities overlapped the lives of the employers and the employed. In most cases, the employers were the owner–managers who had founded the firm and had a trade background. Their work was a way of life for them and far more than simply a source of income. He saw that many of them did not seek growth to any extent. Working in the same Ministry at the same time, Mr N. could not share the work norm of Mr M.'s 'director' approach without introducing any direction to guide business activities intellectually towards maximizing any objective. He wanted employers to find a stable business environment in which they could pursue comfortably whatever the direction they wish to take together. Neither his efforts nor his *kacho*'s administrative techniques, however, brought the desired results. None of the total 60 firms accepted administrative guidance during his time in the office.

When the annual *ido* or job rotation, came to his *kacho* after two years in the office, he left to work in another department. Twelve months later, in December 1983, Mr N. was transferred to a new appointment in the Economic Agency, leaving those 60 firms he had tried to help.

In 1992, when he came across one of his colleagues who was working in the same office, he enquired about those 60 firms and was told that eight had left the industry since his time with them. Fifty-two were still operating as before, although under slightly improved trading conditions that had come about as a result of the general recovery in the national economy after the 1978 recession.[15]

Sale of LPG, 1991

Mr N. was given a second chance to experiment with administrative guidance in 1991 when he was promoted to the position of *kacho*, office director. His task was to supervise the refining and the sale of liquid petroleum gas, LPG, with the aim of maintaining price stability in the face of a possible disruption in the supply of crude oil from the Middle East. A *kacho* appointment gave him relative flexibility in selecting his approach to the task. The interruption of shipping from Kuwait disrupted the import of LPG and the Ministry feared that about half of domestic demand would be rationed, leading to price rises and panic buying as news of the interruption to shipping reached the domestic market. At the time Japan did not have a way of stockpiling LPG as it did for crude oil.

By then economists had learned from the oil crises in 1973 and 1978 what damage could be done to the economy when panic buying by consumers and an unwillingness to sell by producers controlled the market.

At this critical time, Mr N. was asked to formulate an administrative mechanism to control the price of LPG. Without panic buying and possible greed for instant profit on the part of importers, the Ministry was of the view that there would be no major increase in the supply price if the source of imports had to be moved from Kuwait to other areas. His office was asked to find ways to keep this price rise strictly within limits.

For some time the oil-refining industry had been under the careful observation of the Ministry so that the government had accurate and up-to-date information about production capacity, investment level, production methods, price levels and business performance of each firm in the industry. The Japanese people understood the country's dependence on imported crude oil and knew that any disruption would swiftly bring disorder to the economy.

Mr N. began his work by compiling detailed charts of the price changes of LPG over the preceding two years so that he could see the industry's trading and production activities in a normal period. He asked each importer and distributor to present their cost structure giving detailed breakdowns of each cost component (refining, marketing, international and domestic transport fees, interest and insurance cost, administrative and overhead expenses, and so on). His request was met within 24 hours, and he was able to project the effect of a disruption in supply on the market price. Such direct public intervention was tolerated in an atmosphere where the maintenance of market stability was a priority.[16]

With the information accumulated in the Ministry, he asked representatives of the 50 firms in the industry to assemble in his office to discuss the situation and the future prospects of the supply of LPG. Mr N. demonstrated the accuracy and comprehensive nature of the information his office so far had collected. On this basis he asked the representatives to keep the price rise within the limit of any unavoidable cost increases, and that the businesses absorb part of the cost increases through their *kigyo doryoku*, or managerial effort, a notion of obligatory duty to government in the face of a national economic crisis. The business representatives agreed and in this way increases in the price of the gas during the second oil crisis were avoided.

Mr N.'s experiences with the electric furnace steel making industry in 1978–80 and LPG in 1990–92 enable me to make a number of observations about Japan's business conduct in order to evaluate the notion of administrative guidance as it was adopted to restructure ailing industries.

Administrative guidance evaluated

Some may see in Mr N.'s story a tendency in Japan to practise 'government-led' behaviour in conducting economic and business activities. Others read into it a view of Japanese business making a group-oriented decision in investment and trade. I want to make two observations about it.

First, it shows how government and business follow an intellectual style in solving problems. They like to solve them through logic, seeking rational explanations for their causes. Second, in making a managerial procedure, in practice, they are searching for an effective avenue for rescue.

Intellectual approach

In an effort to capture the distinctive characteristics in the planning approach between a 'centrally planned communist society' and a 'market-led liberal democratic society', Charles Lindblom argued that the former makes efforts to plan with the assumption that 'there are men in the society wise and informed enough to ameliorate its problems and guide social change with a high degree of success'.[17] By contrast, he says, such a strong assumption is absent from the latter and the citizens in the society think that 'no individual or group in the society can achieve with a high degree of competence. They are fallible in crippling and dangerous ways in dealing with society's problems and in guiding social change.'[18] He equates his first model with a 'centrally planned communist society' such as China. He calls it an 'intellect-led' society characterized by knowledge-based features.

The second model he equates with a 'market-led liberal democratic society' like those we see from time to time in the West. He calls this society a 'preference-led' one and shows the importance of political process (rather than knowledge) in its planning activities. In short, the former describes 'planning by design' and the latter 'planning by preference'. He argues that because of the very different capabilities of planners in those intellect-led and market-led societies, equally different forms of plans and public administrative activities will emerge across different country economies.

I do not see Japan fitting comfortably into either model. Terms like 'mixed model' and 'planned market economy' have been coined to capture Japan's position. How does Japan manage to hold a 'middle' course? In search of an answer I want to examine, by following the experiences of Mr N., how planning is practised in Japan.

I believe that it was through an intellectually guided approach rather than through market-consulting efforts that bureaucrats in the Ministry and managers in the electric furnace steel-manufacturing industry were able quickly to alleviate the business difficulties they experienced in the depressed state of the market in the 1970s. I want to illustrate how business has promoted this intellectually guided approach rather than simply following government guidance, as some observers have suggested, in an attempt to describe Japan's economy as 'government-led'. Business managers understood the importance of economic knowledge and market information collected through officially organized studies, and consulted econometric estimates of market trends. Businesses themselves organized study committees and surveys. But it did not end there. Firms organized many subsequent meetings in which they discussed and evaluated the findings. These activities took place frequently during difficult times. In this way, firms approached the problems as 'whole-industry' ones and subsequently sought group solutions.

It is noteworthy to observe in this Japanese industry that all the managers of the firms concerned, regardless of the nature of the business difficulties experienced, took part in the surveys and studies. The government responded to this 'intellectually guided' approach by forming consultative councils and study groups in the Ministry with the aim of developing policy formula and guidance mechanisms to solve or alleviate problems.

If it is the 'intellectual approach' through the use of 'information' that Japanese business and the government follow, and if it is the information that they consult that brings them together, then it is important to understand what kind of information it is; how it is collected; how it is used; and what kind of society and business structure will emerge from it.

Firms in Japan seek specific information in their need to make investments and other business decisions. The information consists of facts and figures that help practising managers view business activities as they are actually taking place. Managers in firms expect such information to be 'central', and to provide them with a long-term picture of business conditions.

I have noted that, in the depressed years of the 1970s, electric furnace steel-making firms made an effort to collect such information. This work appeared to increase in intensity as firms experienced difficulties at an accelerating rate. Managers in firms like to review such information in a group with other members in the industry and share it with their competitors so that they are able to observe how others assess and evaluate it. The managers value any follow-up study findings as much as the information itself. As noted above, Mr N. remembers that when his office organized these meetings virtually no managers missed them.

The group evaluation of information takes place with the aim of each industry to assess its own position – its performance, its problems and the nature of any business difficulties – relative to that of its competitors, and to be able to see the big picture of their industry, the national economy and the international context. This is a characteristic feature of Japan's business culture and a basis for the effective working of 'indicative' planning in the economy.

For a long time Japan has made regular efforts to collect facts and figures. Subsequently, it has made it a public duty to disperse information widely among industries. When Japanese businesses show their preference for following an 'intellectual approach', they do not expect the information to be perfect or complete. Officers in the Ministry are not viewed by business, on the one hand, or see themselves, on the other, as particularly wiser than those in business. Intellectual competence itself is not a required quality in Japan for public administrators who help business or planners. Public administrators are effective in helping businessmen because they are well provided with public information and are positioned so that they can get a bird's-eye view of business and economic activities beyond the data collected by businessmen.

As I have said, in 1980 Mr N. was busy organizing discussions between senior administrative officers in government and managers from each firm. He saw many close consultations between the *kacho* and each manager invited to the office, when the *kacho* could demonstrate his experience and superior knowledge of the industry. Some assumed an elite power and public authority. Mr N. felt uneasy, fearing that he was witnessing the formation of a 'manipulative society'.

Observing little reduction of excess production capacity in the 1970s, many economic researchers concluded that the Ministry's policy of intra-coordination had contributed little to price stability, efficiency of resource allocation, or the reduction of excess capacity in the industry.[19] This conclusion is acceptable if we are evaluating technically how the objectives of administrative guidance and industrial policy for restructuring the industry are promoted and with what results.

Responsible behaviour sought in industry

Our second observation is about a general expectation in government of 'responsible' behaviour among competing business corporations.

From the beginning of 1959 to the end of 1971, the Ministry organized several meetings with the purpose of coordinating investment in the electric furnace steel-making industry. There was a cooperative response despite the fact that the administrative help was given on a non-compulsory, non-regulatory, non-binding basis.

I don't believe that we should be too hasty in interpreting this case as a sign of the emergence of 'responsible' behaviour in business in general. To understand why it happened, we need to examine how business followed an 'intellectual approach' and sought 'central' information that appeared to have led them to view their own individual activities in the context of the economy and community. It should lead individuals to appreciate, though to varying degrees, the value of reviewing their own behaviour in terms of 'social consequence' and 'social obligation'. Some may dismiss such speculation as 'naïve' and 'idealistic' and, even accepting the basis of it, bury it under Japan's traditional and cultural background.

Rather, I would like to explore the nature and development of this observation so as to find a way to construct a better future economic society. In such a case the risk may arise of building a manipulative society in which ideals are manufactured by knowledgeable government élites. They may have reduced the economic and human freedom of individuals in their efforts to build a productive economy, or at least discouraged their efforts to implement their own entrepreneurial devices in the changing trade and business environment. I wish to know how to build a civilized society in which the spirit of cooperation works without producing stifling conformity.

In the LPG industry in 1971, we saw Mr N. ready to experiment with an approach that would manufacture a value system that balanced public and private purposes. He focused on raising the sense of responsibility among managers. He provided public knowledge with the aim of leading individuals to behave as public-spirited citizens.

His overall aim in providing public guidance is to maintain stability in the economy and industry so as to give individuals security in the workplace and in life so that their efforts to plan to improve their standard of living could be continued undisturbed. His approach, *in practice*, was to give public guidance to managers so that they could see themselves in the big picture. With this he aimed to let businessmen see the importance of people's rather than their own interests; and to make his argument acceptable to business managers and let them behave accordingly he tried to introduce the concept of 'role' perception. That is, he tried to create roles in society to bring out the desired personal qualities in managers in each firm. If this could be achieved, he expected the managers to behave in a 'public-minded' and 'socially responsible' way. This, he believed, would stop them from putting the prices and/or shifting the cost increase on to others. He was aware of a danger of creating, as we stated above, conformity in business and economy, but his aim was to place a greater importance on providing people with freedom in life than on economic freedom.

The idea of creating desirable personal qualities in industry through public planning was not original.

Let us take the case of the iron and steel industry (this is the other industry we referred to earlier as modern, large-scale shaft furnaces, which differ from Mr N.'s electric open furnace iron- and steel-making) in the 1960s and 1980s. This example is the one that Mr N. and his colleagues often refer to as the 'ideal model'. The 'model' appears to them to lie in the solid establishment of an industry association that represents the interests of every operator from Nippon Steel, the leader of the industry and a giant in the national economy, to the oligopolists of Kawasaki, Sumitomo and NKK, down to the smaller smelters.[20] Its structure is stable in that each firm ranks consistently in terms of sales, profit and the number employed. As if to demonstrate the worth of its structure, the industry behaves in an equally 'orderly' and stable manner. An economics professor once said, with a hint of sarcasm, that the Ministry appreciates the 'virtue' of the industry because it follows the Confucian virtue of 'keep appropriate elder–younger relations' and 'know your own position and ability' and behave accordingly.[21]

Many economists might like to join the professor in looking at the government's approach. In the language of business in Japan, however, such a virtue has traditionally been pointed out as an 'ideal' pattern of conduct in which large established firms take on leadership to guide and protect smaller firms to secure the well-being of the industry. Each firm is expected to understand its relative position in the industry and act on that understanding.

Officers in the Ministry have a strong wish to see a harmonious market. They prefer to see an industry made up of a few firms whose market shares are divided in a stable manner, whose relative positions in terms of sales, profits and other operation resources are steady, and where there is 'orderly competition' with efforts to keep bankruptcies and other disturbances to a minimum. In order to secure such market harmony, bureaucratic devices for limiting competition and restructuring have frequently been implemented. From the 1950s and through the 1960s, to encourage mergers, vertical and horizontal groupings, inter-firm operating agreements and public control agreements were often introduced into the steel industry as part of the industrial policy of the Ministry.

What we see happening in the iron and steel industry in the period is a good example of the strategy that the Ministry formulated to build a stable industry structure that is expected to encourage harmonious market behaviour regardless of trading conditions. This public industrial strategy found ready support in business in Japan in the 1950s and 1960s when its industry was struggling to promote international competitiveness for growth of the national economy. In particular, the problem of excessively strong, cut-throat competition observed in the industry was a concern for many in business and government. A stable investment and trading behaviour was sought and the orderly behaviour in the industry that emerged was welcomed.

Mr N. understood that such commendable behaviour was built on two bases. The first was the public securing of central knowledge and information, and the second, the building of a set of images of the roles that individual members of the industry are supposed to play. Thus managers, even if they are ordinary, selfish people aiming to maximize profit for their own firms, will find themselves obliged to function in a responsible manner.

It is easy to dismiss this approach of the Ministry as based on 'bureaucratic ideology' which has its origin, as the economic professor suggested, in the old feudalism (thus in contrast to the individualistic and democratic norms of today respecting the motivation and interest of individual people) and argue further that that is created by an intention to conform and manipulate society to suit the administrative convenience of government. Instead, I propose to explore the spirit of the approach by asking if there are any ways for us to solve the 'incompatible gap between self interest and general and social purpose'.

Boulding has introduced us to the role theory of the social psychologists.[22] He said: 'Even a single individual does not usually have only one value ordering.' He argues that there are two different bases for ordering in the value system. One is 'personal value' ordering and the other is 'social value' ordering. The actual behaviour of the individuals is determined by yet another overall ordering that decides which of the two value orderings is to be dominant over the other in response to circumstances.

How far are we able to understand the actual work mechanism of the Ministry, which appears to create a new value system in business individuals through the skilful dissemination of central information and the building and distributing of role perceptions? With the help of Boulding, let us try to understand the hierarchy of value systems in the minds of business managers when Mr N. tried to provide them with public administrative guidance in those two industries discussed earlier.

First of all, let us understand that those managers have a 'personal value' ordering in conducting their own business. Take the LPG industry in 1991 with Mr N.; there are two possible choices that individual managers might have considered when receiving administrative guidance, say guidances A and B. A is the choice to put up the price of their liquid petroleum gas and transfer to consumers the expected price rise during the embargo problems as well as take the advantage and make a windfall profit out of the disturbance. The alternative choice is B, which suggests a more socially responsible approach. With choice B, they make the effort to estimate exactly what cost increases might be needed and see if they can find ways to reduce it through productivity improvement.

In contemplating which way to go a manager may think: A is better than B for me, but B is better than A for my family, or for my staff and workers in my enterprise, or for the industry, or for the national economy, or for the country, or for the world, and so on. So his concern may become larger and more general, addressing the interests of larger and larger groups of people beyond his individual self.

This means that people may have a number of value systems, one, for themselves, two, for their family, three, for their company, four, for the industry, five, for the national economy, six, for the world, and so on. Then a question arises about the pattern of the manager's value systems. He may, under some circumstances, say, 'A is better than B for me but I think B is better than A for the nation. But considering the circumstances in which I operate my business I will select what is better for me, not what is better for the nation' or alternatively under other circumstances. Or he might say, 'A is better than B for me but I think B is better than for the nation. Therefore I will decide to follow A for the benefit of the nation at the cost of my own welfare.' The latter is an example of individuals sacrificing their personal interest for the sake of the interest of larger groups. This is the way that Mr N. worked in the LPG industry in 1991.

We may go back to yet another earlier argument given by Lindblom. We see in his 'intellect-led' society a knowledgeable élite that demonstrates its competence to educate the rest of the population in correct theory and practice on social organization, government, policy and political participation so as to encourage cooperation. He observes that such an education consists of two characteristic features: 'ideology' building, aiming to influence a larger and more general audience; and the preference for using 'scientific' and 'fact and observation based' knowledge about society.[23]

It is my observation that to achieve this, Mr N., through the use of his 'scientific' and 'knowledge based' approach, introduced a set of role perceptions to guide managers to adjust their personal value systems to fit into their allocated roles and thereby accept social value ordering.

8
The Intellectual Planner: Mr K., Type A Officer

Career path

Mr K. joined the Ministry in 1977 at the age of 22 on graduating from the Law School at Tokyo University with little preconceived enthusiasm (so he recalls) for dedicating himself to *koeki*. He had not thought much about what working in a public organization such as a government ministry might mean compared to working in private business, practising law as a solicitor, or researching and teaching in a university.

Fifteen years later, in 1994, during our first interview, he spoke about his personal beliefs and professional plans, discussing how he might contribute to the development of Asian economies, convinced that he might have a useful role to play.

Childhood

Mr K. was born in 1955 in a suburb of Shizuoka as the only child of an owner–manager of a dry-cleaning shop. The year of his birth clearly places him in the post-war generation, which was free from the hardships of poverty in the pre-war and immediate post-war period. Many customs were still observed in personal relations and business, but people were beginning to make changes as they steadily accumulated wealth. Mr K. was born during Japan's period of high growth and subsequent economic prosperity. It was an exciting time, when people actively discussed their ideal society and sought ways to build it.

A survey conducted by NHK (the Japan Broadcasting Corporation) reported how the thinking and behaviour of people in Japan had changed by the end of the 1950s, when Mr K. was at primary school.[1] It observed that people nominated 'maintaining good health' as the most important prerequisite for a happy life. Previously it had been material provisions. The naked desire to secure daily necessities was expressed in workplaces by demands for wage rises and job security, and angry protests against the feared loss of the national political direction to US dominance quickly receded as a major concern. But by this end of the 1950s the general public began to show its approval of the way the country had promoted industry.

In this survey, the majority (estimated as large as 80 per cent) expressed a positive view of Japanese culture and tradition. But when asked what they would do if they were in need of money, they said they would go to social security rather than seeking the support of relations and friends. Principles and practice in life began to go in different directions. Of parents surveyed, 70 per cent said that they would like to see their sons and daughters develop their own talents rather than make efforts to show 'balanced' behaviour and fit well into society – again showing a move away from the traditional Confucian teaching. This is in contrast to the responses given in the earlier survey of 1928, when only 43 per cent of parents were reported to have appreciated the importance of the individual person.

The findings tell two different stories. At a national level, the Japanese had become patriotic, holding their country, its culture and economic development in high esteem. At an individual level, they were ready to cast off some of their old customs to enjoy modern comforts.

It is worth remembering that Mr K. was born when Japan's national economy was undergoing a transformation from capital-scarce ($K < L$) to capital abundant ($K > L$).[2] With virtual full employment across industries and workplaces, the differential of wage and work conditions between large modern industrial firms and their smaller competitors quickly dissipated, freeing people from lack of equity at work and home.

The construction boom, coming just before the 1964 Tokyo Olympics, had effects which reached even Mr K.'s little town. As a pre-school child, Mr K. saw a large modern supermarket next to his father's dry-cleaning shop replace a family grocer shop, tall concrete steps with a shopping arcade underneath replaced the timber stairs of the local station, and the little piece of waste land next to a local temple in which Mr K. used to spend hours with neighbouring boys playing hide and seek turned into a 12-room motel. In all such construction activities his father involved himself in varying forms and extents as a shrewd investor.

Neither of his parents had had much formal education, but his father had the sharp business sense to develop the site of his little laundry shop as a basis on which to build a real-estate business in the early

1950s. He had enough information networks among his trading friends to back his speculation and soon found he was quite good at investing.

The building boom that Mr K. and his father witnessed was not limited to the small town but extended all over the nation, making it the largest building boom in the country's history. Within five years, for example, between 1959 and 1964, the number of houses built in Japan rose 2.5 times, and the price of land rose nearly three times. The figure I quote here is the national average and includes remote areas and agricultural districts. In Mr K.'s already urbanized town, not far from Shizuoka, the third largest city in Japan in those days, the price rise of land must have been much higher than those figures suggest.

Towards the end of the 1960s, when Mr K. moved to junior high school, the family had already accumulated quite sizeable wealth. Soon a three-storey concrete building was built to replace the laundry shop – housing the family on the top two levels while the ground floor was allocated to the dry-cleaning business with a modern open shop front. The new building stood high overlooking the moat guarding old feudal Shizuoka castle.

Looking back to his boyhood days, Mr K. feels extremely fortunate to have been given the freedom, through material means, time and his parents' trust, to do almost anything he chose in study, sport, choosing friends and organizing his life. He could buy any books he liked, go to any films, theatres, concerts, visit the shopping centre in Shizuoka and the nearby Tokaido towns, holiday with friends, climb Mt Fuji, boat around the Fuji five lakes, ski and visit remote places. He maintained excellent school records so that his parents had no worries about which high school and university he would be able to get into, a matter that many parents in Japan take very seriously. At the same time he was not much interested in chasing girls and could not tolerate much alcohol. He remained a carefree, model boy in the eyes of his parents and their friends in the neighbourhood.

In 1970 he entered a prefectural state high school known as one of the top schools in the Tokai eastern Japan area. Entry into the school led him to meet and mix with some of those who would later became colleagues in the Ministry, friends in other ministries and senior officers in the nation's leading firms and banks. That is, at the age of 15 he entered on a path that would allow him to become part of an 'élite'.

Tokyo University Law School

But before joining the élite group he had to get to one of a few top prestigious universities. Tokyo University appeared to offer him the best prospect. He and his parents thought it best he went to Tokyo to try his potential in this large city from where the nation's leading talents were drawn. He was good at mathematics at school. Upon this strength he sought an entry into the Maths Department of the University. He passed the stringent entrance examination in April 1973 to become a Todai (Tokyo University) student.

In July, however, he visited the student counselling office to ask how to go about transferring himself to the School of Law in the next academic year. The previous three months, attending maths classes in the university, were long enough for him to be convinced, sadly, that he did not possess a 'natural aptitude' for mathematical studies. Having observed how the top students in his class studied the subject, some even entering the national maths competition to win prizes, showing their much higher understanding than Mr K.'s in the field of pure mathematics, he came to the conclusion that his high performance at the secondary-school-level maths would not guarantee him progress at the advanced level of the field. He did not want to spend the rest of his life struggling to keep up with those who are blessed with the 'natural talent'.

What were the alternatives? Study at the Economics Department, School of General Studies or School of Law appeared within his choice. He had little specific idea which one he should choose except that he thought more prestige appeared to be attached to the Law School than the other two. In these circumstances, he decided to aim for the Law School.

He studied hard at humanities and social science subjects because they were a prerequisite for entry into the Law School, but had escaped his attention throughout his schooling. There were a few others around him who wished to obtain a transfer from the Maths, Science, Medicine and Engineering Departments to the Law School. With them he attended classes nominated by the University to bridge the disciplines. He had to begin everything from the very basics. It was hard but he remembered how he was pleasantly surprised to discover the great attraction of Japanese social history and economics.

He succeeded in transferring into the sought-after Law School in March 1974 and began studying public law, aiming at a position as a solicitor or a public service opening for his future career. Again, why the specific choice? Possibly, at the time, both career paths appeared general enough to allow him to develop his future career in life. As noted at the beginning of the chapter, he recalls that he had virtually no aspiration towards offering himself for the *koeki* public purposes. To be more precise, in the second year of university at the age of 19, he had not yet formed any clear view as to whether he had any aptitude for whatever field of study might develop either his personal benefit or help him make his own contribution, if he wanted to, to others in society.

Personally, he was already becoming ambitious, with a high evaluation of his own capability, hoping to achieve something that would make his life worth living. But he did not know, at that stage, what and how it should be promoted.

First oil crisis of 1973

In 1974–75 many bankruptcies occurred and the national economy, which until then had enjoyed continuous high growth throughout nearly three decades, suddenly ceased its expansion as if it had permanently exhausted its potential for further development.

When he returned home for summer vacation in 1974, Mr K. saw that some of his father's friends and business acquaintances had fallen deep into financial difficulties due, apparently, to investing and expanding business too fast on borrowed money. The recession, however, worked favourably for his father, who could take over their debts to acquire and expand his already large holding of properties.

Despite business recessions in the post-oil-crisis years, in looking back we may remember the 1970s as a good time, when 'affluence' had arrived in the country and its GNP and national income per head rose to the standard enjoyed by most Western economies.[3] It is also important to observe how business and the general working public responded and countered this economic recession and 'shock' and 'crisis'.

It was not only the reduced speed of growth in the national economy but also a considerable loss of economic stability that affected the business and daily life of people.

A sudden shortage of many goods and services arose in almost all markets, leading to explosive price rises.[4] To make matters worse, panic buying followed. People proclaimed that the crisis amounted to the equivalent of the immediate post-war hardship just short of three decades before. Yet, at the same time, many people saw and reacted to this national crisis quite differently from in 1945.

Vivid memories and actual experience of the recovery of the war-devastated economy (throughout the 1950s) and the subsequent expansion and development of the national economy (in the 1960s), industries and corporations, worked to help people to think and act quite positively towards the economic crisis of the 'oil shock'. It may be more apt to say that many, particularly the young, took the chaos as a challenge, with the result that all economic and business matters attracted more of their interest. Mr K.'s shift from the Maths Department to Law School may be explained, though perhaps not consciously on his part, by this rising current of 'economic crisis' in the 1970s.

In his final year at the University Mr K. bought a few shares at the Tokyo Stock Exchange, using part of the monthly allowance his father sent to him for his study. The purpose, he explained, was to follow those ups and downs of stock values at a time of turmoil. He found considerable intellectual excitement in guessing why and how the movements in values of certain companies brought eventual and general changes in national economic performance.

The Ministry and adjustment policy

We discussed in Chapter 7 on Mr N. how the Ministry in the mid-1970s was preoccupied with delivering policies and administrative services to assist business to adjust to a reduced growth mode of the economy. To recapture the economic scene of the time, we observe that during the previous decade the Japanese economy had made a transformation from its previous high-speed to a steady and slow-growth economy (the average annual growth rate of the economy declined from 11.0 per cent in 1965–70 to 4.4 per cent in 1970–75 with a slight improvement to 4.7 per cent in the 1975–80 period). We observed that many policy devices were implemented in the Ministry to help industries and firms adjust their investment and production activities to the newly transformed basis, leading the administrative work in the offices in the Ministry to be highly complex technically and quite time-consuming.

How did individual officers in the Ministry manage to live throughout this time of 'adjustment policy'?[5] Many of our interviewees remembered the time as 'negative and gloomy', and the tasks they had to carry out extremely 'trivial', given their accustomed way of thinking that policy writing is for economic growth and industrial development. With little opportunity for growth and expansion in the economy, they saw their public duty as insignificant and not worth their toil. They saw the duty given to them as 'time-consuming', because it was purely 'administrative' work aiming to assess varying interests so as to adjust and mediate their conflict, and bring about a balance acceptable to all. Officers were extremely unhappy to find that in the process their public administrative work had become highly political: they had to use an ad hoc approach without any long-term principle or target to aim for. This was quite a new experience for all the officers. They lamented their misfortune in being forced to go through such tasks: few economic bureaucrats before them had ever encountered work of this kind throughout the Meiji–Taisho–Showa fast-industrializing and developing Japan.[6]

To make the matters worse, each office across different bureaux and departments was going through an extremely busy time in managing these unfamiliar 'trivial' tasks. They received numerous visitors from industries, who came to make petitions and lodge complaints in order to receive priority attention from the Ministry in competition with others. Mr K. remembered how heavily clerical assistance was drawn on from newly joined junior groups such as himself to help seniors in their need to devote their days to administrative work for those 'conciliatory' matters. He thought how that heavy load that seniors and juniors together must attend to gave outside observers the misleading impression that the Ministry was engaged in an extremely important national plan. Yet, misleading though it was, it worked to attract many young graduates from his Law School. They sought a position in the Ministry in 1977, expecting to be called at any moment into the national programme of rebuilding the economy.[7] Mr K. was one of those enthusiastic youths.

Entry into the Ministry, 1977

Mr K. entered the Ministry in April 1977 on graduation from the University. Twenty-one others were recruited into the Ministry that year. Therefore, it could be said that he became a member of the nation's élite class. It was still a time when high expectations and a general feeling of trust about working as a bureaucrat particularly at the central offices in the national government, was uppermost in people's minds. Many of his school friends, relations, neighbours and his father's friends came to congratulate him upon this achievement. They said how proud they were of his success in becoming a bureaucrat in such an important ministry as MITI, from where he would soon direct the activities of the national economy and guide the development of business and industry.

The government to voluntarily limit car export

Then Mr K. saw his *kacho*, the section head, sitting at his director's desk making numerous phone calls all day long to directors and executives and the industry representatives of car-manufacturing companies. He was discussing the need of the industry to restrain its export activities and at the same time to increase imports of cars and auto parts with the aim of reducing Japan's trade surplus, particularly *vis-à-vis* the USA. The discussion began to take the form of a public lecture, explaining the need to achieve Japan's trade balance against other trading nations, particularly the USA, in order for Japan to be accepted as a responsible trading nation in the international economy. Good performance of industries such as the auto-manufacturing industry in the world export market is required so as to make sure that Japan maintains good relationships with the world economies. It is no longer possible for the competitive auto industry of Japan to drive its export promotion without paying heed to the well-being of its counterparts in the US and other economies. The world economy has got to the stage where industries have to keep a spirit of *kyosei*, cooperative arrangement for the prosperity for all, so that strongly competitive ones refrain from export activities in the world market to leave room for less advantaged competitors to find market share. That is now the official attitude that the Ministry decided to follow.

As for the US economy and Japan's trading activities with it, the *kacho* appeared to imply that the American economy is accumulating a trade deficit because of their export industries, such as the car industry, are ailing and losing market share both at home and overseas to the Japanese. If Japanese car manufacturers refrain from their export activities, as he pleads, it will help American car-manufacturing firms maintain their sales and contribute to the American economy. Expanding the US car industry will save it from unemployment problems and thus assist the reduction of the nation's mounting trade deficit.

After delivering the lecture, the *kacho* entered into a detailed discussion of how much the business representatives on the other end of the phone would be prepared to reduce their exports of cars and, at the same time, increase imports of auto parts and accessories which they could import from the US sources – could it be 10 per cent, 20 per cent or more? On hearing not very cooperative responses, he then began to adopt an arrogant tone, telling them that this policy is on the national priority agenda of the time. Mr K. also observed the same *kacho* make more phone calls to those ex-officers of the Ministry who had been placed as chairmen and in other top positions on the boards on those car-manufacturing companies through the *amakudari* post-retirement appointment system.

Those *senpai*, old boys, were asked to work once again, as in their active time in the Ministry, to 'serve the country' by way of solving this specific problem of the trade war with the US automobile industry.

Mr K. saw this *kacho*'s behaviour as absurd, foolish and damaging to the dignity of the staff in the Ministry. He thought it absurd because he does not see why Japan should be responsible for the USA's economic problems. Their rising problems of internal and external fiscal deficit are the outcome of their own choice of economic management. The Japanese economy should not be blamed in any way. The export success of the Japanese car industry into the US market is the result of the careful and hard management efforts of each of the car firms in Japan itself. Mr K. believes that such efforts should not be interfered with either by his own Ministry or any government agencies, even on request by the counterpart in Washington. This was the voluntary gesture of a hasty fellow in the Ministry who believes, so Mr K. has been told, that it is now time for the Japanese to feel obliged to help the US economy and repay whatever past favours that the country had done Japan for its post-war recovery and so on.[8]

However obliged to the past kindness of the Americans, however much Japan wished to behave in a thoughtful and gentlemanly way, Mr K. thought it foolish to believe that the Japanese could inflict an appreciable impact on the performance of the US economy, which is twice the size of that of Japan, with rich accumulation of capital and other economic resources. In his view, such a belief overestimates the capability of the Japanese economy to solve the problems of the US economy. This behaviour involves a great risk for the Japanese, particularly the Ministry as an economic ministry, with its past high reputation in controlling and guiding business and industry, in that it might appear that they are not reliable or trustworthy when, as feared, the attempt fails to deliver the promised assistance to the Americans. He thought it wrong and risky to make economic policy strongly influenced by such diplomatic concerns, particularly when the latter is mixed up with a soap-opera type logic and sentiment.

Paris

In 1984, after seven years' training and observation of the working mechanism in the offices in the Ministry, Mr K. was sent for a year to Paris to study the French economy as well as administrative organization in France while working at the JETRO office in Paris. In Paris he joined a colleague who was there to take up the more senior task of connecting the Ministry with the networks in the EU countries. They often spent time together in the foreign city discussing each other's experiences and learning.

The senior person had much to say about his bitter and frustrating experiences working in the Ministry in the days of adjustment policy in the 1970s, and he told Mr K. how he had actually been asked by his bureau head to perform a similar task as the one Mr K. had observed earlier in his *kacho*'s telephone calls to car manufacturers. They had numerous occasions to discuss both administrative views and industrial policy matters, seeking to identify the future role of government, the Ministry's future activities, and the comparative assessment of the quality of Japan's bureaucrats and their relations with the community and politicians with those of France. In the process he began to see the quality lacking in the Ministry that led it to fail to understand what forms of policy and planning would be required in future. He saw the reason in the Ministry's inability to collect and collate adequate information that showed how the Japanese economy and society was changing. This, he claims, is due to the fact that the Ministry remained oriented for too long towards growth and efficiency.

He remembered the time when the Ministry, dominated by the public administrative mind, was preoccupied with how to deal with the mounting pressure coming from the US government to check Japan's successful export performance. He thought no effort had been made to review why the problems arose and what solutions must be found to serve the welfare of the Japanese economy and not so much to respond to American convenience. He found the Ministry unwilling to move out of the self-congratulations mode of their past contribution to its industrial growth-oriented policy.

It is true, he thought, that the policy has made a contribution towards building modern industry on the original semi-industrial basis, but it is foolish to stay in this mode when the original mission is accomplished. How to structure the Ministry and lead them to manage their affairs in a progressive manner, always ready to take up new issues, became his lifelong concern. How should people – politicians, government policy writers, academicians – be equipped to move on to a higher quality of desire and purpose along with the accomplishment of the past ones? While asking this question he described Mr M. as his superior senior officer with a good civil personality and Mr N. as his decent, honest and hard-working colleague, for they were serving the established regime and the conventionally accepted/practised approach in the Ministry. He viewed their work as to mend as well as possible the gaps appearing in the working of the regime. However, he considers their work adequate enough to counter the emerging problems in the economy in its fast transision from a poor developing to an affluent developed economy. He began to expand his concern further by trying to establish how the economy as a whole is conducted. That is, he began to ask what people will seek when their basic material needs are satisfied. Lately he has seen his parents begin to show boredom, having secured a little fortune around them and established some social status in their little circle. Without enough education they appear unable to think things through further and explore opportunities they might take up.

Mr K. came home to Tokyo in 1985 to move between offices, working on industry-specific policy matters and business and national economy-wide issues through the Ministry's usual bi-annual *ido* appointments. In 1993 he was sent abroad to Asia to take up a *sangyo-chosa-in* business and industry information commission for the Ministry.

Observations made in Asia

While in Hong Kong from 1993 to 1996, Mr K. visited various parts of Asia in order to further his understanding of the economies and business practices in Asia. He tried to make friends and acquaintances in Asian business and among expatriate managers and workers from Japan in order to gain what he believed to be a 'real and inside image of Asian business' to replace and supplement the official understanding in the Ministry. He wrote as many survey reports as he could manage. The writings were sent to the Head Office in Tokyo to be printed in one of the Ministry's regular publications.

Before his visit to the economies in the Asia-Pacific region Mr K. read Lester Thurow's 1992 publication, *Head to Head*, in order to have an introductory understanding of the world economies.[9] A colleague of his, who had been sent to the USA by the Ministry, introduced him to the book. Mr K. read the book and found that it explained with economic logic roughly what he had believed.

Economics textbooks have traditionally explained that an economy can grow fast and develop its industry more easily than its competitors when it is provided with fertile land and rich natural resources. Natural resources, capital accumulation and the development of modern technologies, and the skill to effectively use them, are seen as prerequisites for developing economies to secure before beginning their industrialization programme.[10] Inadequate provision of these will handicap the economy *vis-à-vis* its competitors in the market.

Thurow argues that this understanding is no longer relevant in a world economy where 'new' developments have taken place in the last century, resulting in the alteration of the composition of resources essential for conducting industrial activities. The 'new' developments were first seen in the coming of the green revolution and material science revolution, which together reduced considerably people's need for land space and natural resources to produce goods and services.[11] Thurow argues that capital is still necessary to begin economic and industrial activities but its inclusion in the start-up strategy of industrialization has become less important than previously.

The growth of multinational corporations results in global sourcing of capital, thus allowing second- and third-world economies to build industries even with capital-intensive facilities. Hence it could be argued that the classical notion of the sources of strategic advantage should be altered to take account of the reduction of the role and importance of those four traditionally valued productions. With this understanding, Thurow proposes the need to write a new theory of competitive advantage on the basis of people and their intelligence, instead of on physically endowed natural resources and other accumulated production resources.

By calling this new source for economic growth 'man-made resources', he forcefully concludes his argument by stating that economic advantage can be *created* and thus economic growth can be induced. I explained to Mr K. that it was exactly what the Japanese have promoted. I put to him my argument given in Chapter 1: it was through building human resources in the economy that Japan engineered the industrialization of the country.

In 1994 Mr K. was asked to work in Asia as the Ministry's resident researcher of Asia-Pacific economies and business contact. He established his office in Hong Kong. He selected this location for its easy access to almost any part of Asia, as well as its close reach to Tokyo.

His first personal experience in the place pleased him immediately. He was accepted by the local people, got on well with almost everyone without them sensing that he was anyone other than an Asian doing a little business there. No one wondered if he was a bureaucrat from the Ministry travelling around with a government budget to conduct economic and business surveys.

What image of plans and policies was he aiming to develop during his stay in Asia? I will outline below the development of his thinking both during his stay in Hong Kong and his subsequent travels around Asia.

During his contact with those parts of Asia he made several observations on how people work there.

Vietnam

One period of observation was in Vietnamese textile factories – a pygmy-type operation – in which many young female workers (possibly of only 14 and 15 years of age or even younger) were producing woven silk cloth with extremely complicated patterns and designs. To Mr K.'s eye the cloth closely resembled in appearance some expensive products in Japan. There they are either woven by skilful, highly paid, specialist weavers for expensive high-priced speciality kimono markets or with the assistance of computer-guided design patterns in a separate workplace for less exclusive but still expensive traditional kimono markets.

In those Vietnamese factories, however, the female workers work in a most dextrous manner, with the utmost concentration of their minds and eyes in order to make up for the lack of long years' training at studios and schools. They do not have the advantage of training in the use of computers and custom-built modern sewing machines. Labour is making its own contribution to the effective use of capital and technology. It is cheap, and thus may be mistakenly called 'cheap labour', but it is certainly not shoddy. With skills and work motivation and careful attention to tasks, its quality is high.[12]

One day the factory manager told Mr K. that he had been puzzled over the way the girls in his mill work.

The manager is a Japanese expatriate sent from Osaka head office of the factory. His principal duty in Vietnam was to establish a quality production line in the plant within four years from 1994. To achieve the task entrusted, he decided to guide the mill-girls to conform to one standard level, to produce exactly the same quality in texture, colouring and design, using a piece of textile that had been brought in from Osaka as their model. Every week the product was sent back to Osaka for inspection and, while waiting for scrutiny and approval, the manager made efforts to reduce to zero the number of cases that failed to reach the required standard. The exercise was mostly technical and he was happy to make good progress within 18 months.

His puzzle began to emerge. He began to notice output from the production line that had additional quality – a better product. This was despite, as noted, his strict managerial direction to the workers to produce exactly the same products, no worse and no better. Under this managerial guidance those mill-girls could not expect to receive any further rewards for their work if they made better quality products and added value. That is, employees would not be recognized or appreciated for their effort in making better quality products. They see the effort as simply a diversion from the requested standard, thus risking some punishment.

The Japanese manager asked who made those non-standard products with added extra quality. Many workers were identified. They were asked how and why they introduced extra value to their products.

Their answer was simple. They said they were not aware of adding the extra. They said they were simply making an effort to produce the same products following the model example, and they expressed an admiration of the already high quality embodied in it.

Hong Kong

Another observation came to Mr K. in Hong Kong on a more personal basis in 1997. He was asked by a young lady to keep an eye on her toddler when he was having a smoke one afternoon, watching the bright setting sun on a beach in Honk Kong. She wanted to rehearse her five-minute presentation at a Japanese affiliated factory where she worked as an assembler of a table calculator. She had composed her speech explaining how she had managed and developed her own method to provide effective leadership to the employees, thereby reducing production costs by 7 per cent within the last two months. She asked Mr K. to listen to her speech, and to give his comments and suggestions so as to improve her presentation. She performed her presentation earnestly, believing in the meaning and worth of her toil. It moved Mr K., leading him willingly to participate in her rehearsal, thinking how this girl might present herself to impress her plant supervisor from Japan. He put himself in the position of this Japanese supervisor and thought hard about what words should be added to the speech to give it sharpness and how it should be spoken to get maximum appreciation from his fellow countryman. Mr K. was doing his utmost to mobilize his understanding of the business culture and social approval of his own country in search of an effective touch to be added to enhance her coming performance. He remembered a feeling of excitement that was equal to the one he had had a long time ago when he had played a small acting part in front of visiting parents at the end of the academic year in his primary school.

Writing industrial policy

Creating value

Mr K. examined those observations in Vietnam and Hong Kong. First he wanted to explain why the mill-girls in Vietnam produced higher than standard quality products despite the fact that they were hired to produce only standard products. He saw in this extra effort a creation of value; namely he saw that their specific behaviour demonstrated that they have an urge to create value. The urge appears to have emerged *spontaneously* and for this reason Mr K. formed his belief that it was a natural instinct of people.

In order to evaluate the acceptability of Mr K.'s view, I give below some of the previous observations concerning the work norm in Japanese factories.

First, an economic historian, Banno Junji, describes his observations in a fountain-pen manufacturing plant in Japan in 1920. He tells us that, one day, workers from the shopfloor began organizing regular after-work meetings to share their daily work experience. Before long this led them to discussions about how they might improve the quality of products, reduce the waste of materials, increase energy input, and organize their time so as to rearrange and integrate the work processes. This resulted in each process of production having a clear purpose, within an efficient cooperative work practice. They believed they had found a way to save production costs, improve quality and design a worker-friendly procedure. This effort emerged on an entirely voluntary basis, through spontaneous initiatives by individual, semi-skilled and not highly educated or highly paid employees.[13]

A second observation of employees' effort and behaviour, made by Kumazawa Makoto, is, on the other hand, presented in a more critical light. In his study, published in 1995, he argues that quality control activities that began to be promoted widely among manufacturing plants in Japan during the high economic growth period of the 1960s and 1970s were not entirely driven by the happy readiness and willingness of workers. He argues that the workers in Japan took part in the activities and promoted them, not because they enjoyed taking part but because they worked in an environment where they were obliged to work hard to contribute to the success of the corporation, in order to receive a large income. Workers had become more aware of the need to gain increasing amounts of income every year so as to keep pace with the ever-rising standard of living and the need to satisfy material and commercial needs which dominated society in that period.[14]

A third study, by Hazama Hiroshi, explains that the strong work ethic of people in Japan, in general, is due to the fact that many ordinary workers are forced to and feel strongly obliged to work hard. They feel under pressure to keep up with a general mode of work led by groups of 'workaholics' within the specific social framework, employment systems and work practices of Japan.[15]

These three studies do not reach a consensus on why people in Japan work hard. But their observations project a common image of how Japanese work. They try to work in an organized way, directing their own individual intellectual contributions to bring efficiency into their workplace so as to produce better-quality goods and services at a lower cost – two aims that are difficult to achieve at the same time.

How does this interpretation relate to Mr K.'s claim about people's value-creating behaviour?

With Mr K. we may ask, should we leave working people to promote their own exploration for creating value? Should we respect the natural spontaneous nature of the work drive for value creation because it is where people will find satisfaction in work? If this is so is there any need to interfere in order to promote the effort further, direct it to a certain goal and shape it using industrial policy and public administrative guidance?

To assist such a study we give below a summary of our understanding of this work behaviour for creating value:

1. When people work and create value following their own instinct and desire, it is natural that they will find happiness in their work. This happiness may be greater than that gained from having a larger income, particularly under the economic condition of people's basic economic needs being securely met, as seen in Japan today.
2. We should value this work behaviour because it comes about through people's discovery of their own 'capability' and their effort to develop it – that is an act of self-development.
3. We note that this observation of work effort/initiative is made at different times and within different economies: one in the high economic growth period of 1960s and 1970s and the other in the early industrial development time of the 1920s in the Pilot fountain-pen factory, as seen in Chapter 1, and also in less industrially developed economies in Asia, Vietnam and Hong Kong, as described by Mr K. This fact leads us to ask if it demonstrates, as Mr K. believes, that people have a desire to initiate and to make value following their own innate instinctive motivation. Is this true with most people,

not only those entrepreneurial champions but also ordinary people, who live in an economic society?

4. In the context of the above understanding, how do we review industrial policy promoted by the Ministry in the past – particularly through the approach Mr M. called 'match-making' (discussed in Chapter 6)?[16]

To resurrect the work approach promoted in the Ministry, we remember how administrative officers like Mr M. promoted industrial growth. Armed with large public economic information, Mr M. went out to industry trying to locate emerging signs of entrepreneurial plans. When business and investment programmes in the embryo stage were found, the officers subsequently selected some of them to be paired up in a suitable manner and introduced to each other so that they would eventually come to establish a partnership and cooperate in business activity.

Many factories and corporations were established through such an approach. Industrial policy brought growth to industry and the national economy throughout the 1960s and 1970s. It served the needs of the time, when the country was seeking economic growth. My question is this: today in Japan, in a post-industrial, affluent society, where people seek a quality of life in which they wish to explore their potential and develop themselves, is this approach appropriate?

5. In addition we ask how should government act in the future considering its wish to contribute to the building of a good economic society?

Back in Tokyo

In 1998 Mr K. was asked to come back to Tokyo to head the Ministry's newly established office to promote Japan's position in the Asia-Pacific region. The appointment allows him to make further observations about the specific nature of business and of economic development in Asia and of increased contacts between people in Asia.

I have recently continued discussions with Mr K., reviewing the industrial planning approach of the Ministry, asking what contribution it has made to the development of the industry and what future role it should promote. I discuss my thoughts in the next chapter.

9
The Society-consulting Planner, Mr O., Type B Officer

By 1991 Mr O. saw the Japanese economy as having reached a high stage of development where it could easily afford to introduce new policy initiatives that would aim to improve the well-being of people through the raising of living standards and quality of life. He hoped to achieve this improvement by reducing standard annual working hours. He wished to see individuals in the working population provided with more free time so as to lead a relaxed lifestyle and explore their own life, be it enjoying family life, engaging in leisure and hobby activities or gaining further training and education.

He read many novels and writings on social history in Japan to find out that it is only in the national industrialization effort since the 1920s that people have begun to follow a lifestyle devoid of comfort outside the office and factory. He made a special study, reading autobiographies and biographies of how the pre-Showa Japanese lived before the 1920s and learned how those people lived closer to the land and nature, allocated more time with people around them and explored many activities outside their main professions and work.

He sees today that Japanese people are relatively well provided with material comforts but lack living comfort: their way of life is stressed because of the long hours they have to work. Although rapid economic growth and industrial development have brought increasing wages and salaries that were estimated, given the official exchange rate, as one of the world highest by the mid-1980s, the population still continues to work for long hours and in an intensive manner as if they were still struggling in a developing economy.

Mr O. is not completely sure how people in modern industrial society will be able to become happier and more contented with

169

their own life, as well as making an effort to improve themselves, when more free time is provided. For some time people in Japan have spoken about the need to correct the warped trend of mind and spirit that has developed in the national industrialization effort since the Meiji Restoration and modernization of society. People have worked like dogs. Mr O. acknowledges that some say the problem of how to restore these dog-like people to live as humans is better left to writers of literature rather than to economists and public administrative officers. He does not accept the view. Precisely because the deterioration of people's quality of life has come in the process of industrialization and through the promotion of economic activities, he thought a correcting device should be sought exactly in the industrial and economic dimension.

In this chapter I discuss his concern and the efforts made to bring 'quality of life' and 'betterment of living' to the population. Economic thinking in Japan has traditionally oriented itself in its maximization goal towards 'more and faster', leaving the concept 'betterment' outside active discussion. I wish to observe how economic planners in Japan will react to maximizing those new goals when this approach meet a challenge.

To think about 'quality of life' with regard to their high level of living standards and the desirability of reduction of work hours was not new in 1992. Many suggestions and policy proposals have been made, as seen in the Maekawa Report of 1986.[1] When looking at statistics reported of the total hours worked in industries in Japanese workplaces, a reduction appears to have been made. What should be noted is that, despite the Maekawa Report which appears to have secured support among the population, and the official report of the reduction of work hours, in reality in 1992 people's actual perception was that they were not actually working less, or enjoying more free time and relaxed living with reduced work pressure. They knew they were actually working outside the official office hours, taking work home at the weekend and staying on in the office and factories over and above the officially recorded schedule. This extra working was carried out on a voluntary basis and thus escaped official counting. Why was this so and what should be done to correct this behaviour?

In this chapter I follow the activities and experience of Mr O. in his attempt to bring a real reduction of work hours for people with the aim of seeing the population provided with comfort in life, and room for individual effort to take place for living a full life.

Personal background

Mr O. was born in 1955 in Nagasaki at the beginning of Japan's high-speed economic growth. His father, to start with, was a company accountant in the local office of a construction company. The father's career developed and income went up along with the expansion of the company. He rose to become a chief accountant and then a financial director of the company, which grew from its local basis to operate in a nationwide dimension. The family shifted to Tokyo when Mr O. was in primary school, with his father now working in the company's head office in the national capital. The family's financial state rose exponentially every year. He remembered his experiences of moving family house several times, each time into a larger place in a more prestigious street. His family's lifestyle had literally followed the rise of the nation's GNP.

Mr O. does not think his childhood was a particularly happy one, although in anyone's eyes he had one of the most generously, materially and mentally, provided childhood. This fortunate environment, however, made him cynical. He saw many shameless fights among already wealthy relations over further wealth. At an early stage of his life, he concluded that people with wealth are less happy, driving themselves to become selfish people who are not prepared to extend care to others around them. So, he views his childhood as not happy because he was surrounded by unhappy people and in his childhood he was not been able to find ways to make himself happy either.

Despite such a personal view of people and their lifestyle, he has managed, in his adulthood, to be a contented person, building a closely related family of his own. He describes himself as a 'family' person, allocating more time and interest to life at home. I observe him to be a happier person than the other three of my case studies (presented above in Chapters 6, 7 and 8).

As a youth, apart from high living, he has enjoyed freedom both at home and school throughout the pre-Ministry period. His father was always busy with his work and was seldom at home for family. So most matters of housekeeping and guidance of the children were left with the mother, of a rather weaker character. She had to handle the two extremely independent sons. Both were good at school but never followed the traditionally respected type of career. Both successfully entered one of the most prestigious private boys' high schools in Tokyo. Neither showed any interest in collecting 'A's in school reports. Instead they spent most of their time and energy either playing soccer for the school or the guitar for private bands. The two shared many interests and became very close brothers.

In his final year of the high school at the beginning of the 1970s he and his brother (Mr O. was 17 going on 18 while his brother was 16) found themselves in the centre of the rising campus disturbance that had originated in university campuses in Tokyo, spreading within a few years to universities in local prefectures. Students became highly conscious of the importance of the country's political independence in relation to US dominance. The critical view of government led students to demand to see education at schools and university free from bureaucratic control and guidance. The protest movement spread further down to high schools, including theirs. At Mr O.'s school in particular the disturbance took place in a most vehement way. The school decided to make a strong protest against the control and intervention from the Ministry of Education. Being the top renowned high school, it decided to take the lead in conducting debates over how far individual schools should be allowed to determine the purpose and direction of education. The headmaster made a demand to the Ministry of Education to let his school develop its own textbooks. Up to then the Ministry of Education had authority to approve textbooks so as to ensure that all the high schools in Japan followed the same curriculum.

Subsequently more problems developed when the headmaster of Mr O.'s school refused to follow the bureaucratic guidance from the Ministry on the structure of the school's entrance examination questions. The headmaster ignored the bureaucracy and composed the examination questions, to be followed by interviews to test candidates' ability to think independently and to express their ideas and argue in order to let others hear and be convinced their argument. They aimed to test the extent of candidates' individuality and capacity for imagination.

Not many questions were included in order to test knowledge. The Education Ministry considered that the school's approach and the selection of the subject matter included in the examination and the interview meetings were quite outside the publicly endorsed curriculum.

It had been the approach of the Education Ministry that the purpose of education in the country up to university level was to secure a nationally agreed-upon body of knowledge (particularly in Japanese and social history) and academic skills (particularly in maths) instilled in students' minds by the completion of high-school education. The school was asked to conform to the national curriculum. It was asked to refrain from acting otherwise, whatever high reputation this particular high school enjoyed and how many eager candidates wished to enter the school in their expectation of receiving the 'better' and 'unique' instructions that the school was known to have provided throughout its long history. The headmaster objected to the request from the Ministry, arguing that the school was not evaluating the amount of knowledge but the academic judgement and imaginative thinking of the candidates.

The headmaster, subsequently, was suspended from teaching. Many students including Mr O. and his brother, supported the headmaster and initiated many protest movements, thus inviting riot police to charge into the campus.

As a part of his gesture to support the protest, Mr O., with many other classmates, skipped classes and stayed at home for a couple of months in the autumn of 1973, which otherwise should have been used to prepare for the entrance examination to get into a university. Despite this, he managed to enter the Law School of Tokyo University in 1974. But again, in his final year, he decided not to sit for the final examination and deferred graduation for two years to enjoy the extra time of freedom.

During the period he travelled to the USA and Asia for a few weeks, took casual jobs at hotels and cafés for pocket money as well as staying home doing nothing in particular. Both his parents were annoyed by his 'irresponsible' behaviour but could not change his mind. In all, he spent two years before taking up his career as an independent adult. He could afford to behave like this knowing his family could well afford to support a son not on a payroll.

Thus it was that in 1980 he entered the Ministry. He found himself one of the oldest among the newly recruited. He was 26, while most of his colleagues were 22 or at most 23.

Why the Ministry? He thought at the time he would have no chance of getting a position in private business corporations, given his past activity in campus politics and only average academic results, together with the fact that he was two years older than others, making him not really fit well in the Japanese management system that practises lifetime employment and a seniority promotion system. Only positions in government appeared to be open to him.

He thought himself extremely lucky to find a position in the Ministry. First, the year when he sought employment was a relatively good year of business expansion. Many good graduates from good universities with good academic records sought positions in business corporations for better pay, leaving public service positions with less attractive remuneration provision as a secondary preference. Second, he had good luck at the job interview. An old boy from his high school led the interview meeting as the *kacho hosa*, deputy head of the personnel department. They spent most of the time confirming how they both appreciated the greatness of the personal character and professional conviction that the headmaster showed. Mr O. was convinced that it was only with the support of this senior that he got a position in the Ministry.

He also tried two other ministries, the Ministries of Construction and of Employment, to supplement his chances of getting employment. As if to prove his conviction correct, both (despite the fact that they are usually ranked below that of the Ministry in the public service world) rejected him at their first screening.

The *Jitan* proposal

The 1992 study

At the beginning of 1992 Mr O. was asked by the head of his section in the Industry Policy Bureau to write a report to discuss if it was time for the Japanese to promote a *jitan*, reduction of work hours, programme. The Ministry wished to examine exactly what level of working hours could be reduced without risking a considerable loss of international cost competitiveness of Japan's export industries. He was asked to examine all possible ways and areas in which the proposed *jitan* policy influenced the performance of the industries and the national economy.

He had been already promoting such a study privately, and this initiative became known to people in the section. The invitation from the head of the office allowed him to take advantage of what he had already examined.

Long and intensive work developed in Japan through the period of high-speed economic growth. Working hours in the industry throughout continued to rise extensively with the official launch of the 'Double-national income' economic plan in 1960.[2] The annual total working hours in 1960 was recorded as 2,432 hours (see Figure 10.1 in Chapter 10 where I give further discussion on the working hours of the people in the post-war Japan). Not much doubt has been raised by workers or trade unions whether such intensive work was necessary to bring the high rate of growth of GDP and labour productivity for the achievement of the economic plan.

As the economy grew and industries developed many jobs were created and the labour market in Japan for the first time in its history became, as seen in Chapter 3, labour-scarce. The economy was in a situation of full employment by the mid-1960s. Despite securing a bargaining position in employment markets, workers decided to behave very cautiously, directing first their absolute priority to securing their employment before demanding the betterment of their work conditions. A few more years had to pass until the mid-1980s, when trade unions began to make initiatives to bring improvement in working conditions and work practice in an organized and systematic way.[3]

The economy was expanding at a rapid rate to enlarge the scale of operation for almost all industries. With intensive work effort and the benefit of increasing operation scale, labour productivity rose exponentially (over 10 per cent every year throughout the 1960s, with the rate approaching the 20 per cent level in the years up to 1973). It was not difficult for the employers to agree a large wage rise under such buoyant conditions. Workers could have demanded a reform in work places to improve general work conditions. Instead they decided to demand the benefits of the high economic growth and rapid rise in labour productivity only in the form of payment. Many workers responded favourably to the request from employers who asked them to work long hours beyond the normal scheduled practice. They expected the time had at long last come for them to improve their living standards through the high rate. The employers' strategy was to meet the boom by employing overtime so as to economize on new capital investment. The intensity of work rose as demand for their output rose faster while corporate investment lagged behind. Deterioration, not improvement, of work conditions became general in all workplaces and was further aggravated by the deterioration in the living environment through an increase in industrial pollution, congestion on roads and in living areas. It is no surprise to see that there arose very rapidly among the general population in the community an acute desire to detach themselves from the economic growth mode. A slogan, 'Damn GNP', arose.[4]

A new era was emerging, challenging an evaluation of the industrialization effort and the results it had achieved. People began to seek an alternative economic system for the national economy and to management practice at workplaces. This new development was indicated in the national survey that asked what people valued most in life in 1971.[5] For the first time a number of people said it was decency, comfort and peace (expressed as *kokorono yutakasa*, richness in heart) that were more important than a materially rich life. This contradicted the preceding trend observed through the 1950s and 1960s when people, without hesitation, responded by saying that their preference was for wage and salary increases rather than a reduction in working hours).[6]

In practice this 'change of mind' among the population had not met any effective response before the economic recession came with the arrival of the oil crisis in 1973. Working hours rose throughout the 1970s. They rose at and often above 22,000 hours, with annual working days exceeding 230–40 days (see Figure 10.1 in Chapter 10 below). The improvement that had been coming to workplaces in Japan was wiped out in the chaos of this oil crisis.

When Mr O. was asked to write the report on the *jitan* enquiry for his office in 1992, the government was still in the negative mode of the post-oil-crisis period. It was not sure if public initiative was desirable in the promotion of the reduction of working hours. It was not convinced if the aim could be managed within the confines of the capability of the national economy and of industries.

In practice Mr O. was asked to compile his report to show whether the economy would be able to provide workers with shorter working hours without experiencing a reduction of labour (and total economic) productivity. The report must examine the influence of the reduction on the international competitiveness of Japan's exports and thus reduce the growth potential of the economy as a whole. This is the concern that the government had. Mr O. had a different view on the issue. He thought the important concern of the proposal was how to bring *jitan* to the Japanese economy. The examination of the capacity of the economy seemed to him a secondary concern, so that the core question is to estimate 'by how many hours should the *jitan* be promoted?' and not 'whether it should be promoted or not'.

Mr O. organized a small team consisting of three young officers in his section in the Ministry to carry out the task. Soon he saw the need to involve more people from other ministries in search of information and knowledge that were not available through the network of his own Ministry. He found the study required, in particular, macroeconomic national accounts and labour and employment statistics. He wished to direct the study by analysing the national economic basis and not be confined to an enquiry on 'industrial policy'. He believed it to be the correct approach, given the nature of the enquiry that asks about people's lives and their living standards. The enquiry should raise questions about the allocation of economic resources in the country, building of infrastructure facilities such as transport, houses and cities, over and above employment patterns and their system, work arrangements in factories and offices and payment of rewards.

He gained the support and cooperation of three officers whom he had met at high school. Two were working at the Economic Planning Agency and the remaining one was at the Ministry of Labour. They managed to gain permission from their own offices to take part in Mr O.'s enquiry on a part-time but regular basis. The study group originally met twice a week over lunchtime, but the practice expanded soon to work after office hours and at weekends to, as Mr O. joked, 'contradict the very objective of the proposed study'.

The 1992 policy proposal

At what level of working hours should the reduction of working hours be aimed? The Ministry suggested, as a rough guide, the equivalent level observed in the USA, at the time, of 2,000. In Europe the hours are reported to be much less than those in the USA. When suggesting 2,000, the Ministry expressed its view that this initial level should be aimed at only as a starting guide so that Japan should make a continuous effort in the future to approach the European standard, if not a better one.[7]

In 1992 the officially recorded working hours in Japan on their own estimation was 1,958, but when estimated on the same bases used in the USA and European countries it was generally suspected to be much nearer a level of between 2,100 and 2,200 hours. They were much longer hours compared with advanced industrial economies: slightly above 1,600 hours for West Germany and France and at about 1,900 hours for the UK. Mr O. set the target for his policy effort to achieve the level for the Japanese reduced to 1,800 hours by 1996 from the current 2,100 hours in 1992. He aimed for the level to become eventually among the world's best, but began with a comparable level to that in Europe and better than that in the USA.

Will this target be possible? His approach was to set the target that should meet adequately the aim of the policy programme, that is, to provide comfort and betterment in people's lives. He wished to establish an appropriate *jitan* level in the economy so as to enable the working population to live a 'good' and 'full' life. He expressed his belief that it is important to set a high target level rather than a manageable one, for the enquiry is not about managing the economy better, but making the economy better. He began his enquiry with a strong conviction that the Japanese economy, given its industrial development and accumulation of wealth supported by modern technology and managerial know-how, should aim at providing its population with an equivalent, if not better, level of comfort as observed in the best economies elsewhere.

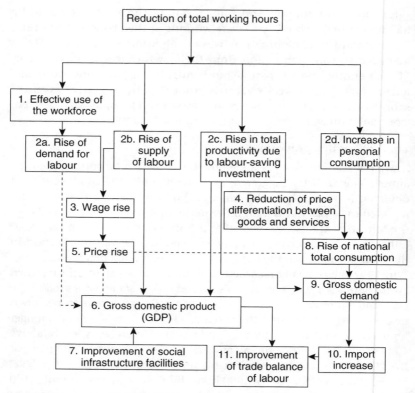

Figure 9.1   Effect of *jitan* reduction of total working hours on the national economy[8]

Thus his main concerns will be directed to see what reforms should be introduced to the economy and workplaces to achieve the desired practice which he believes has been long delayed in Japan. Since the original request from the department came to him to estimate the possible extent of the reduction of work hours without risking productivity loss in industry, Mr O. has had to make a special effort to gain approval and support for this approach from his department and later the Bureau and the Ministry.

He began his study with three specific enquiries to estimate the capacity of the Japanese economy. He asked (1) how far would its *jitan*, affect the production efficiency of the economy with target level of the reduction of 300 hours within four years from 1992 to 1996, namely to see 2,000 hours worked in 1992 reduced to 1,800 hours by 1996? (2) in what ways and where will this *jitan* affect the operation and performance of the country's industry and business? and (3) what specific results would be expected to take place in the national economy when the *jitan* is introduced to the proposed extent? To be more specific, he wished to forecast an evaluation of the growth capacity of the economy in the *jitan* environment. He wished to clarify how the lower labour input through the proposed reduction of working hours would affect the cost structure of export industries, and to estimate the resulting overall growth rate of GDP of the national economy.

We discuss how he conducted the enquiry following his study plan presented in Figure 9.1. The numbered points in the text correspond to the numbers in the figure.

Demand and supply of employment and the effective use of the workforce (1 and 2)

Given the current structure of industries and production and employment practice in business, a public promotion of the reduction of working hours is expected to bring to industries an increase of employment with a reduction of the work intensity of individual workers. This is good news.

However, Mr O.'s study indicated that, given an emerging shortage of labour, which predicts a steady decline of the supply of labour in the economy in the future, this public promotion of *jitan* will be only possible through active investment efforts of employers aiming to modernize their production facilities for effective use of labour. How ready were business to take up new investment programmes?

It has been a regular exercise of the Ministry to administer a survey of patterns and extent of investment plans every year. To the delight of Mr O., the survey indicated that most corporations across all sizes of business had already considered this need for new investment and began programming plans for the coming years in 1996 and 1997. They were beginning to build labour-saving facilities and develop management devices as a standard and ongoing management strategy regardless of the introduction of the promotion of *jitan*.

This is quite a contrast to the practice up until 1992, when business tended to meet increases in production through increases in overtime and employment of workers on an irregular basis. Such a stop-gap device is expected to be replaced by business promoting efforts to restructure their production to be oriented towards high value added production away from traditional labour-intensive activities. Mr O. expected that the transformation would take place gradually with continuous effort for several years to come. It is expected that the proposed target of the reduction of working hours (by 1.3 per cent annually) will be promoted throughout the 1990s to see the target level of 1,900 hours. He expected that this would be achieved by the end of the decade. It is good but the progress, according to his estimation, will be much slower after the year 2000. With some public policy assistance he expected the *jitan* would progress further to make the Japanese economy become the best-practice example in the world. He was excited by the potential. What policy devices could be used?

In search of adequate policy devices to be introduced post-2000, Mr O. conducted intensive interview surveys with management in the manufacturing industries. He found that the initial reduction of working hours would be more rapidly established in offices rather than production plants, reflecting the rising understanding of management that this was more likely to increase labour productivity.

Additional supply of labour, and wage rise (2b and 3)

Long hours of work together with casual employment arrangements that have been practised for some time in the employment of female and senior workers will be challenged. The extent of the shortage of labour is expected to increase generally in the economy so as to create demand for those people operating outside the standard workforce as casual helping hands.[9] This itself is a good thing in that employment opportunities are created for those not yet in the workforce. What should be taken care of is the possible concern that they will be drawn hurriedly and casually to workplaces before the establishment of supporting arrangements for their employment. There will be a risk again of seeing them hired on the basis of their 'cheap labour' and 'flexibility' in coming to work. Mr O. strongly wished that the labour market in Japan should not repeat in the process its traditional system of double-structured employment.

However, Mr O. was relieved when he saw that the labour market in Japan had been changing from that operated in those old days, so that the source of such workers was fast drying up, as the rise in their wage level indicated. Without waiting for the *jitan* many industries found it necessary to structure their employment system and work schedule to improve the employment of those female and senior workers and draw higher productivity from their work.

A general rise in wages took place at a rapid rate throughout the early part of the 1990s, reflecting the speed of rising labour shortage in the economy. Mr O. wished to examine such expected increases in wages and the difficulty in labour supply as a separate matter from the proposed working of the *jitan*.

Increase in personal consumption (2d)

The increase in free time among the population would bring more leisure activities into the economy. A provisional estimate indicates that a 1 per cent reduction of working hours will cause a 0.5 per cent rise in household consumption.

Jitan and the national economy

In order to estimate the expected effect of *jitan* on the general activity of the national economy, Mr O. was able to consult various econometric models of demand and supply in the economy.

The Economic Planning Agency developed econometric models to project national economic activities. It was directed to forecast economic changes for eight years to year 2000. Mr O. and his study partners expanded their study period (to 1992–2000 from 1992–96) in their need to use the agency's macroeconomic data. They estimated the total effect of the proposed policy on the national economy when the total working hours were to be reduced to 1,800 hours by 1996 from the 1992 level of 2,100 hours. When this comes about, GDP will at the most be expected to be reduced by 0.2 per cent in the first couple of years from 1992 to 1995 but it will be made up by a subsequent increase, not reduction, of 0.5 per cent.

This is expected to take place on the assumption that the total consumer market will expand because people will spend more when allocating their free time outside working hours for leisure and for their own purposes. What has actually taken place in the economy from 1992 to date? The working hours have been reduced from 1,958 hours in 1992 to 1,700 in 2000, with the maintenance of the rate of economic growth (measured by net GDP) at 1.1 per cent. Since his target was aimed at 2,000 hours by year 2000, the performance could be said to be better than Mr O. had planned to achieve at first in 1992. But in reality the result failed to meet the target. First, by 2000 many industrial economies in Europe had made improvements in reducing working hours. The leader in this was Germany, with 1,449 standard working hours with 68 hours worked as overtime. Dutch workers are reported to have worked only slightly more than 1,300 hours while maintaining a higher GNP growth rate than in Japan. The others, including France and the UK, also had a better record in the year 2000. The USA is the only country where workers worked for longer hours than Japan, particularly with many overtime hours.

As for actual work practice many studies, academic, government and popular journal reports, indicated that it is customary practice for workers in Japan in offices and factories not to take holidays and time off although these are officially provided.[10] We cannot explain this behaviour to our satisfaction. Some said that workers feel obliged, through fear of losing employment, to keep up with others who are more willing to work. Others think Japanese workers have not really learned how to value and make use of free time. Yet others even claim that the observation should not trouble us much given the fact that work intensity in the workplace in Japan is not altogether high.

The study finding was tabulated and presented as a policy proposal from the Ministry to the Parliament in January 1993. Despite the correctness of Mr O.'s estimate, as found later, the House did not respond positively in 1993: without economic and econometric estimates of its own, it cast doubt on the accuracy of his statistical information and the acceptability of his economic assumptions. Only members of the Japanese Communist Party were supportive. The proposed policy was abortive.

The reduction of working hours, 1994–2004

What progress has Mr O. made with his *jitan* study and policy proposal since 1994?

Figure 10.1 in Chapter 10 below will show the working hours practised in Japan from the high economic growth period in the middle of the 1950s to date. A couple of observations can be made.

First, the high-speed economic growth that was promoted in the post-war years of the 1950s was achieved with considerable use of long working hours among regular as well as part-time workers. A case of an extensive use of sweated labour in the effort to generate international competitiveness in many of the industries can be argued. A national practice of 'social dumping' based on driving workers to work unreasonably long hours cannot be denied. A question should be asked as to how far the working population benefited from economic growth and the rise in labour productivity beyond the obvious rise in hourly payment.

Second, let us note that despite the traditional behaviour observed among the Japanese (by following Figure 10.1 below), there was some progress in the reduction of working hours for a couple of years in the post-1973 period. We see also that the reversal soon came in 1975. This was the time when the labour market had already secured full employment for several years since 1965 and many workers were taken into regular employment positions. A puzzle arose as to why, despite such favourable conditions for employees emerging in the labour market, we find no strong sign of demand or desire among the working population for an increase in leisure time as observed elsewhere in other economies with the rise in income. Let us consult the national survey to understand the patterns of people's preferred lifestyle.[11] The survey was conducted in 1975 at the time when progress in reduction of work hours halted and a reversal was emerging. The survey tells us that people listed their priority demands to government as 'building more houses, improve roads and transport, living facilities such as water and city sewage, particularly in major cities as Tokyo and Osaka, to cater for living environmental problems and increase public parks and education'. We also read responses that suggest that the majority of people in Japan at the time began to develop concerns over the purpose of work. Namely, many began to ask, in their own individual and personal ways, what satisfactions they get from work, as if to begin asking the value of 'good working conditions'. Yet on careful examination of the response, in the light of other information, we soon find that in the concept of 'good working conditions' only half of the people surveyed see 'free and leisure time' as a necessary element. Even those who saw the value of free time understand its value and role in terms of returning to work from holidays fresh in mind and recuperated from fatigue.[12] They did not see, even at the time, the value of 'free time' itself.

Third, the reduction of working hours that took place in the years from 1960 to 1982, however, was, as we saw, reversed as soon as the economy met difficulties in the oil crises in 1973 and 1978. We know how various managerial efforts were later observed as the 'Japanese management techniques' to guide business in Japan to survive the difficult times.

Similar to the rapid economic growth of the 1960s, the economic boom of the 1980s provided employees with considerable wage rises (on average over 10 per cent per annum during the period). But improvement of conditions at work came only in the form of the provision of a standard employment security and regular and faster promotion than previously, modernization of work facilities, and a more employee-friendly work environment, for example flexible working arrangements (office hours start at 8:00 am for some workers while at 8:30 and 9:00 for others to respond to the requirements of employees). The provision of more free time, however, did not come to workers. In fact the *jitan* was interrupted despite the economic boom that continued in 1984–91. In this high boom employers operated the workplace at full capacity and employees welcomed working for long hours for extra payment. When consulting those of the official record it is said that the actual working hours rose much more than the officially reported standard and overtime hours shown in Figure 10.1.[13] The workers in the economic boom sought higher wages in preference to comfort at the workplace and in life. We wonder why workers in Japan did not use the advantage of working in a boom time with a labour shortage to gain shorter working hours, as counterparts in other industrialized countries achieved. Once again, Mr O. asked, why this special behaviour? This worried him.

2000 to date

Let us note that in 1990 and 1995 working hours in Japan are estimated to have been reduced only by 1.4 per cent annually while labour productivity rose by well over 4 per cent. The subsequent years to date saw a widening gap between the two. We may claim that the Japanese economy continued its traditional path towards growth and efficiency but without quality of life in its newly found depressed environment in the lost decade.

After having conducted a thorough survey as given above, and making such discouraging observations, Mr O. came to suspect that he had to seek an explanation outside the economy. He came to suspect that the reduction would not come through the normal working of economic and employment markets. He thought some outside force must be introduced into the economy so as to alter the pattern of employment and work practice. He felt that public planning would be needed so as to direct the benefit of economic development into improvement of the quality of life of the working population. Let us follow his effort.

Previously some economic historians reported that in Japan the result of economic growth had not brought much improvement in the provision of free time for general workers. They said that economic growth and industrial development have been promoted, virtually always and exclusively, to bring wage rises and not so much an increase in free time. They also observed that an increase in free time in history has almost always been brought about through government initiatives.[14]

At this moment I have not enough information to suggest whether this is specifically due to Japan's social culture or because of the economic need that has imposed hard work upon the population, as discussed in Chapter 1 above, in building the industrial state as a late-industrializing economy on a economically backward basis and without much endowment of natural resources. What we are able to note, however, is that the promotion of *jitan* in the post-war years, particularly in the rapid economic growth time from 1960 to 1974, has been once again directly initiated by government, for example, by the establishment of many public holidays.

The 1996 study

Mr O. decided to continue his study with his group privately. It was to be organized without the official support from the Ministry now that the 1992 report was compiled and presented to the Parliament for its negative evaluation.

In 1996 the group began their examination of new strategies. They decided to conduct two enquiries.

They wished to ask that, if *jitan* could not be promoted as quickly as they hoped, then what alternative devices in the economy should be introduced to, in effect, provide people with more free time?

From their own personal experience of spending long hours in crowded transport carriages every day to and from home to their office in the Ministry, a reduction of commuting time by way of building houses for individual workers seemed an effective way to provide free time. They began to construct policies for housing with this particular purpose.

To begin the task, Mr O. asked those two members in the study group from the Economic Planning Agency to tabulate how to redistribute the national annual budget to the building of good transport facilities and houses for the comfort of the working population. The purpose is to reduce the commuting hours between the home and workplace of the average working population. It has been estimated that most people in Japan, particularly office workers in cities, are forced to spend considerably long hours travelling, often exceeding 90 to 100 minutes one way by changing from bus to train to subway and so on. Such extended commuting hours reduce the welfare of individual workers themselves directly through physical strain and also in depriving them of time together with the family.[15]

The study group asked how much public spending is required to build a standard house as observed in Japan that would be acceptable to individuals (given size, hours of sunlight per day, availability of water and sewerage, public transport and easy access to other services such as child care, hospitals, schools and shopping facilities and so on). The study examined a variety of scenarios by gradually upgrading the location of new houses so as to reduce commuting hours by half, i.e., from the current 90 to 100 minutes one way to, say, 30 to 45 minutes.

As soon as the enquiry began, the study team found that during the economic boom period in the mid-1980s until the end of 1991 the number of houses with upgraded facilities as defined above in fact increased much faster than the rate of the growth of the economy. This is good news.

However, the supply pattern of houses during the period was hostile to the average working population wishing to acquire convenient housing for the improvement of working and living conditions. Statistical estimation indicates that the Japanese economy of the period was structured in such a way that when the growth rate of the national economy rises by 1 per cent the working population is forced to wait for an increase of 0.25 per cent of years for them to save in order to finance the required down-payment and monthly repayment on a housing loan. In essence, it illustrated that economic growth in Japan will not solve the problems of people in their effort to obtain adequate housing despite their working hard and gaining more income and saving for the acquisition of housing. It indicated that economic growth and active business conditions would work to deprive them of free time.

What would happen if government decided to increase tax revenues so as to increase, say by 5 per cent, national budget spending without altering the pattern of allocation? Their estimate indicated that only a small improvement would be achieved. In particular, the improvement will be virtually nil in the area of housing. For example, 1 extra per cent rise in public budget allocation would bring a 0.3 per cent increase in the total number of houses newly constructed and only a 0.1 per cent improvement in the extent of facilities (like water and sewerage) and service networks (public amenities such as public hospitals and for child care) for residential purposes.

When traditional patterns of budget allocation do not alter (which has been the case throughout the three decades since the beginning of the 1960s), any increase in the budget allocation in an upturn of the economy is likely to be absorbed by improvements in education and training for vocational purposes, expansion of transport and communication networks, services for business, defence and general public administrative services. There is no denying that the economic system in Japan appears, thus far, to have been essentially structured to allocate a larger public budget to the improvement of facilities for further economic growth and productivity, leaving the need to provide more free time and improve well-being of individual people as a secondary concern in the decision of public budget allocation. It may be acceptable when the aim of the nation and the public economic objective are directed to economic growth and industrial development as before, but when the aim shifts to welfare improvement of the population the pattern of this public budget allocation needs to be altered.

Basically the problems should be discussed in the political arena. However, Mr O. continued to ask if there was any way to counter them through industrial policy. He wished to see what drives Japanese workers to be obliged to work such long hours in comparison with their counterparts in other industrial economies. Why, in the labour-scarce economy now in operation, is there the same strong pressure as previously imposed upon workers to conform to the convenience of employers?

Industrial policy

With this question Mr O. went out to study how people work in car-manufacturing plants, which are understood to be the world's most efficient. He tried to follow the work schedule for each stage and process of operation in various auto-parts-producing plants and their assembly factories in order to see how the parts were produced and delivered to parent plants so as to understand the role and function of each stage in building the final product. He wished to follow the progression of work to make the final product, a car, that is said to be internationally cost-competitive and of high quality to satisfy users both at home and abroad.

The purpose of his visit was to examine where workers could be possibly spared work without loss of their effective operation and the quality of the final product. Originally he expected to find no such waste, given the reputation of the working of the 'lean production technique' of Japanese management.

To his surprise, when he put himself in the position of a consumer, he could not help finding many unnecessary parts, decorations, design and services that could be omitted without risking the satisfaction of general consumers such as himself. He has owned and driven several cars of different makes and nationalities both in Japan and abroad. He thought it might be possible that he could be seen as an easy-to-satisfy consumer going for a standard product for less price, not representative of average customers. Yet his observation led him to a general judgement that the car makers under his observation could be said to be driving the operators to work to deliver a 'perfect' car with 'perfect finish of paintwork', many and varied extras for smokers, children, ladies with their needs to comb their hair and fix their make-up, hang dresses, clothes and place portable phones, writing equipment and road maps, protect eyes from the glare of sun and headlights, and so on.

Policy for business

Are all these necessary? He asked this question when he found that many of those extras that he viewed as non-essential were in fact not included in the ranges that were made for customers overseas. Those extras are specially for the domestic market. They are of course nice extras, meant to give advantage to the product over that of competitors. The important concern is to seek a balance between extra working hours of the people in plants and the additional competitiveness that is expected to be appreciated in the market. He could not help but see many of the extras coming from the 'fastidious' approach of the makers with little genuine 'quality and technical requirement' for a car to function as expected. A car is not an art object, yet the workers are driven to perform as artists!

Why so? He asked the question again so as to acknowledge the continued existence of the traditional problem in Japanese business. It is the pressure of competition in the market, observed as problems of *kato-kyoso*, excessive competition.

He came to understand that in the highly competitive market of the car industry management is under pressure to differentiate its products, believing that adding many parts and services to dress up the final product makes them better than others in the market. Competition in markets and business should not be elevated to the extent of loss or hindrance to the welfare of individuals at the workplace. The approach and the structure of business and the market must be revised.

Old discussions within the Ministry in the 1950s through to the 1960s appeared to be resurrected once again to examine the specific nature of this *kato-kyoso*, excessive competition, observed in recent times in the economy that has developed and accumulated wealth. Mr O. wanted to find some regulations to introduce to supervise the use of working hours in effective and meaningful ways in the production process and in service and distribution activities in industry. He saw it is a public duty and role to regulate business to limit such practices. He has tried to voice his concern in the Ministry but has failed to find support. Influenced by the popular mode of reducing public intervention, the Ministry was reluctant to introduce any regulations.

Throughout 2002 and 2003 Mr O. continued, privately, his study effort with his team. He believes in the importance of the study. He also believes he has acquired knowledge and experience whose relevance he was keen to evaluate in a real-world situation. He is keen to promote economic planning and write policies – a task he wishes to undertake in close communication with the behaviour and demand of people in economic society. For this reason I classify him in the category of an 'intellectual and society-consulting planner'.

Before concluding this chapter I wish to remember our parallel experience made earlier by Kawakami Hajime in the 1920s as discussed in Chapter 3. The economy in Japan then was still at a developing stage, providing people with only low income. Yet in time we began to see an emerging group of more advantaged wealthy people who brought their power into the working of the economy to use their services for their personal convenience and comfort. Kawakami's concern, as we discussed, was that most economic resources were used to satisfy the welfare of that limited number of advantaged people. Today, after four decades of industrialization and building of wealth in society, those served by the economy and able to claim the use of economic resources are expanded to a larger, in fact general, mass of people. As the popular dictum in business marketing textbooks says, 'consumers are the king', and industry and business are all making efforts to respond to the whim of 'the king'. This, in itself, should be viewed as good news if one believes that the economy has come, at last, to serve the ordinary general public. But in reality, as Mr O. discovered, the rise in service to satisfy those ordinary people is made by themselves at the cost of their own welfare. Once such a mechanism of a particular form of consumer satisfaction is explained we must ask if we will continue to want to gain that 'satisfaction' offered in the market and created and devised out of pressure-ridden hard work at the workplace and through distribution networks.[16]

Part III
Conclusions

10
Economic Development and People's Satisfaction in Life

Introduction

How do the Japanese people see their economy, their life now, and its future prospects? How do they evaluate the way their economic society is structured and its activities conducted? Do they feel that they are securing life satisfaction? These are large questions that can only be discussed by searching for a deep understanding of human nature and desire.

This challenge is larger than any that conventional economic thinking alone can hope to respond to. However, I wish to contribute to this enquiry by taking advantage of two research opportunities provided by the Japanese economy. The first is the fact that there is a rich record of industrialization now available in Japan for our study. The second is the fact that the country has reached a new stage of economic development from which the Japanese are carefully evaluating their past efforts, with the aim of updating their programme so as to set a new course for the future.

Many researchers have observed how Japan has grown from an industrially developing and low-income state to a nation with a modern economic capacity that provides the people with a relatively affluent and comfortable lifestyle. In the preceding chapters I have made my own contribution to this conclusion. Researchers have also observed that despite this apparently successful economic achievement, individuals in Japan today do not find that their lives are 'full'. These individuals have found that their desire to gain economic comfort inspired their hard work through many years. On attaining this economic comfort, however, they have come to see that it is limited and as the provider of happiness and satisfaction in life. This chapter observes the gap between the achievement of the national economy and the failure and discontent of individuals in their lives.

Japan is not alone in perceiving this gap. Many industrially developed and affluent societies have already experienced this dilemma. This makes it easy to dismiss the situation in Japan as yet another unavoidable 'post-materialistic' trend resulting from the people's antipathy to the nation's preceding period of hard competition and struggle for 'economic growth and efficiency'. Instead, however, we must seek ways to salvage Japan and these other economies from their states of inertia, if we are to begin the next stage of progress.

I wish to study the case of Japan and seek an image of a 'better' economic society, with the help of the accumulated records noted above. My question is: how do we build a truly 'good economic society' on the foundation of previous industrial efforts? Galbraith, among others, argued for the importance of building an ideal society on the achievement of post-industrial affluence.[1] Galbraith's image is defined as possessing such 'good' characteristics as economic 'equity', 'stability', and 'freedom', which encourage people to actively seek their self-development and that of others. I need to clarify my own definition of 'good economic society' for Japan. This definition should emerge during the course of my examination of Japan's current problem.

The task of this chapter is to examine the nature and the extent of the gap between national economic achievement and individual failure to find happiness. The subsequent task of proposing a way in which to construct this desired 'good economic society' will be addressed in the next chapter.

I seek to gain lessons from Japan's past experiences of economic development. The worth of this study of Japan will increase only when it is evaluated with the aim of furthering the understanding of human desires that, if not disciplined, will lead to self-destruction – whether in terms of cruel competition or destruction of our environment.

In Chapters 3 and 4 we saw how leading thinkers such as Kawakami, Fukuda and Fujibayashi observed the shortfalls and dangers of the nation's industrialization strategy. They strongly objected to its treatment of people as mere economic resources to drive its growth. Subsequently, as seen in Chapter 1, the government formulated employment and management policies to develop people as a productive 'human resource'.[2] These thinkers urged the need to revise the national industrialization strategy so as to obtain an image of 'good economic society' in Japan. This 'good economic society' was to be built in a balanced way and as a large productive economy that worked to secure international political independence of the country as well as to facilitate people's aspirations towards making themselves better individuals.

Despite this early warning, the Japanese economy has continued to maximize economic growth – ignoring the individual needs of the population. Given the situation at the time, in which very few economic resources were available to achieve the country's industrialization, this warning was given, regrettably, without any actual constructive plan to build a 'good economic society'.

We should not underestimate the warnings of these thinkers.[3] Though they went unheeded at the time, they have stayed with people and are now recollected in the present climate of modern economic affluence.

The structure of the chapter

This chapter consists of three sections. The first discusses how people view their economic progress and standard of living. How do they evaluate their economic progress in relation to the increase of their life satisfaction? I examine this through the Life Satisfaction Survey conducted by the government. I follow the way in which people's happiness increased steadily as the economy developed, and social affluence grew up to the mid-1980s. I ask what has taken place since this time. I also question what ideals and desires people have today – and how they expect to fulfil them through economic means.

The second section examines reasons for the halt in the increase of life satisfaction since 1984, despite ongoing economic growth.

The final section provides the basis of our enquiry relating to how we are to begin work on building a 'good economic society'. This discussion will be covered further in Chapter 11.

How contented are the Japanese today?

Satisfaction survey, economic growth and people's satisfaction in life

In 1972, the Japanese government decided, through the Economic Planning Agency (EPA), now incorporated into the Naikaku-fu, the Office of the Prime Minister and the Cabinet, to conduct a national survey of the standard of living and living environment of Japan. The government understood that the high-growth economy that had developed throughout the 1950s up to the early 1970s had brought a considerable rise in living standards. However, the government also became acutely aware of the side-effects that this economic growth had caused, such as the general deterioration of natural and living environments. It was the government's wish to understand exactly how people viewed and evaluated previous economic growth and industrial development in terms of satisfaction in life – namely, personal and individual feelings of happiness weighed against emerging concerns about the economic environment and living conditions. At the time, the government was able to draw on general support from the population for their public planning and administrative approaches that had been promoted since the end of the war. They wished to create further activities to promote social progress via public planning. The proposed survey was developed for them to learn how best to promote these further activities. The government was proactive and ready to refine its previous methods in order to expand its public planning approach into any new areas for the improvement and reform of its economic society.

The preferred approach of the Japanese government was to ask people directly how they saw their living standards, by putting to them a series of economic and socially related questions. The survey asked questions about how people assessed the worth of their household income; what availability of daily free time they had; the standards of their employment conditions and the nature of their work practices; the extent of their life satisfaction within family, with friends and neighbours, and within society in general; the availability of education and training for themselves and their children; the availability of housing facilities; the standards of health care and public amenities provided; and the nature and the extent of natural and living environments in general.

Upon examination of the survey results, government subsequently decided to enlarge the survey efforts by introducing further questions and conducting it on a bi-annual basis. The official title of the *Kokumin Seikatsu Senkodo Chosa: the National Survey of People's Satisfaction on Life* (henceforth the Satisfaction Survey) was established.[4] The second survey was administered in 1975. Today, in 2004, we have 12 survey results for our study.

Many changes have taken place in the economy and living standards of the people since the initial survey of 1972. Despite this, however, it was decided that the survey should keep its original format as far as possible. This is because successive governments held to the belief that it is important to conduct the survey on a consistent basis with the aim of accumulating records of the results over a long-term period.

The survey now consists of two parts: Phase I and Phase II. The former is a survey with core questions. The first of these core questions asks people how contented they are with their lives compared with 12 months previously. They are requested to nominate one of the following in response: 'highly satisfied, fairly satisfied, satisfied, not satisfied, or extremely dissatisfied'. The Phase II survey began in 1982. Questions for the Phase II survey are formulated after the government has carefully evaluated the findings of the Phase I satisfaction survey and identified issues and areas where government policy efforts are called for. The supplementary questions in the Phase II survey are formulated in order to address the priority areas for constructing public plans and drawing up economic and social policy measures.

People's life satisfaction from 1947 to 1984 (Phase I survey)

The origin of the survey goes back as far as 1947, when the government conducted an economic survey in drawing up a post-war reconstruction programme. The government wished to gain an understanding of how people were beginning to reorient their life and work in the post-war environment. They wanted to gain information about what forms of assistance were needed in order for the people to resume their normal peacetime way of life. The survey was carried out in the form of a direct enquiry addressed to a group of randomly selected people. It asked how people saw and evaluated their living standards; what improvements should be made immediately; and what direction public programmes should take in the future. Figure 10.1 shows the accumulated survey results of Phase I. Table 10.1 shows the issues identified in Phase II of the survey.

Figure 10.1 includes information on the economic growth record and people's annual working hours. This allows us to examine the Satisfaction Survey in light of economic performance and progress. Our examination will focus on the post-1975 survey results. The trend before 1971 should serve as a supplementary reference to enrich the main post-1975 study. The results for the period between 1964 and 1973, though shown in the figure, should not be compared strictly with the post-1975 results, because of the different basis on which the survey results were collated.

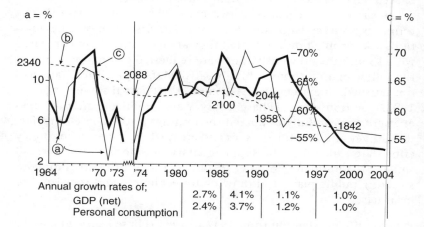

a   Net annual growth rate of GDP per head
b   Total hours worked
c   Satisfaction index

Annual growtn rates of;				
GDP (net)	2.7%	4.1%	1.1%	1.0%
Personal consumption	2.4%	3.7%	1.2%	1.0%

Figure 10.1   Rise in income, working hours and life satisfaction

Table 10.1   Issues identified

1985	'lifestyle preference in the ageing society',
1986	'the internationalization of the economy' and 'the widening of economic and social inequity'
1988	'how people use "free time"'
1990	'concentration of population and economic activities in Tokyo'
1992	'the "low birth rate" and the expected labour shortage in the future'
1993	'development of old-age society'
1995	'living in affluence'
1997	'lifestyles of the female population'
1998	'comfort and security in life'
2000	'taking part in voluntary activities'
2001	'family and daily life'
2003	'Seikatsu *tatsujinn* (master of living)'[5]

Let us study the survey results and ask what the Japanese have revealed about their own well-being (happiness and feelings of contentment in life). Have they become happier with the growth of the national economy and the consequent increase in their incomes?

We asked at the beginning of this chapter how people in Japan today live, appreciate their lives, and look to their future. I now make the following observations:

1. Up to the mid-1980s, there was a positive relationship between economic growth and satisfaction in life in the minds of Japanese people. People were appreciative of the rise in their incomes because they assumed that this rise would enable them to purchase increased comfort in life. Thus appreciation of economic growth was expressed as a rising feeling of contentment. Other supplementary information available in the survey shows that the rise in income led the same people to harbour increasingly positive feelings towards the future of the country and society. This was the case despite frequent fluctuations in the performance of the national economy. The figures reveal that the level of people's satisfaction rose continuously from the mid-1970s to reach a peak in 1984. Thus the majority of the people at the time (65 per cent of those surveyed) are reported to have said they enjoyed a rising level of contentment every year, up to 1984.

2. This high state of national happiness occurred despite the general working population's gradual and continuous increase in working hours. From the middle of the 1970s up to the time of this peak period of satisfaction in 1984 (as indicated by (c) in Figure 10.1), not only working hours but also work intensity increased for both regular full-time employees and those working on a part-time basis. Payment for work throughout this period did not increase sufficiently to compensate for this rise in work hours and intensity. In fact (as seen in Chapter 4), wage rises were generally restrained in labour markets in the second half of this period, under the national need to control price levels in the economy after the oil crises of the 1970s. Despite this, many people appeared to have approached long hours and intensive work positively, saying that they found that working and living during this period felt vigorous and exciting. In fact, they even said that they enjoyed higher morale and an increased interest in their workplaces and lives. Long hours and intensive work are usually understood to indicate a deterioration of working conditions and, hence, the loss of quality of life. The working population of 1974–85 responded to this situation positively. Why is this?

3. Some explanation may be found in the fact that at that time the Japanese economy was enjoying high praise from overseas. Many

observers, academic and practising economic and business managers across the world, began to appreciate Japanese economic management and management practice as so cost-competitive and dynamic that they should be studied and followed internationally as a model. In practice, many of Japan's businesses were expanding their production bases and transplanting their much-praised management techniques into host economies. It was not only managers in affiliated companies but also those in competing firms who studied and eagerly adopted the Japanese way of conducting business, believing that it would lead to an increase in their growth and cost-effectiveness. The workers employed in many of the affiliated plants, at the same time, were also expressing their positive view of Japanese management, claiming that they were receiving better and more humane treatment from their Japanese employers.[6]

4. In addition to such successes in business, the national economy was achieving a high record in economic results. Statistically, the level of Japan's real income per head and the hourly real wage paid to workers in manufacturing plants became the highest in the world (measured by the official exchange rate of the currency) for the year. Also, the national total accumulation of assets and wealth held overseas was reported to be the world's largest, surpassing the records held by the traditionally globally rich Americans and British. Despite rapid capital export by direct investment, Japan's trade surplus accumulated rapidly. We saw that the building of trade surplus was as bad as building trade deficit and would soon bring the problem of trade friction to Japan. In the meantime, however, people saw in the building of trade surplus proof of an increase in the international competitiveness of the nation's exporting business. Some even saw in it an assurance of the worth of their culture and their effectiveness in conducting the economy and promoting social development.

People's life satisfaction by 1985

The continuous rise in people's life satisfaction came to an abrupt halt in 1985.[7] The level of life satisfaction in Japan has failed to rise since. For the first time since the beginning of the survey – possibly throughout the history of the economic development of the country – people began to express feelings of reservation towards the simple rise in their incomes. There had already emerged a 'Damn the GNP' movement at the beginning of the 1970s, but never before had so many people expressed their lack of appreciation for their increasing incomes and living standards in such a general and continuous way. This groundswell came as a new experience to the Japanese. A change in economic thinking had developed among people that led them to an awareness of the importance of issues and aims in the wider fields of society and life beyond mere economic concerns. This change began through the speculation boom and its subsequent collapse from 1985 to 1991. During this period, people saw how rapidly the basis of the economic equity that had been carefully built up through the many years could be destroyed. It gave the population the opportunity to evaluate the hitherto neglected issue of the purpose of economic effort in life.

The speculation boom of 1987 to 1991

Beginning in 1991, the Japanese government introduced many fiscal and monetary policies in order to revive the economy after the collapse of the speculation boom. The scale of public funds injected into the economy rose with the introduction of each new policy. Realizing that the ailing economy could not be cured by the administration of medicine in the form of monetary and fiscal policies, the government decided on a reconstructive operation of the economy itself, through the aggressive promotion of the free market approach. Despite these public devices the economy remained in a depressed state, with the growth rate remaining between 2 and 4 per cent. This is a result of the government's persistent failure to understand the people's change of economic thinking and thus its failure to find how to stimulate activities of the ailing economy in the chaos of the post speculation period. The government has since continued in its misguided economic efforts and its waste of public funds. The state of the economy remains depressed and the level of people's satisfaction continues to decline (follow (c) in Figure 10.1). We examine these changes in the people's economic thinking and behaviour in the next chapter.

Quality of life and life satisfaction

Quality of life

Despite the fact that people are finding themselves relieved of the daily worry of securing essential needs in life, other new concerns have begun to bother them. The two surveys clarified these concerns as being in three areas. These were: the maintenance of 'good health' for themselves, their ageing parents and relations; the enjoyment of a 'happy family life'; and the securing of 'good employment and work'. These may be said to be universal concerns for all people in developed and developing economies at any point in history. They are not limited solely to Japan today.

However, we shall study these concerns in the context of how they arose in the process of economic development. This will help us to gain an understanding of the emerging pattern of the Japanese economy in its post-industrial affluence. This pattern becomes evident when we look at several interrelated emerging characteristics of Japanese society; the new development of people's economic thinking expressed in terms of economic value; and the changes in the people's preferred approaches to economic management.

The first emerging characteristic of Japanese society can be seen in the increase of the number of people who are expressing their concern over the importance of the maintenance of good health. This is a result of the country's increasingly ageing population. The average life expectancy in Japan is the highest in the world. This fact is good news in itself but is tempered by rising medical expenses as more advanced and cost-intensive health care is becoming available. People are concerned that their individual efforts of careful budgeting of family expenses to build savings and asset holdings may no longer be effective. This has led people to the view that health care matters must be promoted under further public arrangements and organization.

The second relates to the importance of family. At the beginning of the 1970s many people had already begun to note that having a happy and well-maintained family was an important, if not the most important, basis for happiness in life.[8] Japanese society has since moved to relinquish previous customs and forms of family maintenance. Many see the resulting loss of the traditionally close-knit family as the cause of the drop in people's well-being today.

At the time of writing this in 2004, however, the Phase II survey is still in the preliminary stage of seeking new understandings about this issue before formulating any public programmes. Many people have suggested that family is a matter that should be dealt with by individuals and because little can be achieved through public policy, whether economic or social. Since 1980, the official view of the government has been that the public is disinclined to take part in active public initiatives that deal with the maintenance of the 'happy family'. At the same time, however, the government has begun to restructure the education and schooling of early-age children to increase their understanding of how to live harmoniously with their elderly family members, combined with efforts to re-educate parents on how to build good relationships with the younger generation. Thus far no specific economic policy measures have been introduced to counter the concern of the fast deterioration of families. Only a few propositions have been made to re-structure government social policy. These were made based on the understanding that some of the government assistance that provides seniors in the family with age pensions, health assistance, and other regular pecuniary handouts to seniors, work to destroy part of the traditional feelings of virtue and obligation that band children to their parents and reduce precious intimacy within families.

The third emerging characteristic of Japanese society relates to work. Work has always been an important issue – if not *the* most important issue – for the Japanese. Lately, people have begun to evaluate work in terms of its long-term capacity to provide them with opportunities to develop their talents and respond to their wishes to develop themselves. More people, in particular the young, see wage rates and the tradition of finding a job with a reputable and established employer in order to secure life long employment and the steady rise of career, as less of an immediate concern or important issue. Engagement in part-time irregular occupations, or frequent 'job-hopping', has become a preferred practice for workers who seek opportunities for long-term fulfilment. This new phenomenon has yet to become the dominant trend, but its rate is accelerating. A decline in the importance of immediate material gains, expressed previously in terms of people's wish to seek higher income for present employment, has been gradually replaced by the wish of people to secure welfare throughout life. Since the 1992 speculation boom, people have begun to think and behave based increasingly on a long-term perspective.

New role for government

Some people see this change in the people's economic thinking as a post-materialistic phenomenon that is expected to arise after society has reached a certain level of affluence. In an affluent society where most people are freed from the daily toil of securing basic necessities for living, it is expected that they will seek living improvements and provisions beyond the subsistence level. This is certainly the case in Japan. The people's demand for quality luxury items is ever increasing. I should note, however, that this observation should not stop here. With the arrival of affluence several new phenomena emerge.

By responding to the Satisfaction Survey and nominating the above three major concerns in life, people are beginning to acknowledge that these concerns are shared throughout the country. The Japanese people view these problems as typical in today's society. They are large issues that cannot be easily solved through individual efforts of 'self-help'. This way of approaching the particular issues of health- and family-related problems has led people to build feelings of unity, an appreciation of the value of sharing their experiences, and of seeking solutions together on a cooperative basis. In this development of communal thought, I see a new perspective towards the government is forming. That is, people regard the government as an institution possessing vast technical information and administrative resources – a central body to which they may direct their problems, however individual and personal – for finding solutions.

It is a new way of viewing the government that is distinct from the previous ways. This is a new way of viewing government that is distinct from the preceding view of one in which government was expected to provide guidance and assistance to individuals in the form of benevolent handouts.

In this renewed assessment of the role of the government, public servants are expected to serve as 'public servants', true to the term, on demand from individuals so as to serve and respond to their specific needs. In addition, the government should redirect its public administrative and planning work from its previous concentration on economic growth and efficiency, towards larger areas that encompass people's life activities. I expect there will be an increase in the role and contribution of individual people themselves and not government who will come to direct Japan on its course of nation building. To achieve this, proposals have been made to decentralize public resources and authorities to local governments and community-based organizations.

It is therefore no great surprise to observe that lately, people appear to be entrusting the government with more responsibility in its role as the central body that coordinates individual concerns and attempts to find effective national community-wide solutions. We saw how this arose in our earlier observations regarding the 1970s in Chapter 4. This was when the Japanese people realized, for the first time, the limitation of 'self-help' as a solution for the problem of the deterioration of the environment.[9] People came to be convinced that a unified public effort was evidently the only means of alleviating this problem. Let me further explain the emergence of this popular conviction.

The 1972 and 1975 Surveys clearly indicated that this was the people's understanding. They reported the people's willingness and readiness to accept an increase in income tax to pay for the cost of building countermeasures to the problem of environmental deterioration.[10] Furthermore, a decade later in the Phase II Life Satisfaction Survey of 1987, the survey response is reminiscent of this earlier observation from 1975 (though not in the same context of environmental problems). The people perceived the new problems of health, family and work as being part of the same 'large-scale/beyond-self-help' category, and expressed their willingness to carry a part of the cost, if necessary, for solving these problems.

We saw above that the people's wish to work *with* the government is a newly emerging mode of thinking that has developed among the population. In this new mode of thinking I see the beginning of people making their own effort to shape an ideal economic society. The Japanese people have begun to see the importance of promoting planning activities by using the government as their agent. It is therefore the people themselves who will come to steer Japan on its course of nation building.

I believe this is a significant change that will alter the general economic paradigm of Japan. It is taking place in the form of real activity that is leading people to gauge the worth of their individual talent and ability to take advantage of the situation today. The building of family savings enables people to be more adventurous and discriminating in their decisions to set the future course of their work and life. Young men and women, in particular, have become more progressive about following this new approach. This generation has begun evaluating the various life patterns, job opportunities and forms of employment that were hitherto unavailable to people in the previous traditional way of life.

It should also be noted that this has occurred, not only through the rise of affluence in the country, but also through the development of the economy and through the rapid expansion of industrial activities that have become apparent since 1980. These achievements created both a large number and variety of jobs for the working population. Women workers benefited in particular, with the increasing provision of job openings and career choices. Many women – single, married, with or without children – began to see varied employment opportunities.[11] Government planners have come to appreciate the value of the widening of lifestyles and work practices in Japan. It is now encouraging individuals to seek employment that fits and satisfies them most. The government hopes that through the best allocation of resources higher productivity will be created in the economy.[12]

The rise of economic freedom

Lifestyles

For the Phase II Surveys of 1985 and 1997, the government put questions that examined the increase in variety of lifestyles. Some of these lifestyles are quite new and differ from traditional approaches to life. For example, people now do any of the following: they marry; maintain *de facto* relations; have children; practise a 'two-income-without-kids' lifestyle in order to enjoy increased free time and disposable incomes; live independently; support their parents; are instead partially supported by their parents; continue to work on a regular lifetime employment basis; work on a part-time irregular basis moving nationally and even internationally between jobs; seek further education and training for career development or for personal enjoyment; and so forth.

The important point to note is that the Survey found that, in most cases, the wide range of observed lifestyles and work practices was developed as the result of careful considerations of the pros and cons of each of the alternatives. The most carefully considered choice is the choice between the welfare of the present and that of the future.

Volunteer works

It was also found by the 2000 Survey that an increasing number of people engaged in non-paid volunteer work. People reported that they derived excitement and satisfaction from undertaking activities based on altruism rather than from pecuniary considerations and self-interest. The assistance of the public service through participation in community service activities, such as building parks and other public amenities, cleaning up cities, assisting teaching staff in schools and colleges and helping care for the sick, the young and the old, is beginning to be seen by people as valuable and necessary. Their activities are now expanding overseas. Indeed, many Japanese people are reported to be travelling overseas in their desire to help needy people, particularly in neighbouring parts of Asia, and in Africa.

The rise in the number of volunteers began after the Kobe earthquake of 1995. This disaster is said to have inspired more people to see the value of working for others through active participation in volunteer work. By 1994, the number of NPOs (non profit organizations) in Japan had rapidly increased to almost three thousand. In 2001 the government decided to commemorate that year as 'the Year of Volunteer Activities'. This was in accordance with its wish to see new forms of work and human relationships develop to respond to the emerging desires of people to seek various patterns of employment beyond those traditionally practised.[13]

'Freeter' syndrome

The last observation to be made regarding recent years concerns a rising phenomenon among young people.[14] This is what has come to be labelled the freeter syndrome. The term is derived from the German 'free *Arbeiter*', but its actual meaning has been broadened to loosely describe a new generation of people whose motives for and behaviour towards work and life. Freeters are people who have yet to decide on fixed employment or career paths. In English NEET (not in employment, education or training) describes roughly this group of people. But for Japan's case it may be more apt to call the group 'not in regular employment, education, or home duties.[15] They are a generation of people who have established certain lifestyles because they do not see any alternative, as yet, to satisfy their purpose in life. Freeters wish to keep their choices open until they find suitable directions in life and work. They do not know themselves how long they are prepared or able to postpone this decision. In the meantime, some stay at home, leading idle lives financially supported by their parents who have built savings through their hard work in the high economic growth period of the 1960s and 1970s, while others hop between part-time jobs whenever the need to gain income arises and/or suitable job opportunities crop up to entertain them. Some studies show many of these freeters, on the other hand, appear to lead this life of freedom with their purposes relatively focused. These freeters experiment with many and varied forms of employment to test their talents and aptitudes for work. They also attend various educational and training courses to gain knowledge and skills in financial planning, engineering, electronic R&D activities, social care, medical services, agricultural activities, volunteer activities and overseas aid programmes. Many freeters are reported to attend these courses not so much to gain formal qualifications as to learn activities in Japan's newly developing fields. That is, they are seeking to understand the future direction of development in their own country, so as to locate where and how they may be able to work and live with satisfaction, or travel overseas in order to learn the ways of other countries.[16]

The rate of unemployment in the total work force in Japan has risen in the last several years to 6 per cent, the highest level of the last four decades. As to how many of Japan's jobless have fallen into the

self-imposed unemployed category of the freeter, it is difficult to estimate. Some estimates claim that the proportion of unemployed is
higher than 30 per cent of the total unemployed and is approaching
the 40 per cent mark.[17]

Why one becomes a freeter, what one is, and what an increase in
their numbers might do to the national economy are important questions. As yet, no one has definite answers. We do know that many
freeters have stated that they do not wish to undertake the kind of
employment which would force them to follow similar life patterns to
those of their parents (many of whom were born between 1945 and
1960). Freeters fail to see the worth of gaining the life experience of
their parents' generation. They therefore await new opportunities.
Many of the older generation, on the other hand, find the freeter attitude to be lazy and irresponsible. They see freeters as taking advantage
of the current affluence of Japanese society – an attitude that will not
be tolerated in the future when the stock of national savings is
reduced. Some people worry that the rise in freeters will lead to the
deterioration of skills, particularly in the manufacturing fields. These
people fear that the coming generation of people will be without adequate ability to secure a productive economy and a progressive
society. Others believe that this problem is not entirely the fault of
young people. Rather, it is due to the lengthy recession that has prevented young people from gaining work in secure job environments
that provide education, training and even encouragement to develop
themselves into human resources, as was the case in the past.

The government conducted its research in order to assess the nature
and extent of the 'ranges of lifestyles', 'volunteer activities' and the
'freeter population'. The results were published in the 1999, 2000 and
2001 White Papers.[18] The evaluation of the emergence of the phenomenon is not uniform among government and economic observers.
Some see it as only temporary, arising from depressed economic conditions. They see the decline of employment opportunities during the
economic recession and the changes in employment practices as being
owing to employers, who, in their efforts to restructure business by
rapidly revising the traditional long-term employment system, have
forced their employees to adopt to consequent new forms of work and
life patterns. These observers expect the population to return to its previous forms of life and work as the economy resumes its former
dynamism. Little importance is attributed to the new behaviour of
people as an indication of the emergence of any new approach to the
economy. This is the basic view of the current government, which

promotes financial and monetary policies in order to revitalize the economy. When these policies fail, the government invariably promotes deregulation of the economy to stimulate investment to industries and increased consumer spending, and thus invigorate national economic activities. The question is, will there be any improvement in job markets?

Emerging new type of people

I do not accept the current government's view of the economy. I believe the economy is experiencing a new stage of development that is affecting people's economic behaviour. People are beginning to behave differently from previous patterns, habits and customs. Further studies should be conducted to understand what exactly this development in the economy means and where it will take the Japanese in the future. I believe it is important that we begin our study centring on the 'new type of people' who are promoting these new phenomena in the spheres of employment and life, instead of viewing them as 'outcasts'.

Instead of understanding this new behaviour in relation to the economic slump, I propose to study it through an appreciation of the present rising economic freedom. That is to say, I believe that people, now that they are freed from the pressure of immediate economic necessity, are taking the time to consider choices in life and evaluate all possible avenues for the future as well as the present. This is what Japan's 'new type of people' are doing. I call these people the 'new type', because of their new type of attitude. These people find themselves living in a new environment which allows them to (a) evaluate the environment and conditions in life and the economy; (b) develop and cultivate themselves in order to gain full advantage of the expected development of opportunities in the future; and (c) make further efforts to alter and reform the environment to their benefit. I therefore expect the relationship between people and the economy to be transformed with the increase in numbers of this new type. In future, people will actively go forward to seek maximum benefit from the economy and their own required form of economic welfare and personal 'happiness', instead of passively waiting to receive handouts.

When people require their economy to improve the quality of their life, the relationship between the people and the economy is expected to enlarge into all fields of human aspirations to satisfy them. Throughout its development, this is how the economy has come to serve the people. This development has enlarged the role of the economy beyond its former objective of achieving growth.

It is not clear how many people in Japan have acquired this new manner of thinking today and are ready to behave differently by taking advantage of living in this 'affordable' way. It is difficult to give an accurate estimate due to the lack of adequate information. However, an increasing number of reports and observations about people who choose to remain free from binding themselves to certain career paths, forms of employment, marriage, and family building is available.[19] It is even more difficult to envisage how the Japanese economy will change with the rise of new economic thinking and the new breed of people in the future. I shall continue this discussion in the next chapter.

Before concluding this chapter, I would like to consider briefly the present situation in relation to the argument that Fukuzawa Yukichi put forward regarding the future direction of his country on the arrival of the Meiji Restoration towards the end of the nineteenth century. He tried to explain why and how the Tokugawa regime that had lasted for two and a half centuries had at last been overthrown. Fukuzawa located the cause of the overthrow in the increase, though gradual over the period, of people's dissatisfaction with their lives under the *ancien régime*. He observed that people had sought something new to liberate them from the existing, stifling feudal society. Eventually, this liberation came when the people's individual negative feelings became a unified force that was shared among the people in the context of their general understanding of their own daily lives – that is, the building of people's 'wisdom'. This wisdom was gained from the people's realization of the shortfalls of society and from their repeated feelings of dissatisfaction with life. The Meiji Restoration occurred when the regime was no longer able to suppress the country's growing resentment. Thus the old way yielded to the beginning of Japan's modernization and industrialization.

Does the Satisfaction Survey expresses the possibility of the coming of a similar scenario for Japan today, as Fukuzawa observed a century ago?

11
Planning the Future

At the beginning of this book I talked of Japan as being a resource-poor country. By 2004, however, the country had become affluent, with its people economically well provided for. The Japanese people have not only eradicated most problems of poverty, but are also enjoying the benefits of increasing economic freedom. For many individuals, the possibility of being able to actively explore the potential to their own lives is emerging. Nevertheless, as discussed in Chapter 10, today the majority of Japanese find themselves unhappy, their economy poorly structured and their society stifling.

Many observers are pessimistic about the future of the Japanese economy. I believe that, more often than not, it is in difficulty that things reveal their true nature. By drawing on the observations and discoveries that I have made throughout this book, my final question will be to ask what the driving force of the economy has been – and where this force will take the economy in the future.

Reasons for failures in the economy and society in 2004

The golden ages

During the 50 years following World War II, the economy experienced two peaks of prosperity. The first came towards the end of the 1960s after the high economic growth period, dubbed by some as the 'miracle' era. The second peak occurred between the latter half of the 1980s, the period in which the Japanese government gained high praise internationally, and claims to have developed an innovative and highly effective economic and management technique.

On both occasions individual people expressed their appreciation of Japan's economic achievement. They expressed contentment with

211

the way things were going in Japan. The two peaks at both periods in the Satisfaction index, in Figure 10.1 above, confirm this. The people approved of the way that a modern productive economy was being built in the country, allowing them to enjoy good lives.

They were satisfied and expected this satisfaction to continue into the future. They did not, however, make efforts to progress towards betterment. At both times, the Japanese failed to capitalize on the opportunity that presented itself to build a truly 'good' economic society. They failed to make effective use of the large amount of economic assets, knowledge, techniques and experiences that had been accumulated in the Japanese economy on its path to reaching these 'golden ages'. They failed to understand the importance and the real meaning of these times, and missed the chance to consolidate the large opportunity.

It is true, as we noted in Chapter 4, that many ideas for economic and social reform and for progressive proposals and activities had emerged during these peaks in the economy. Many people began to experiment those reform ideas in various parts of the economy and society in general with their aim focused to see an effective use of the accumulated wealth and technology thereby to build a truly 'good' economic society in Japan. The installation of production facilities to counter the rising destruction of the environment was also discussed. Unfortunately, such initiatives could not attract the support of the general public. The majority of people still thought that it was not yet time to 'indulge' in ideas of reform. They wished to continue as they had been doing in order to ensure the ongoing growth and development of the economy, before moving towards further improvements in the quality of their lives.

In the first instance, while uncertain how to proceed – that is, whether to progress in search of the further betterment of life or to secure the improved economic comforts gained thus far – Japan was greeted with the sudden rise of import and crude oil prices from the Middle East. The economy plunged into the oil crisis of 1973, curtailing any chance of beginning the next stage of its progress and development. The crisis sent Japan into panic mode. The people feared that their industries, the very source of their golden age, would be destroyed. The general trend of society and the direction of the economy reverted towards economic growth and expansion by the mid-1970s, but the economy would never regain its previous state of rapid growth.

The Japanese people failed again in the 1980s. Once again, they did not make appropriate use of the assets and knowledge accumulated in the economy to provide a better life for the population. This time, the cause of the problem was not external. The failure arose from the poor behaviour of people within Japan. Government, business and community members failed to behave in the civilized manner expected of citizens living in the economic comfort and security that the country was now able to provide. The people behaved selfishly and greedily, forgetting Japan's traditionally respectful, industrious and balanced approach to life. These people began wild speculation activities, leading the national economy to fall into the chaos of speculation throughout the four years from 1987 to 1991. The economy experienced a large-scale boom. As shown in Chapter 2, in the economic White Papers of the time the government single-mindedly returned to the growth-oriented approach, businesses became preoccupied with hunting around for speculative opportunities (that is, windfall gains in property and share markets and expanding ownership and control of business in many parts of the world) and individual people participated in many kinds of money-making activities in search of quick gains. A large amount of money (estimated to be equal to the size of a year of Japan's GNP at the time) was said to have changed hands during the boom within the country and overseas. During these four years, national income and capital formation in business are reported to have expanded by 30 per cent. When the bubble burst, the 30 per cent expansion was found to be not real.[1] The expansion was only on paper and did not create much true economic value or social improvement.

The Japanese not only wasted the rising opportunities for the betterment of people's lives, but also invited the destruction of the socio-economic basis that had been built through the efforts of the people to develop themselves as productive human resources through education, mission-oriented skills, and hard work to build assets in the economy.

The deterioration of the economy and the pessimism that people began to feel for their life and for their future prospects, noted in Chapter 10, are the consequences of this failure. It is my intention to explain how this failure occurred, and I hope to identify an important mechanism to explain it. That is, by locating and examining this failure I will be able to explain how the Japanese economy operated in its growth and development post 1945. More importantly, by undertaking this exercise, I plan to arrive at practical propositions to guide the economy in a better direction.

Life purposes and economic objectives post 1945

Many economic historians studying the Japanese economy cite the general population's hard work and readiness to engage in economic efforts as major factors in the country's rapid achievement of industrial development. I appreciate that these factors have assisted greatly the effective working of the government's planning and policy-writing efforts in bringing rapid economic growth and industrial development to Japan. The Japanese people – at least during the period studied in this book – not only worked hard to take directions from management, but also considered how they could best contribute to the progress of the economy. They are therefore economically minded as well as economically oriented.

I wish to examine how the hard-working attitude and characteristic willingness of the people to develop themselves as productive human resources have worked to drive the economic development of post-war Japan. I have chosen to call this drive the 'economization ethos', meaning the willingness to commit both physically and intellectually to work.[2] This 'economization ethos' is the force within a person's mind leading them to take up an economic activity in a certain way and in a certain desired direction. It is the internal motivation that drives individuals not only to work hard, but also to actively engage in economic activities. It is observed as a social and economic phenomenon that is supported by a group of people expressed as distinct at a certain time in society. It is not simply the work motivation or the moral basis that encourages people to work. By calling this force an 'ethos', I wish to emphasize the importance of social, cultural and spiritual elements shared by people through their common experiences in developing this particular ethos. It is the most important driving force of the economization efforts of the people, and by extension, the driving force of the national economy.

The ethos is built on four points. These are the individual's:

1 view and understanding of the economic and social environment of the time;
2 cherished image of ideals that he/she wishes to see in his/her economic society;
3 evaluation of his/her own capacity and role in making a contribution to the improvement of the welfare of others through the sharing of this cherished image of ideals; and, on a more practical basis;
4 life objectives, embodied in the promotion of an economization effort.

The relative importance of these four concerns differs between periods in economic society, reflecting the economic environment and the extent of economic advancement in that society. It also differs between individuals, reflecting the personal and professional experiences, personalities and educational backgrounds of the individuals in question.

I have focused on white-collar workers, leaving the discussion of blue-collar workers to appropriate previous research observations. I have chosen to examine office workers as their greater freedom encourages them to use their own initiative, judgement and professional education and training, compared with factory workers, who are generally placed to work under the instruction of managers. This initiative is a major element of the driving force of the economy. Also, it should be noted that I have more contacts and direct experience relating to office workers than to factory workers.

Table 11.1 demonstrates what constitutes Japan's driving force. It shows: (1) what the people's work ethos consists of; (2) why this ethos has formed as has been observed; (3) how this work ethos has developed during this period (how economic motives held by individuals have developed into the work ethos of the country); and (4) that the economic wills of the people and the aims of society are not the same – that is, the simple aggregation of the former do not sum to the latter. I wish to note this gap and explain how this caused the failure of the economy.

Column I of the table indicates eight generations of active working adults of 30 to 50 years of age. If we take the first period of 1946–50, we can see that the generation in question were born between 1906 and 1916 (shown in column i) and became 30–50 years of age in the immediate post-war years beginning in 1946. The date of their births makes them the pre-war generation. Their education was therefore in the traditional mode of emphasizing the importance of 'building a modern independent country, rich with its own culture through the promotion of industrialization'. Many of this generation were sent to the front to fight directly in the war in the Pacific, or contributed to the war effort at home and abroad. The extent of this experience and the way it influenced the determining of their work efforts in the recovery of the economy varies between individuals. Despite this, there emerged a general force that can be seen as guiding the economic effort of the post-war reconstruction period.[4] The wartime experience gave the Japanese a perception of the enormous superiority of Americans in their capacity to produce economic resources.

This perception led this generation to first understand the foolishness of attempting to fight against such economic superiority with

Table 11.1   **Generations of working people and their economization ethos**

I *Period studied*	*II* *Generations of working people*		
	i *Birth dates*	*ii* *Economic and personal experience*	*iii* *Images*
1 1946–50	1896–1920	Building independent country through strong industry; war experience	Industrial soldiers
2 1951–55	1901–25	Development of and promotion of light industries; democratic approach in society	
3 1956–60	1906–30	Promotion of heavy industry	'Corporate men'
4 1961–65	1911 –35	Promotion of war industry; advancement of militarism in society	
5 1966–70	1916–40	Promotion of war industry; direct war experience	
6 1971–80	1921–50	Living under a general liberal atmosphere of 'Taisho Democracy' (alternatively meaning something as 'people as the baseism'[3]	'Economic animals'
7 1981–90	1931–60	War economy; destruction; post-war reconstruction of the economy; democratization of society	
8 1991–95	1941–65	Road to economic growth	Bubble people
9 1996–2003	1948–73	High economic growth	
10 2004 and beyond	1954–74	Living in affluence	With economic freedom

Japan's paucity of resources. Subsequently, this realization led many people to see that the only way for their country to recover from the defeat and humiliation of the war was to make their own work effort – that is, to make human hard work supplement the short supply of Japan's economic resources. As we discussed in Chapter 1, an idea that sees the need in Japan to develop people into human resources and work effectively in organized and co-operative manners of their own has developed so as to supplement the short supply of economic resources. I argue that this specific idea and effective practice of it has served as a powerful driving force of the reconstruction of the economy.

Sangyo Senshi

In his study of the work ethos that appears to have driven the rapid growth of the Japanese economy during the 1960s, Hazama labels the generation of people that contributed to this achievement *kigyo senshi*, or corporate soldiers. Hazama suggests that many in this generation of people came to work in factories and offices as if to continue fighting the war in the Pacific. The reconstruction of Japan, Hazama argues, is thus an economic 'war' against the West. It should be noted that this reductionistic ethos of the *kigyo senshi* alone is insufficient to aid us to fully understand the economic efforts that were made during this period. However, it is important to note that a common sentiment arose among many people based on their experience of fighting the war. To appreciate the importance of this sentiment, following Hazama, I label the 1946–55 generation of working people *sangyo senshi*, or industrial soldiers (column II (iii)).[5]

In sum, immediately following the war, the Japanese people made a cooperative work effort to rebuild their war-ravaged nation. This work was coordinated from a common desire to recover Japan from the humiliation of its defeat and prove the country's worth. Many ideas were proposed as to how and what shape of new country should the people desire to have and be able to construct. Some suggested, for one, a rebuilding of Japan in the model of Sweden and Switzerland, which are distinguished by natural environmental beauty and peace-loving lifestyles.[6] It was when the Economic White Paper of 1948 was drafted that people came to consensus support to the reconstruction of the country through economic activities. The Paper proposed an economic planning of the national economy and argued that the ruined country would be recovered through pulling together the work efforts of the people. Most of the population understood this logic and decided to follow the Paper's lead.

Chapter 4 illustrated the implementation of this economic effort. In that chapter we saw that the life objectives of individual people, which were initially diverse – ranging from the practical need to secure food, clothes and housing, to the national desire to reduce Japan's dependence on American economic aid and American social, political and other guidance – were integrated into one national programme. This national programme focused on the swift reconstruction of the production basis of the country, so as to provide for the basic needs of all the people, thereby bringing order and stability to their lives. This made sense to everyone as the answer to the life objectives people had at the time. A work ethos was built by integrating the daily objectives of the people. This work ethos became the aim of society. Subsequently, Japanese planners decided that the aim of society should be promoted in the economy.

Kigyo Ningen serving for corporations

The post-war work effort brought economic results. In the second and third periods of 1956–65 and 1966–70, new working generations emerged, free from the inferiority complex of the previous generation. These generations were brought up in the relatively liberal social atmosphere of the Taisho (1912–26) period. The importance of the national slogan 'build a strong economy for national independence' held less meaning for these generations. Many people from these two generations began to see their individual roles in society and in the economy as more closely related to their individual needs in life. They began to work for the benefit of their individual corporations rather than for the nation as a whole. Their continued hard work and active economic efforts notwithstanding, the new generations' efforts were directed at helping the corporations they worked for achieve success and expansion, with the expectation that they would gain economic rewards in return. These rewards came in the form of higher pay and work conditions, generous corporate welfare systems for the employees and their families, and a high status in society. Employers also made an effort to design management policies in order to respond to the change in work attitudes of employees. The result of this effort was the development of a system that came to be loosely called the Japanese Management System.

These generations built an economic ethos based on their rising confidence and respect for their own skills, and the workability of their approach to economic management. These generations greeted Japan's yearly performance with satisfaction, as it confirmed the effectiveness of their economic activities. As covered in Chapter 4, the aggressive 'National Income-doubling Plan' was written on the basis of this rising confidence. This economic plan integrated the people's newly emerging work aspirations into an economic ethos. This was despite the fact that most individuals had yet to clearly understand the economic capacity of the country. This resulted in Japan becoming the world's second largest economy at the end of this period.

The term 'corporate men' was coined to describe the approach observed among this generation of workers (generations 3 and 4 in the table). The aggressive attitude of 'fighting' for Japan's national confidence that had been apparent in the work ethos of the preceding working generation was replaced by a new 'composed' attitude. It is important to note that though the people no longer saw the need to 'fight', due to their renewed feelings of self-confidence, this self-confidence only re-emerged from seeing proof of their skill in adopting and developing modern technologies in their workplaces for efficient production, in the form of Japan's good economic record. However, the Japanese people were well aware that these industrial technologies were still coming from overseas – most notably from America. This motivated the Japanese to continue to work even harder to catch up with the wealthier Americans. The Japanese workers committed their utmost to their work, sometimes overworking at the risk of their health and even their own lives ('*karo-shi* syndrome'), in order to make the operation of their companies internationally competitive – and thus win growth and expansion for these companies in the world economy. As is to be expected from this situation, people quickly became materialistic and self-serving, seeking economic gains for themselves.

Then there was an economic crisis in 1973. The prices of imported crude oil, the basic source of energy for the country, escalated. Japanese industrial firms were threatened with the need to meet the sharp rise in production costs, which led them to lose their international competitiveness. People saw this as an important testing time once again for the country, not unlike during the Meiji period, and at the end of World War II.

The corporate men quickly came to the consensus that the utmost effort should be made to save the Japanese economy by discovering ways to reduce production costs in both the factory and in the office. Once again, people were united in working towards finding ways to economize energy use in industrial, office and home activities, as well as in developing technology to build energy-saving tools and mechanisms. Saving the economy was undertaken as the task that would save the country. The motivation of corporate workers to put in hard work and promote economic activities was pushed even further. These efforts created many innovative management practices, as demonstrated by, for example, the development of lean production methods in automobile factories and the quality control systems implemented across the majority of workplaces.

The result was a large cost reduction in most manufacturing factories and the general improvement of production efficiency in the economy. Thanks to the concerted corporate effort, the country continued to accumulate wealth and enrich individual people and their families. Once again, the people worked cooperatively. This return to the previous way of working took place with the common purpose of saving the economy through the economic use of energy. However, this joint cooperation this time was promoted only as a technical device and did not restore the basis a common attitude towards work and life.

The Japanese people worked hard in order to save the economy from losing its international competitiveness, and to build its national wealth. What their effort lacked, however, was the basis from which to think forward to imagine what would be a better economic system and improved approach to living. In the absence of a progressive mentality, the people's hard work was limited to their individual workplaces and stopped short of developing into a unified social work ethos. The self-serving thoughts and behaviour of the people during this period failed to help them find a common ground on which to base future economic activities. As discussed in Chapter 1, the earlier condition of the economy operating under a resource-poor economic environment in a $K < L$ condition had ceased. However, the working population and the nation's work ethos continued to operate on the basis of the preceding $K > L$ shortage of economic resources.

The idea to reform Japan's economic system and build a good economic society for the betterment of people's lives came and went in the brief period between the pinnacle of the first golden age and the panic of the oil crisis in 1973. The cause of this failure of Japan was not the external factor of the international oil crisis. Rather, it was the poor quality of its work ethos – poor quality in the sense that the people failed to seek to progress their lives.

This unfortunate situation is evident in the survey results that were presented by the NHK, the national broadcasting organization, in late 1978. The NHK asked the population for their views on life satisfaction. The majority, nearly 70 per cent, who responded to the survey reported that they were still closely following the traditional approach of seeking life satisfaction in work. They saw this as appropriate and felt happy with developing themselves as productive workers and efficient managers of offices, so as to contribute to the industrial development of the country. As for their approach to work, more than 80 per cent of those surveyed expressed their conviction that 'they should always strive to improve themselves at work'.[7] We may take this to imply that they expected to achieve life development by becoming good workers, given the popular thinking that had emerged through the development of the 'quality control' movement that one produces good products when one is a good person oneself.[8]

While the accumulation of economic wealth continued, the economy remained destitute of any collective, progressive aspiration. The people continued to work hard. They worked with increasing intensity for long hours to bring efficiency to factories and offices, seeking, as the NHK survey illustrated, life satisfaction through work. Little sign of progress in people's thinking and attitudes towards work and life developed. They failed to see the rise of an opportunity for them to take benefits out of the development of the economy that progressed into a higher K>L to a K<L stage.

Economic animals

The economic White Papers of 1980 and 1981 were not effective in altering the work ethos of the time. They could not convince people how inappropriate it was for them to continue to seek growth and efficiency in the economy and selfish materialistic objectives in life. It was outside Japan where some economic and social critics have come to observe that the economic environment for Japan was improving from its previous resource-poor state. They saw that the country's high economic growth has brought fast accumulation of capital and improvements in production and economic management. They further observed that the Japanese people, despite this newly available level of economic provisions and comfort were not promoting living an improved life by seeking relaxation and pleasure outside the field of simple hard work to the extent and the ways that would normally be expected. Seeing that this expected behaviour did not result, they decided to brand the Japanerse people 'economic animals'.[9]

Behaving like animals or not, the Japanese themselves in this period failed to see the importance of themselves aspiring for their betterment. Most of the people in this work generation were born long after the war and were brought up in the subsequent high economic growth period. In our search for a work ethos that was the driving force of the economy, it must be conceded that there is no clear basis on which to form one. That is to say this generation, the traditional value of serving others, the spirit of *koeki*, was replaced by egoism. People no longer saw the importance of community, cooperation and mutual sympathy, and, as a result, perhaps were no longer happy.

When mutual feelings are lost it is only natural that the basis for forming an economic ethos and, thus, the driving engine of the economy are also lost. Without an economic engine, the economy ceased to develop, only expanding through the speculative movement of money. This is how the economy threw itself into the speculation boom.

Living in a phantom world of 'Japan as No. 1'

The concerted work efforts of corporate men brought a large cost reduction to most manufacturing factories and the general improvement of production efficiency in the economy throughout the second half of the 1970s. The people became accustomed to estimating everything in economic terms.

The Economic White Papers of 1980 and 1981 were not effective in altering the work ethos of the time. They could not convince people of the impossibility of finding the life satisfaction they sought in mere growth and efficiency in the economy, and selfish materialistic objectives. The people did not welcome warnings when the economy was seen to be thriving. Instead, they chose to hear only what they wished to hear. On a monthly basis, the daily newspapers and business journals proclaimed to the people that Japan had become World No. 1 in this field, or on that basis. Examples included news that the annual production of cars in Japan had become the world's largest in 1980; the export value of Japan's industrial goods had become the world's largest in 1985; the foreign capital held by Japanese banks had surpassed that of the other international capital exporting economies of the world such as the USA, the UK and many other European countries, placing the Japanese banks at the top of the world's rich list by holding foreign assets all over the world, in 1986; Japan had become No. 1 in terms of GNP per capita, with holding the world's largest sum of foreign currencies in 1987, and so on.

The constant news of high economic results as such led the Japanese people to believe that their economy had become the world's most powerful, the richest in capital assets, the most industrially technologically advanced, and the most efficient in managerial know-how. Misled by this belief, they failed to remember the original message that had guided the previous generation in their past economization efforts. This message was that Japan lacks economic resources. Much hard work would be required to overcome this limitation before people could begin to concentrate on their aspiration to improve their way of living.

The economic environment has changed, allowing the economy to operate in a capital-rich condition, yet most people in Japan fail to understand the capacity this achievement offers them. An important question to ask now is whether Japan is going to repeat yet another, third failure to take advantage of a golden age.

'Economic freedom' and the new generation of working people

Many of the current young generation of people in Japan feel that they have lost sight of the objective of promoting economic activities. This generation is alienated from the economy and does not actively contribute to the economization ethos. In order to recover the energy of the economy, the Japanese people must assist each other and share this ethos. The aimless elements of this generation complain that they can see no clear image of a 'good economic society' to which they wish to contribute (lost in apathy?). They have their individual objectives in life, but they are unable to relate these to the objectives of others in society. They confess that they feel at a loss as to how they should make themselves useful in building Japan's desired 'good economic society'. We should not dismiss these people as lazy or parasitic, because they are merely riding on back of the wealth that has been accumulated through the hard work of the preceding generations. We should appreciate the current observation that their promotion of various lifestyles and work approaches is a sign of their search for an answer (putting out feelers?). We should take note of Fukuzawa's observation, cited at the end of the preceding chapter, and think how to guide the growth of these emerging efforts.

To facilitate the birth of the necessary 'economization ethos' by which to recover the driving force of the national economy among the current generations of work people, it is now absolutely necessary for Japan to find an image of a 'good economic society'.

In search of proposals for the future

The following is a list of what we have discovered during the course of this study:

1. The aims of the economy
In an economy that has matured, with industrial development and the accumulation of affluence, our economic aim will be to maximize the 'happiness' of people. The preceding aim of increasing material provisions for the people should be replaced by this new aim. We may give this new goal the general term 'quality of life'. Its achievement should be sought through the development of individuals into

complete human beings by their understanding of their talents and capacities, and their exploration towards self-actualization.

2. The role of the economy

The role of the economy is to provide people with the opportunities and adequate facilities to enable and encourage their initiative for exploration. Job opportunities, essential economic, social and educational provisions, and a civil environment for living, studying and socialization with others, are all required for people to explore the higher aims of life.

3. The role of government

We expect that people will attain 'happiness' through this exploration. We expect that people will promote this exploration throughout their lives.[10] We expect that a public body – central government; local authorities; community-based institutions and the like – will be able to build the facility that we have noted above, on a large scale and on a regular, stable, long-term basis to benefit the population as a whole.

Activities the government should promote now:

- The Japanese government should continue its study of life satisfaction. It has accumulated experience in examining how economic development brings life satisfaction to people. In addition, through such surveys, the government is able to provide opportunities for the people to consider how economic development might bring satisfaction to their lives; in what ways and to what extent it should engage in directing the economy for their benefit, and provide them with the chance to compare their own perceptions with those of other people. The aim of this would be for individual people to think for themselves what life objectives they might wish to pursue within the economy, and how and where they might work and live, in cooperation with others in society.
- The government should take the initiative to draw a clear and exciting image of a good economic society for Japan in the future. It will be able to achieve this task by following its past experiences of writing 'vision policy' throughout the 1970s and 1980s into the first half of the 1990s.

Exploration into a new frontier

Past experiences should be studied to gain guidance in creating a better future – to build a 'good economic society'. Two observations must be made about the Japanese work ethos and how it works to develop the economy.

The first is the importance of having a work ethos that represents the aims of the people through the promotion of economic activity. This ethos is built out of people's life objectives and work motives. Life objectives and work motives alone, however strong in the individual's mind, will not work as effectively as the driving engine of the economy. These objectives and motives must be expressed in a concerted form, drawing sympathy from as many people as possible. In order to build a work ethos from the collective objectives and motives of individual people, people must learn and value each other's objectives and motives – and resonate with them. This 'resonance', this feeling of commonality, is the binding force that unites individuals in economic society and inspires many to work together in that society. It arises through shared objectives. While some people may continue to work individually in their economization efforts, it is expected that many people will desire to work cooperatively with others when they see the value and quality of their objectives. Economic development will be promoted through the sharing of objectives and by working on a cooperative basis. Any economization efforts that are made without mutual sympathy for the efforts of others may create economic growth and efficiency, but not economic development that improves the lives of people. This was illustrated in the case of the speculation boom.

During the boom, people sought individual gains; that is, they acted individually, for individual purposes alone. The boom drove the growth of the economy for a period of four years – but for no longer. No real development of the economy was made out of the boom. Despite large sums of money circulating around the economy, its real economic output was surprisingly small.[11] The bubble burst when people realized the emptiness, and perhaps the 'vulgarity', of the objective that they had been separately seeking.

In explanation of the rise and the fall of the boom, some critics have suggested that government monetary policy was inadequate in checking the rise of prices, particularly real-estate and corporate shares, at an early stage of the boom.[12] Instead, my argument has been that the lack of progressive aspirations among people was the greater cause. Growth and efficiency allow economic society to build economic resources. However, if people cease to create value in their work by using these economic resources because they fail to find mutual aims and make efforts to work cooperatively, those resources remain idle. These idle resources only serve to feed the greed of the people and soon destroy the working mechanism of the economy – as we saw in the case of the Japanese economy following the speculation boom.

The second observation about the Japanese work ethos is that now, in 2004, the young generation of people appear to be experiencing difficulty in finding joint social aims. I have observed that this generation lives in affluence and is therefore allowed and encouraged to explore many possibilities in life. They are not without life objectives or work motives of their own. What the people of the new generation are seeking, but are unable to find in society, are mutual objectives that they can share. The people of this generation are not provided with opportunities to resonate and cooperate with each other. They are alienated – free to explore diverse activities but without a common aim with which to direct their efforts to work and economize. No work ethos can be created and no driving force is found to promote economic activity. Thus the economy remains in a state of stagnation.

Again, it is important to emphasize that the problem is not a lack of individual objectives and motives. In any economic society there have always been a certain number of people who have been unable to find life objectives. In examining the case of Japan today, it would not be correct to state that the young generation consists of a greater proportion of such unfortunate people than was the case in any of the previous generations. If anything, the current generation have shown themselves more anxious to progress from this unfortunate state, as was demonstrated in the recent rise of varied lifestyles undertaken by them. It is not true to suppose that it is because the young generation do not have a common experience to unify their objectives that they are unable to form a mutual work ethos. This is the generation that has grown up in an affluent society. This affluence has provided them with the opportunity to pursue varied lifestyles of their choosing – such as travelling, working and living overseas – and to evaluate the rising worth of their own culture in the eyes of the world.

In short, this generation's experience is new and different from the experience of all Japan's preceding generations. For this reason, they are indeed a new generation of people who possess a new type of personality. The older generations should provide support for their successors in this unfamiliar world.

As a member of the fourth generation, I wish to draw on the wisdom of hindsight that allows me to look back to evaluate how the older generation worked to build the country after the war and to look forward to understand the coming of generation of people with their difficulties and potentials.

In previous chapters we saw how many important Japanese economic decisions originated as defensive responses to 'external threats'. In response to the demand that it forsake its traditional isolation and open up to the industrially advanced Western world a century ago, Japan engaged in its national industrialization effort. When Japan was defeated in World War II its independence as a nation was threatened. To counter this threat, Japan quickly rebuilt the basis of its production and provided stable living conditions to its population. In the 1970s, the oil crisis threatened the continuous operation of Japan's productive industry. In response, management and workers collaborated on a joint effort to restructure and strengthen business to withstand the anticipated damage of the rise in production costs.

Today, in 2004, for the first time, the cause of the economic problem is internal. The Japanese people have no clear direction as to how to counter this problem. However, the country must undertake this task today. It is my desire that the young generation will actively ask what contribution Japan can make towards the increase of welfare in the world. This will raise the self-esteem of the people.

Past experience shows that, in practical terms, Japan's approach should be directed to achieve the following three missions; (1) the wise and economic use of resources, with the aim of controlling and preserving the natural environment and the maintenance of the living environment, in the process of the further industrialization and urbanization of our cities and villages; (2) the design of workplaces and employment practices to save people from becoming alienated; and (3) the eradication of poverty from the world. These three missions have been selected based on the fact that the Japanese people have made previous efforts towards the achievement of these goals. I outline them below.

The natural and living environment

People in Japan have realized painfully the importance of the natural and living environment. The Japanese people may be said to have been the first to suffer from the harmful results of their continued thoughtless acts of damaging the natural environment, through the country's effort to develop its industry through the 1950s and 1960s. Throughout this period Japan failed to check its increasing damage to the environment: first through ignorance, and subsequently through total disregard, due to its preoccupation with industrial development.

When the damage they had inflicted became too obvious to ignore, the Japanese people mistakenly chose to counter the problem through the promotion of scientific and engineering counter-techniques, instead of refraining from the economic activities and overconsumption that were the cause of the problem. It took people a whole decade to realize that the solution lay in prioritizing the curtailment of economic growth – with the development of environmentally friendly products and livingstyles, and the promotion of anti-pollution devices as measures to supplement this priority objective.

Much progress has since been made towards this aim, with attitudes having changed greatly. People now value the natural environment and wish to maintain quality of life by living in a good environment, rather than through the mere rise of standards of living. Active discussions are taking place today in government and business as well as in the community at large to support the basic principle proposed in the Kyoto Protocol. The Japanese people are acutely aware of the importance of finding a balance between an adequate level of quality of life for people to enjoy, and the extent of economic activities needed to sustain this level without depleting and damaging the natural environment. It augurs well that people today are more frequently asking what adequate level of quality of life people wish to secure – and that many people appear to be realizing that a promising way to gain a satisfactory answer to this question is to seek ways to raise people's happiness *in the process of* leading life and work in an appropriate way, rather than by raising economic provisions themselves to facilitate contented lives.

Alienation of people at work

Many researchers have observed instances that illustrate the Japanese people's preference for doing things on a community basis and through cooperation. Management approaches and work practices demonstrate many cases of this. Views are divided on the origin of this preference. Some observers see the importance of village and farm life as the origin of modern Japanese culture, while others point to the logic of achieving tasks in groups, rather than as individuals.[13] Despite differing opinions, this cooperative approach to work has led many management and economic studies observers to appreciate the benefit of allowing workers, particularly blue-collar workers, to engage in their tasks on a humanistic basis. That is to say, these observers appreciate that their blue-collar workers will work more like their white-collar counterparts, by taking their own initiatives, if they are granted more freedom.[14]

The extent to which this interpretation is accepted should be tested by further studies. Meanwhile, however, I wish to propose that practising managers and business leaders in Japan and elsewhere explore ways to install employment systems and work practices that are encouraged by this positive view.

Throughout the internationalization of the business activities of many Japanese industrial firms, the managers of these firms have accumulated much experience to make progress in building good global workplaces in various cultural backgrounds. The generation that is emerging to direct the Japanese economy in the future consists of those with a great deal of experience in visiting, living and studying in foreign countries. Their experience is far greater than that which was gained by any of their preceding generations. I make this proposal with the understanding that the people of this young generation are more prepared to make progress, based on the learning they have gained from their international activities. They have already had the chance to evaluate their ways of doing things in Japan in the comparative context of the world. This generation should seek the direction in which the accumulated economic resources of Japan should be wisely and effectively used for the welfare of people generally across the world. In my view, the international experience of these young people is one of the most important elements of Japan's economic resources.

The elimination of poverty

The elimination of poverty should be one challenge that the Japanese people are ready take. Japan has challenged this task throughout its social and economic history. The Japanese people have accumulated many innovative devices to achieve economic development. The government has written economic and industrial policy and planning programmes, businesses have formulated investment strategies and developed management skills, and families have bent over backwards to promote the education of their children. Many of Japan's national efforts have been promoted to providing the population with basic education, technical skills and training, and progress into advanced fields of knowledge, inventions and innovations. On a practical level, these efforts have been promoted most effectively with the understanding that the Japanese economy will develop via development of new products. That is to say, many business leaders in Japan consider it their core strategy to allocate management efforts and investment funds to educate and train employees both formally and practically, on the job, before any other considerations. Many of the developing economies outside Japan that suffer from problems of low income and inadequate supply of capital will be able to find effective means for their industrialization and the maintenance of their national and economic independence, without necessarily depending on foreign investment.

As a final footnote to this study, I wish to report briefly on how our four officers are living today, at the end of 2004.

Mr M. is 66 years of age. He has completely retired from all executive and administrative appointments in public and private sector organizations. Financially, his post-retirement life is very comfortable. He is receiving superannuation and other retirement allowances from the Ministry, and post retirement *amakudari* appointments to private corporations were arranged for him.

Mr M. looks back on his work experience with satisfaction, confident that he has contributed to the welfare of the people of Japan as much as could be hoped for, given his personal aptitude and capacity. He has worked hard, and with integrity.

Mr M. has damaged his health in the process. Overwork and many public engagements at the Ministry led to an irregular pattern of life and frequent drinking. On his last medical check up, Mr M. was warned by his doctor to take greater care of his health in future.

Mr M. lost his wife to cancer five years ago. His mother also passed away before he could realize his longstanding plan to invite her to move from Fukuoka to Tokyo to live with his family. He now lives with one of his daughters, who works for one of Japan's major general trading companies as a young, emerging executive.

When invited, Mr M. likes to attend all study and discussion meetings that are organized in the Ministry, and to be in close contact with the officers and their activities. He does this for his enjoyment only, and does not claim to be of much use professionally. Looking back on his life-long efforts to work well – both professionally as well as personally – he has realized that the administrative approach and skills that he wished so eagerly to improve have become less and less effective, as the economy has developed.

Mr N. is 51 years of age and is still working in the Ministry. He is the least successful among the four, in terms of gaining good promotions and creating a high profile in the office. However, there is little doubt in his own eyes, as well as in those of his peers, that he is happy for having worked honestly and sincerely in attending to all public duties. He is proud for having closely associated with the ailing small businesses that have struggled to survive by seeking opportunities in the niches left by the larger mainstream operators. Mr N. is happy with his work, because it is an area more likely to be neglected by many of the mainstream high-flying officers of the Ministry.

Mr N. now has a large family of seven. His parents are leading an active life in his old house. However, they rarely visit him in Tokyo. Instead, he receives many visitors from the owner-managers and the employees of the small business that he helped, many of whom have originated from his home town of Nagoya. They come to see him for seasonal greetings to pay their respects, and also to just drop in to let him know how they are, and how they are still operating their workshops traditionally, with the same recurring problems and difficulties.

Mr K. is 49. He is advancing towards higher and more responsible appointments at every bi-annual *ido* occasion, despite his feisty manners and his readiness to frequently disagree with his superiors. His seniors appear to tolerate his attitude and his colleagues appreciate the openness and honesty of his approach. The younger officers enjoy witnessing the heated exchanges between the top seniors and Mr K., who manages to somehow express his views without hesitation without risk of 'demotion', whenever he finds questionable points in the approaches of his seniors. Mr K. does not practice flattery. I expect that he will continue to rise to a position of a certain height in the Ministry (perhaps Bureau Head) but not higher. Nevertheless, he seems to enjoy talking to me about how he will some day direct the Ministry as its Administrative Head, and introduce and practice many of the reform ideas that I, as an academic researcher, propose in our discussions.

He is not a family man, though he is married with two sons. Currently, his main concern now is his father's health. His father is ailing and needs to be cared for in a healthcare institution outside his home, yet the man abhors the idea and makes it a regular habit to leave the hospitals and old people's homes that Mr K. takes pains to find, and for which he pays extra expenses. Recently, Mr K. was having to take a trip almost every other week from Tokyo to the old house in Shizuoka to explain why the elderly man should seek care outside his house, and to urge him to stay at the right place. 'My father is as stubborn as a bull', Mr K. said to me, and added jokingly, 'I've never met anyone as self-opinionated as him – except myself'.

Mr O. is turning 49. As noted, from the outset of joining the Ministry, he did not find any specific personal purpose in working in government. He is another person who does not practice flattery. Unlike Mr K., however, he remains quiet when he finds himself in disagreement with others. This approach has resulted in his being regarded as someone who seems to prefer the company of his close-knit family over that of his colleagues. He has been contemplating leaving the Ministry for some time so as to live overseas with his family – possibly in France. For Mr O. the freedom to choose the right lifestyle is important.

Why France? Mr O.'s wife works as an editor and translator of French children's fairytales. Mr O. fancies taking up a cooking course there and becoming a French country-style cook. He jokes that he would like to teach Japanese people how to enjoy quality of life through eating quality food (simple and healthy, yet tasty), as they cannot see the value of enjoying more free time.

Notes

Preface

1. Some restructuring of central government took place in 2001 and 2002 under the Koizumi government. For the title of the newly formed ministries and their relation to the previous offices, see http:/www.kantei.go.jp/foreign/koizumidaijin/010426/index-h.html.
   I met an additional 11 younger officers in 2003 in order to supplement the core study. This is reported at the end of Chapter 5.

Chapter 1

1. Sakai (1990), pp. 3–27.
2. I shall return to this observation and discuss this argument in Chapter 11.
3. For further information on those activities, see *Kodansha Encyclopaedia of Japan, 1983*, vol. 6, pp. 7–8.
4. Najita (1987).
5. Ibid., see especially chapter 3.
6. Naramoto, Tatsuya (1965), chapter 3.
7. Nishikawa (1989), chapter 3.
8. Ibid., chapters 2–4.
9. See research results by several economic historians: Hayami, Miyamoto, Shinbo and Saito (1989).
10. Thurow (1992).
11. Under the diplomatic negotiations concluded at the Restoration, Japan was allowed on average to levy only 3.4 per cent. For further information, see *Kodansha Encyclopedia*, 1983, vol. 8, pp. 148–9.
12. See, for example, Minami (1986), chapter 1.
13. The speed of mechanization in those industries in the total industrial sector was said to have been the fastest in the world in the time. Ibid., pp. 126–8.
14. We read in the history of industrialization in Japan an observation about government-built model steel plants where labourers manually moved, carried and unloaded coal. The case was reported as an example that demonstrates the ingenious layout that made transporting the coal as efficient as possible. In this way, good design was used to reduce spending on tools and machines.
15. Minami (1986), p. 135.
16. Ohokawa and Rosovsky (1973), pp. 12–8.
17. In the post-World War I boom in 1914–21 employers began to train their workers in a systematic way so as to develop their skills. At the same time the employees began to make specific employment arrangements in order to retain those new skills in the company. This marked the beginning of the Japanese employment system. See, for example, Itami Hiroyuki et al. (1993).

18. Banno (1992), p. 9.
19. Koike (1987), pp. 306–13.
20. Ibid.
21. Kumazawa (1995), pp. 131–4.
22. Lewis (1955), chapter II.
23. Kimmoth (1981).
24. The spirit has been maintained widely in society throughout the years of industrialization from the Meiji period to the present. It has been a social tradition to see many people, even in great need, hesitant or ashamed to receive social security or unemployment benefits, or other help. This spirit has been sustained among people from all walks of life, not just among those in the middle class. Ironically, however, it is diminishing as affluence grows.
25. We should not forget the negative side of the approach. Kumazawa, for one, carefully examines how working people feel great pressure from the constant need to work hard. This pressure deprives them of freedom to enjoy life. Kumazawa (1995).

Chapter 2

1. A part of the argument presented in this chapter based on my previous publication in 1994.
2. The official title of *Hakusho* is *Nenji Keizai Hokoku, Annual Report on the Japanese Economy*, but it was usually referred to as *Keizai Hakusho* until 1991. It is now generally called *Keizai Zaisei Hakusho*.
3. See note 1 in the Preface.
4. The Paper has become less popular reading material in the recent years, at least since the middle of the 1980s, with the successful development of the economy and increased affluence in society. People began to see private business as more important in determining the nation's economic activities and thus attend more closely to business activities than government plans and regulative behaviour as before.
5. There is no official translation that the EPA authorizes.
6. There have been made many studies examining the Paper. See, for example, Kanamori (1990).
7. Kirschen et al. (1964), chapter 1.
8. I have identified and discussed policy cycles in the history of Japan's industrialization. See Sheridan (1993b), pp. 189–98.
9. At this time many overseas publications, particularly in the USA, acknowledged the strength of the skills of government macroeconomic management and business management techniques.
10. Until this time, Japanese exports grew annually twice as fast as world trade.
11. For the views expressed in the Paper, see Kanamori (1990), chapter 14. To follow how the national economic activities took place and how they were viewed by leaders in business, government and academics during the years in question, see Kato (2001), pp. 260–410.
12. For further discussion, see, for example, Hashimoto et al. (1998), chapter 20 and Tanaka and Okada (2001).
13. Sheridan (2002).

14. Hashimoto (1998), chapter 20 and the last chapter; see also Sawa (2000) and Kaneko (2003), chapter 13.
15. Moriya (1990).
16. With the establishment of the Koizumi government in 1991 a change was introduced into the writing of White Papers. The prime minister was to exercise greater leadership in directing financial matters of the national economy, drawing administrative services from the newly formed Naikaku-fu, the Cabinet Office, on the basis of the former Economic Planning Agency (the author of the White Papers). With this change, White Papers came to serve more as a *political bulletin* announcing the direction and the purpose of the government's economic policy rather than the traditional purpose of 'providing the population with an overall basic picture of the economy', as noted at the beginning of this chapter. See Nishioka (2004).

Chapter 3

1. The estimates are taken from Nakamura (1968), p. 30.
2. Najita (1987), Prologue.
3. Boulding (1959).
4. Ibid., p. 417.
5. Sheridan (2002).
6. There are several studies that report how Japanese people have changed their lifestyle and consumption patterns under influences from the West. Some of them observe the changes that came to Japan in a wave-like manner over 10–15 years, where the first change appeared to have come in the first decade of the industrialization period between 1890–1900, followed by the second in the 1920s–1930s. The greatest change took place several years after, and not during the high-speed economic growth time of the 1970s and 1980s. The changes appear to occur with the Japanese with delayed responses from the people. For further discussion on this matter see, for example, Sogo Kaihatsu Kenkyu Kiko *Seikatsu Suijun* (1988). Also many surveys and analyses of household accounts have been conducted since the early period of industrialization in Japan. See Yano Tsuneta Kinen Kai (1991), p. 469.
7. Lewis (1955), Chapter II.
8. Minami (1986), pp. 296–308.
9. Kawakami (1965).
10. I make this observation based on interviews with bureaucrats that I conducted in preparing this book. They were working in the central offices in economic ministries in Tokyo. There are also many writings by leaders in various sectors in society who note how they gained strong impressions and guiding encouragement in their youth from reading Kawakami's book. See also autobiographical writings of selected leaders in business and academia in Japan that appeared in *Nihon Keizai Shinbun* under the columns entitled 'Watakushino Rirekisho'.
11. Yamazaki and Kitsukawa (1995), pp. 95–105.
12. Sheridan (1993), chapter 4.
13. Sugihara (1984), chapter 4.

14. Nakamura (1993), vol. II, pp. 369–71.
15. I was one of the students in the class in which Professor Fujibayashi lectured on the persisting poverty and the backwardness of the economy and society in Japan. The story of distress stimulated us students all the more. We conducted many active discussions in the class and among ourselves, seeking what we should do to improve the conditions in the country. Some of us pursued student political activist careers, became journalists and broadcasters to let the general public understand the state of the play of the country; some even joined *Zaibatsu* corporations, scheming to reform the operation of the corporation from inside. I left Japan by taking up an invitation from the Australian National University to train as a Pacific economy researcher.

Chapter 4

1. In drawing the planning activities in terms of the following three dimensions I gained considerable benefit from the earlier discussion by Tinbergen (1967), chapter 1.
2. Boulding (1959), p. 18.
3. Sheridan (1993), chapter 3. See also Kadowaki (1985).
4. Iida (1998), chapter 3 and Lewis (1955), pp. 376–7.
5. Boulding (1959), pp. 19–20.
6. It is estimated that roughly equivalent to two-thirds of the production facilities remained intact through the war raids. Nakamura (1986), pp. 148.
7. Masamura (1986), vol. 2, pp. 18–36.
8. It is reported that all of this was made possible with the informal support of senior bureaucrats in the Foreign Ministry and some members of the Upper House of Parliament; see Arisawa (1989), pp. 5–6. We also know that the writing of occupation plans and reform and reconstruction programmes of Japan began in the USA in anticipation of the defeat of the country as early as 1943. See Koshiro (1995), p. 185.
9. He is the author of Japan's first Economic White Paper published in 1947 with which the nation's comprehensive macroeconomic plan officially began. See Sheridan (1993), pp. 126–31 for the writing of the Paper and its impact upon the national economy.
10. Tsuru (1993), chapter 1 and (1990), pp. 2–9.
11. See also Koshiro (1995), pp. 1980–85.
12. This was also the diagnosis that policy advisers to the US Occupation Authority reached. The Authority addressed the problem through the introduction of new institutional apparatus known as the three pillars of GHQ's (General Headquarters) economic democratization programmes: land reform, democratization of labour and the dissolution of the *Zaibatsu*. For economic analysis of GHQ's reform programmes, see, for example, Miwa (1989), pp. 182–6.
13. There were more than six million repatriates who returned home from either civilian or military jobs in the countries Japan had invaded, as well as the problems of hyperinflation that led the price level in 1945 to be as high as 300 times the pre-war 1934–36 level.

14. As for the economists, they included Marxians and Keynesians. The free-enterprise approach that forms the basis of neoclassical economics had not been fully developed in Japan at the stage.
15. Nakayama (1979), pp. 82–6.
16. Arisawa (1989), pp. 8–9.
17. Ibid.
18. Nakamura (1981), pp. 34–45.
19. They are those who are not 'gainfully' employed in using all their available time and effort for the work in which they are engaged. Arisawa (1989), p. 133.
20. Many discussions of these problems took place. See, for example, Komiya, Ryutaro (1988), pp. 10–11.
21. The annual rate of growth of GNP was recorded as 17 per cent and 10 per cent in 1959 and 1960 respectively.
22. For more discussion of how the Plan was made, see Sheridan (1993), chapter 7.
23. Nakayama (1979), pp. 103–6.
24. The government was promoting the resigning of the *Anpo* US–Japan security pact, causing large scale protest movements across the country. See Nakamura (1993), vol. II, pp. 563–6.
25. We note here the work of Okita Saburo, who played an important role in the making of the national economic plans as well as influencing the education and training of bureaucrats in economic and foreign ministries. He spoke of his rich experiences and learning about planning of Japan's annexed economy in China while working in the pre-war Teishin-sho, Ministry for Telecommunication, as an electric engineer in Peking. See Arisawa (1989), pp. 3–5.
26. Such a feeling is noted by many of my interviewees who worked in the Ministry during the time.
27. Koshiro (1995), pp. 552–3.
28. The rise in price index for consumer goods and services was estimated at 11.7, 24.5 and 10.4 percentages respectively in 1973. See ibid.
29. *Shunto* is often translated in English as 'spring wage offence' but sometimes referred to as 'scheduled struggles'. It means a strategy of organized labour which is designed to achieve a near uniform pattern of annual wage increase throughout the Japanese industry. For further explanation see, for example, Kodansha, 1983, pp. 188–90.
30. Koshiro (1995), pp. 98–101, 455–60.
31. Koshiro (1995), pp. 472–4.
32. See Sheridan (1993), chapter 8.
33. Ibid., pp. 166–71.
34. Ibid.
35. Nakamura (1993), vol. II, pp. 570–8.
36. The report was compiled under the chairmanship of Mr Maekawa Haruo (hence its popular title), a former governor of Bank of Japan.
37. The national economy continued to grow annually at faster than 4 per cent in net terms from 1986 to 1992 under almost full-employment conditions (the rate of unemployed remained at less than 2 per cent) plus a stable price level (consumer price increase was controlled within 3 per cent level). Personal consumption, however, did not rise.

Chapter 5

1. A large-scale reorganization of the public-sector economy has been taking place since the middle of the 1980s. At the beginning of its third term of office, towards the end of 2003, the Koizumi government said it would continue to promote deregulation of the economy with the aim of increasing efficiency. What kind of economy will develop through this deregulation and reduction of government? What kind of economic society will emerge in Japan from this reform and restructure? Even more specifically, how will this affect the building of manpower and talent for planning work in government? The question is important to our present study. I will provide some data explaining the restructuring of the public-sector economy, but they will be kept to a minimum because my study is not about the reform itself.

2. Such opportunities have often arisen since the first meetings in 1995. Many officers visited Australia on their official duties as well as to have holidays, while, for my part, I have had numerous opportunities to visit Tokyo to assist the Commonwealth and state governments of Australia with their Australia–Japan business, and trade and education matters.

3. I conducted interview meetings with the same officers more than once during the period after 1995. By meeting them as often as they would allow, I was able to study their personal as well as professional development over several years.

4. 'Career' or Class I officers in Japan's civil service organizations are those who have entered public service after passing a stringent senior civil service examination on their completion of study at one of the prestigious universities in Japan. Also there are 'non-career' civil service officers who have qualifications through the lesser civil service examinations; they consist of two groups, Class II and Class III. Those in Class II are usually either graduates of less prestigious universities than attended by Class I officers, or of college or sometimes high schools. Those in Class III are high-school graduates without university degrees. They consist mostly of clerical assistants. In addition there are technical officers working in the Ministry. They hold graduate degrees in science, technology and engineering, mostly from first-class prestigious universities in Japan, and have also passed the relevant civil service examination. For further explanation on those matters see, for example, Tsujii (1984), chapter 5 and Tanaka Kazuaki and Okada Akira (2001).

5. To begin with, a group of close friends from my student days, previously in the Ministry and now working in a large private industrial corporation, helped me arrange the interview meetings. These people were all aware of my wish to research public economic planning and policy issues through interview discussions with officers in government.

6. The total number of senior positions (at and above the rank of *kacho*) in the Ministry is limited. When officers reach senior positions they are advised to leave the Ministry for outside positions (a letter of voluntary retrenchment arrangement). This procedure normally begins when officers reach their late forties and is carried out under the so-called *amakudari* (heaven-descending) system. It has been customary practice, but reform of

public administration carried out in recent years has meant that few retiring officers now find prestigious and high-paying jobs outside the Ministry.

7. The Ministry has followed a policy in the last couple of decades of reducing the dominance of Tokyo University Law School graduates in their intake as well as the proportion of those born or brought up in Tokyo, so as to see more diversity of personalities in their personnel. Despite this, Tokyo University Law School graduates made up not less than two-thirds of the total. A notable development in recent years, particularly since the beginning of the 1990s, is that more female officers are being recruited, though their number is still limited to at most two to or three every year. I counted a total of nine female officers recruited in the 1990s. I tried to see them all, either through interview meetings or other more casual ways, so as to gain impressions of these new types of recruits.

8. The Ministry of Finance and MITI have been the most popular ministries among graduates with social science and humanities backgrounds. Most top scorers in the senior civil service examinations have been attracted to these two ministries. This indicates how management of the national economy and the promotion of industry have been viewed as important to the welfare improvement of the country and the population in general. The selection of other popular offices among new graduates appears to have fluctuated over time, due to changing conceptions of their importance and the extent of influence in the administering of national affairs. It has, however, generally included the Ministries of Foreign Affairs, Home Affairs and Defence. MITI has been popular throughout the post-war years. It may be said that because of the lack of actual resources and its commitment to a trade-or-die policy in Japan since the end of World War II, the Ministry has become a major force in the promotion and management of the national economy, thus projecting a high profile among the students.

9. Schubert (1957), pp. 346–8.

10. Quoting the research findings in Australia, Europe and the USA in the 1970s, Michael Pusey makes an important observation for our study, saying that top public servants in those countries began to act more throughout the 1970s and 1980s as if they were the 'switchmen' of history. He writes that 'top public servants are centrally involved with ministers and elected politicians not only in implementing national and public policy but also in its formulation and, equally, in the brokerage of interests and articulation of national ideals and goals' (Pusey, 1991, p. 2). I sought the officers' view on Pusey's interpretation of the role of civil servants. This topic led to discussion of what distinctions could be made between the priorities and aims of the public service and those of the general public.

11. Yamada (1988) wrote in his autobiological study that he likes to follow 'Gouverner c'est prevoir' as a guiding work principle. I see him as an example of Type D officer.

12. Najita (1980), pp. 4–5.

13. Tsusho Sangyo Sho (2000).

14. Keizai Sangyo Sho (2000).

15. See, for example, Takemura (1986).

16. The GNP grew only by less than 1 per cent during the post 1995 period to date.

17. I find the report rather hurriedly prepared. I suspect this 'vision' was drawn not after a careful study and discussion which was the case with the preparation of the previous 'vision' policies for the 1970s and 1980s. I found through talking to the officers in the Ministry while conducting interview meetings that many younger officers appeared to have read the report more critically than others.
18. It was noted that one of the attractions in joining the Ministry is the high possibility (one out of two) of gaining opportunities to be sent overseas for study with all costs paid provided they resume their work at the Ministry on their return home.
19. I must hasten to note that by expressing such aspiration young officers are not necessarily finding Japan's culture and past achievement higher than those of other countries. They do not express any strong national pride or patriotic feeling towards their nation compared with those one to two generations previously.

Chapter 6

1. For a further discussion of the plan see Sheridan (1993) and Chapter 4 above.
2. I have noted in Chapter 4 that officers in the Ministry, as well as those wishing to join them, view, though loosely, those corporations as almost public corporations and a part of the Ministry itself.
3. The matter was discussed in Chapter 4.
4. There are many such writings published in Japan.
5. Together with the Minister's Secretariat, these bureaux make up the core offices in the Ministry. The Industrial Policy Bureau has always been important because, as its title suggests, it plays a leading role in selecting and determining the nature and direction of short-term and long-term industrial policies. The other, the Consumer Goods Industries Bureau, developed from the office that looked after the development of the textile and clothing industries, once a core sector in the national efforts to expand exports. In more recent years, it has responded to 'quality-of-life' issues, for instance with the development of housing industries and other goods and services industries to enrich lifestyles.
6. By 1988, nearly half of his *doki* (those who had joined the Ministry with Mr M. in 1961) had left the Ministry to take up positions elsewhere following the custom of *amakudari* post-Ministry appointment.
7. This was in fact the response I heard later in 1997 when I met employers and workers from several car manufacturing and machine making firms as well as local business representatives in Fukuoka, where I was invited to give some lectures.
8. 'What was your reaction to the request by your office in late 1990 that you should leave the Ministry?' I put this question to him when starting our discussion about the promotion system in the Ministry and its *amakudari* procedures. He recalled that at the time there were few very senior positions – perhaps three to four – that could be contended by a half a dozen senior officers apart from he. Given his experience, only one or two of these

positions (such as Bureau Head in the Home Office) could be contemplated. As it turned out, he was not chosen to take any of them. He told me that he had to concede that it was his honest view that, given the envisaged tasks in the coming years for the Ministry, he could not help accepting the decision as fair and appropriate. Those who successfully obtained the positions were better suited to the job than he. In his view, the decision did not indicate to him that he was not as *good* as those who were successfully appointed, but rather, that they were *better suited* to the appointment. This is how appointments and promotions have always been conducted in the Ministry. He supports the practice and thus must accept the official decision. Speaking from his own work experience in the years between 1961 and 1994, from his initial recruitment through the training and biannual relocations to various offices and promotions, he evaluated the employment procedures as having being conducted in an efficient and proper manner, giving 'fair and open' treatment to everyone in the Ministry.

9. The *Amakudari* practice was established due to recognition of the following facts. First, a public service career does not give a particularly high income to officers, compared with that obtained from alternative employment. Second, though the retirement age of bureaucrats in government offices is set by the Ministry at 65, career public administrators mostly retire (on recommendation) from their offices in their mid-forties, relatively young with more years left to work elsewhere. This is designed to maintain high standards of public service administration with the aim of retaining only the officers best suited to the small number of senior positions. This is a device that has been adopted to draw on the high turnover of officers, in light of the customary lifetime employment system practised in government offices.

Given these customary practices in government employment, the *amakudari* practice has been promoted in order to provide officers with security and relative comfort in life while they work in public office, with the special aim of protecting them from any temptation of receiving bribery and engaging in misconduct.

However, not all officers retire young. Selected officers who stay in office up to or near the official retirement age of 65, like Mr M., are well provided today with public service superannuation. The *amakudari* system exists to provide them with further additional security and high social status in their post-retirement years. This practice is today meeting with severe criticism from the public. Some say that it is an unnecessary luxury and drain on the national coffers. Others say that the Ministry, as a prominent example, is placing its staff in business corporations to maintain close links and thus retain control of private business activities. There are yet others who maintain that it is the businesses that are seeking to secure their own access to public assistance. It is now said that these comments only reflect the era when the Ministry was concerned with industrial regulations and with issuing licences and approvals through the 1950s to the 1970s.

The actual arrangements of the appointments for retiring officers in the Ministry are made either by young *kacho-hosa* or by senior members of the secretariat for the more senior officers like Mr M. In the senior cases, views are sought from other ex-officers in business and politics. Mr M. was appointed to the board of a company which was a new business concern, having grown from an owner-managed firm with its production and marketing basis mainly confined to local *kansai* Osaka areas to a nationally based one less than 20 years earlier. The board was acutely aware of its lack of good executives who were capable of representing the enterprise in leading business and government circles, particularly in financial circles. They wanted to be able to make investment and R&D decisions based on knowledge of the national and international economies. So Mr M. was particularly welcome to the Board and was given a vice-president position. The position that is specifically concerned with corporate affairs is based in Tokyo. The company's production activities are mostly conducted in Osaka, with some in the USA.

10. Ueno station is the entry point to Tokyo for people from the northern agrarian-based, less developed part of Japan.

11. For Yoshida Shoin's life and activities, see *Kodansha Encyclopedia of Japan*, vol. 8, pp. 345–6.

12. He spoke of seeing the status of the nation rise steadily during his overseas appointments at embassies in Indonesia and Australia and while attending many international conferences and economic and diplomatic negotiation.

13. Bieda wrote in 1970 that the planning of the Ministry follows its objective of minimizing problems of 'externalities' that take place in free markets. He equates the approach with the case of 'the beekeeper and the orchardists' in economic textbooks. Bieda (1970), pp. 55–6.

14. In an attempt to explain how Japan's rapid industrialization took place, Najita points to the importance of a set of ideological assumptions that developed to take the form of mutual respect among top public service administrators. He observes how bureaucrats share this mutual respect, which guides their professional activities in the office as a unified force. He calls it 'bureaucratism'. It is not an ideology, but, as Najita notes, more an attitude towards life which, with an element of paternalism inherited from the feudal past, recommends and demands of the person responsibility and the 'mission' of maintaining national and individual well-being. Najita (1974), chapter 1.

Chapter 7

1. Mr M. in the previous chapter was born in 1938, while the following three officers, Messers N. K. and O. belong to a younger generation. Mr N. was born in 1954 and the other two were born in 1955.

2. It turned out to be 26 positions for the year compared with 25, 19 and 23 in 1975, 1976 and 1977 respectively.

3. It was Itoh (1986).

4. The Ministry promoted the recruitment of female officers from the beginning of the 1990s. More recruits have been accepted with the case of *gikan* technical officers numbering two to three every year. Recruitment of female officers has taken place on an average of two every two years, so that new female recruits are able to see fellow female officers in the Ministry.

5. As noted in note 2 above, towards the end of the 1970s the government thought it necessary to compile such a record, to reflect on the past achievements of the national economy and the contributions made by public

policy. A sizeable budget was allocated to the task with the book taking five years to come together with several dozen authors contributing from academia, business and other communities. Eventually 17 volumes of detailed official accounts of the Ministry's activities were published. MITI (1979–).

6. I discussed on Najita's 'bureaucratism' in Chapter 5 above. See also Najita (1974), pp. 2–3.

7. The size of the Ministry, in fact of the Japanese government itself, is relatively small compared with equivalent organizations in all OECD economies. Muramatsu (1994), chapter 2.

8. He put this observation to some of his seniors for comment, only to get responses such as 'economic problems keep coming back. But it is consoling to see that often we find policy suggestions and devices in out files in the Ministry that have already been formulated by our wise seniors. We have only to consult their wisdom.'

9. The bi-annual transfer between offices has been practised in the Ministry for some time. In recent years more exceptions began to emerge from the need for the officers to approach their duty with more experience and understanding of the issues they are assigned to. Further discussion on this matter will be given in Chapter 10 below.

10. The *ido* and on-the-job training that I observed in the experience of Mr M. in Chapter 6 may be taken as the traditional form practised in the Ministry in the post-war years up to the middle of the 1980s when many changes began to be introduced. For further discussion concerning the practice, see, for example, Kawano et al. (1983), pp. 28–38 and Nishio and Muramatsu (1994), pp. 125–35.

11. See MITI (1979), vol. 14, pp. 7–12.

12. See, for example, Miwa (1990), chapter 10.

13. There were 13 industries that were designated by this law. They include aluminium refining, synthetic fibre manufacturing, shipbuilding, ferrosilicon and liner board manufacturing, cotton and other spinning industries and the chemical fertilizer industry.

14. MITI (1992), p. 72.

15. MITI (1993), pp. 60–62.

16. It is reported that in 1974 as many as 553 officers of the Ministry were assigned to conduct such surveys.

17. Lindblom (1975), p. 26.

18. Ibid., p. 26.

19. See, for example, Komiya (1988), pp. 297–8.

20. The industry structure has altered considerably since the time through the merger of those three smaller firms to build one larger than Nippon Steel.

21. Komiya et al. (1984), p. 13.

22. Boulding (1959), p. 427.

23. Lindblom (1975).

Chapter 8

1. NHK (1979).

2. This transformation is discussed in Chapter 4 above.

3. Compared with Western economies, Japan's GNP in 1963 was estimated to have been much below their standard. For example, Japanese figures were at most 11.4 per cent, 70.4 per cent and 78.8 per cent of those of the USA, West Germany and the UK respectively. A great improvement came in the 1970s. The 1978 estimate of Japan's GNP stood 44.5 per cent of that of the USA but exceeded those of West Germany and the UK by the large margin of 1.5 times and 3.0 times respectively. As for national income per head, Japan reached almost an equal level, 83.6 per cent and 78.3 per cent of those of the USA and West Germany, surpassing that of the UK by 44 per cent. These estimates are based on the official exchange rate of the yen at the time were made. Masamura (1986), vol. 1, pp. 341–2.

4. The period is described as the time of 'crazy prices', when the rise in prices on average was recorded as 37 per cent in the wholesale and 26 per cent in consumer market respectively. A more severe shortage occurred with many of the daily essentials like food and clothing. See Uchino (1983), pp. 201–55 for more details.

5. I discussed the period of the adjustment policy in chapter 4. The discussion in this chapter on Mr K.'s experience aims to give a fuller picture.

6. Meiji period expands from 1868 to 1912, Taisho is 1912 to 1926, Showa is 1926 to 1989 and the current Heisei began in 1989.

7. In that year a greater number and on average better calibre (with good academic records and the high public service entry examination score) of candidates sought entry to the Ministry than in other years.

8. A senior member of the Ministry is said to have personally pleaded at a social function with the representatives from Japan's leading car manufacturing firms to restrain their exporting activities to the US market for the time being until such time as they (the US economy) had fully recovered. This is because, as he puts it in an anecdotal manner, it is neither kind nor commendable to behave roughly and noisily and disturb the sick at the bedside.

9. Thurow (1992).

10. In Chapter 1 I called those economic resources essential economic resources that are required for an economy to conduct its activity and promote its growth. In this I included natural resources, capital and industrial technology.

11. Thurow (1992), pp. 41–2.

12. Their competitiveness is threatening the continuing operation of their counterparts in Japan, leading the Ministry to introduce tariff protection devices against their own capital that was advanced overseas.

13. Banno (1992), pp. 8–9.

14. Kumazawa (1995).

15. Hazama (1996), pp. 159–79.

16. The approach was sometimes called 'public administrative guidance' and not strictly industrial policy because of the way it has been practised in a very *ad hoc* and case-by-case manner.

Chapter 9

1. The report is discussed in Chapter 4.

2. See Chapter 4 on the Plan.

3. Koshiro (1995), pp. 372–80.
4. Masamura (1997), chapter 19.
5. Hazama (1996), pp. 166–9.
6. Ibid., p. 140.
7. MITI, *Sangyo Seisaku Kyoku*, 1991, mimeo, p. 1.
8. MITI (1991).
9. This in fact has taken place since the mid-1990s. Koshiro (1995), pp. 372–9.
10. JETRO (2001), p. 120.
11. See our discussion in Chapter 10 below.
12. EPA (1980), p. 31.
13. In early 2002 I had discussions with office staff working at public employ-
    ment exchange offices in downtown Tokyo now newly called 'Hallo Work'.
    It is difficult to estimate the extent of a suspected gap between the official
    report and the actual extent of working hours. The Hallo Work office is
    making its own efforts to collect reliable information through interviews
    with job seekers visiting its office.
14. Saito (1996), chapter 18.
15. I have been involved in a study concerning this matter. See Castle (1992).
16. During 1999 and 2001 I conducted several interview discussions with exec-
    utives of Japanese car-manufacturing companies operating in Japan and in
    their affiliated plants in Australia. I put the questions and puzzles that
    Mr O. raised to the executives in those companies. We discussed the rela-
    tionship between welfare of individual workers and satisfaction of con-
    sumers and the fact that the two, workers and consumers, are in fact the
    same people. Some indicated that discussions have already begun to take
    place in their board concerning this dilemma.

Chapter 10

1. Galbraith (1999).
2. We observe that their critical minds and warning words have occasionally
   contributed to guiding the authors of various industrial policies in the
   government. This observation is based on my reading of the many autobiographical writings of economic planners and business leaders of Japan.
   These writers often speak of the importance of constructing a humanistic
   economy that serves, when the economic environment allows, the welfare
   and happiness of the people of their country before, as much as possible, the naked desire to industrialize the country through growth and
   efficiency.
3. We should also appreciate the earlier effort to develop a humanistic
   economy in Japan that dates back to the Tokugawa period in the seventeenth century. In this period, many thinkers from diverse backgrounds in
   society, with various intellectual experiences, undertook this challenge. It
   was, however, towards the end of the Meiji period at the end of the twen-
   tieth century when the question was raised, this time in a systematic debate
   as an 'economic 'issue. Some of these writings are mentioned in the notes
   to previous chapters.

4. The survey was made and the results published in 1975, 1978, 1981, 1985, 1986, 1987, 1990, 1993, 1996, 1999, 2000 and 2002. At each survey a total of between 4,000 and 10,000 Japanese adults (aged between 20 and 29) were randomly selected and asked to answer questionnaires. The questionnaires were delivered and the responses collected by hand by appointed personnel. The response rates differ slightly between survey years, but in general the rate has been high, at around 76–80 per cent. For further technical information, see EPA (annual).
5. Published in 2004.
6. Further study needs to be undertaken before such claims can be accepted. In the meantime, see, for example Itami et al. (eds) (1993), vol. 2.
7. To quantify the observed decline of people's life satisfaction we have an additional statistical figure that is compiled annually under 'People's Life Indicators' by government (Keizai Kikaku-cho and Naikaku-fu).
8. EPA (1970), pp. 70–73
9. Previously, in Chapter 1, I discussed the importance of 'self-help' in conducting daily life and promoting life careers in Japan throughout its economic development and industrialization. I quoted a work of Kimmoth (1981) that saw the important contribution of this 'self-help' as the driving force of the Japanese economy. We may note that this tradition still exists in a large part of Japanese society.
10. Satisfaction Survey 1971.
11. Caution should be excercised in noting the rise in women's progress in the workplace itself. It should not be read as an overly positively increase in economic freedom for women. In many cases women are seeking extra income to meet an increase in living expenses and also in the desire to keep up with their neighbours whose living styles are perceived to be rising. Also, we should not ignore the possible negative effects of working mothers on the welfare of their children, who might benefit more from the constant care of their own mothers rather than from that provided by child-care facilities. Further study is required to examine this problem.
12. Kokumin Seikatsuhakusho, 1991, Introduction by Minister Sakaiya Taichi.
13. Ibid.
14. Ota (2002).
15. Ookubo (ed.) (2002).
16. According to the survey conducted by the Japan Financial Planners' Association in May 2003, over 60 per cent of those surveyed gained qualification to work as financial planners. They said that they studied the subject as a part of their voluntary wish to 'develop themselves'. The need to gain a qualification for future employment and promotion was not stated as an important reason. *Nihon Keizai Shinbun*, 26 November 2003. p. 13.
17. Kosei (2001).
18. Naikaku-fu, White Paper on People's Life.
19. Lately, an increasing proportion of people are reported to follow an open-ended life pattern, so that today, those who select 'part-time irregular employment' over working in a 'full-time long-term' position, and those who choose a 'single, without-family-commitment' over a 'married-with-children and with other-forms-of-family' paradigm, are the majority among the coming generation of the twenties to late thirties

age group of male and females of all social, educational and family backgrounds.

Chapter 11

1. Kato (2001), chapter 1, section 9.
2. I am indebted to Hazama for selecting this term 'ethos'. However, I convey a different meaning from his, as I explain above. Hazama (1996).
3. For further information about 'Taisho Democracy', how it has been developed and what activities have been promoted in society in the period, see, for example, *Kodansha Encyclopedia of Japan*, 1983, vols 1, p. 87, 2, p. 84, 5, p. 175, 6, p. 211 and 8, p. 268 and also, Ohokouchi, Kazuo, Kuraitanima no Jiden, 1979, pp. 91–111.
4. Ibid., pp. 13–29.
5. I have replaced Hazama's 'corporate soldiers' with my term of 'industrial soldiers', as my study is about office workers in business as well as government.
6. Koshiro (1995), pp. 180–206.
7. The survey also showed that the response to the first question in America was 16 per cent, and in the UK 15.4 per cent. Hazama (1996), pp. 149–50.
8. Many thought at the time that it was possible to produce quality goods only by having a quality personality. Kumazawa, Makoto, 1995, chapter 5.
9. Yet the annual GNP growth rate in net terms was estimated only at 3.5 per cent. Iida (1998), chapter 2.
10. Long-term commitment is a foreign concept to market competition. In order to encourage individual people to promote long-term commitment as such it is essential that they are provided with the security of relief measures and services against risk of loss in the course of this lifelong exploration effort. It is therefore welcome to see active discussions beginning to emerge in search of formulating effective forms of 'safety nets' in society. For further discussion, see, for example, Kaneko (1999).
11. As we noted the amount of money that changed hands during each year in the boom was estimated as equal to annual GNP. Yet the GNP in net terms increased only by 3.5 per cent.
12. Iida T. (1998), chapter 4.
13. See, for example, Yamazaki and Kitsukawa (eds) (1995), chapter 1 in particular.
14. Koike (1993)

Bibliography

Amano, Ikuo, *Gakureki no Shakaishi, Kyoiku to nihon no* kindai, Tokyo, Shinchosha, 1992.

Arisawa, Hiromi, *Sengo Keizai wo Kataru, Showa-shi eno Shogen*, University of Tokyo Press, Tokyo, 1989.

Armstrong, J.A., *The European Administrative Elite*, Princeton University Press, Princeton, 1973.

Baba, Hiroji, 'Gendai Sekai to Nihon no Kaisha Shugi', in Shakai Kagaku Kenkyu jo (ed.), *Gendai Nihon Shakai*, Tokyo University Press, Tokyo, 1992, vol. 1, chapter 1.

Banno, Jyunnji, 'Seiouka to shite no Nihon Kin Gendai Shi', in Shakai Kenkyu jo (ed.), *Gendai Nihon Shakai*, Tokyo University Press, Tokyo, 1992, vol. 4.

Bieda, K., *The Structure and Operation of the Japanese Economy*, John Wiley and Sons, Sydney, 1970.

Boulding, Kenneth E., *Principles of Economic Policy*, Staples Press, London, 1959.

Castle, Ian, 'Living standards in Sydney and Japanese Cities', in Sheridan, Kyoko, 1992.

Craig, Albert M. and Shively, Donald H., *Personality in Japanese History*, University of California Press, Berkeley, Los Angeles and London, 1970.

Eads, G.C. and Yamamura K., 'The Future of Industrial Policy', in Yamamura, K. and Yasuba, Y. (eds), *The Political Economy of Japan*, Stanford University Press, Stanford, CA, 1987.

Ekins, Paul and Max-Neef, Manfred (eds), *Real-Life Economics: Understanding Wealth Creation*, Routledge, London and New York, 1992.

EPA, see under Keizai Kikaku cho.

Erikson, Erik, H., *Young Man Luther: A study in psychoanalysis and history*, W.W. Norton & Company, Inc., New York and London, 1958.

Galbraith, John K. *The Economics of Compassion*, Japanese edition published in Japan by Tachibana Publishing Inc., Tokyo, in cooperation with Peter David Petersen and Bernard Krisischer, 1999.

Genda, Arifumi, 'Kekkyoku Wakamono no Shigotoga Nakunatta', in Tachibanaki, Toshiaki and Wise, D. (eds) *Kigyo Kodo to Rodo Shijyo*, Nihon Keizai Shinbun Sha, Tokyo, 2001.

Haitani, Kanji, *Comparative Economic Systems, Organizational and Managerial Perspectives*, Prentice-Hall, Englewood Cliffs, NJ, 1986.

Kawakami, Hajime, *Binbo Monogatari*, first published by Kobundo, Tokyo, 1917 now reprinted by Iwanami Shoten, Tokyo,1965.

Hashimoto, Jiro et al. (eds), *Gendai Nihon Keizai*, Yuhikaku Aruma, Tokyo, 1998.

Hayami, Akira and Miamoto, Mataji (eds), *Keizai Shakai no Seiritsu, 17–18C*, Iwanami Shoten, Tokyo, 1989, 2nd print. Nihon Keizaishi, vol. 1.

Hazama, Hiroshi, *Keizaitaikoku o Tsukuriageta Shiso)*, Bunshindo, Tokyo, 1996.

Headquarters for the Administrative Reform of the Central Government of Japan, *Central Government Reform of Japan*, Tokyo, 2001.

Hosokawa, Bill, *Old Man Thunder, Father of the Bullet Train*, Sogo Way, Denver, CO, 1997.

Ihara, Tetsuo, *'Yutakasa' Ningen no Jidai*, Kodan Sha Gendai Shinsho, Tokyo, 1989.

Iida, Fumihiko, *Nihonteki Keiei no Ronten*, PHP Shinsho, Tokyo, 1998.

Iida, Tsuneo, *Keizaigaku Tanjyo*, Chikuma Gakugei Bunko, Tokyo, 1998.

Inoki, Tokutake, *Jiyu to Chitsujo*, Chu'o Sosho, Tokyo, 2001.

Itami, Hiroyuki et al. (eds), *Readings, Nihonno Kigyo Shisutemu*, Yuhikaku, Tokyo, 1993 2nd print, 4 volumes.

Itoh, Mitsuharu, *Keynes Keizaigaku*, Toyokeizai Shinpo sha, Tokyo, 1967.

————, *Keizaigak uha Genjitsu ni Kotaeuruka?*, Iwanami Shoten, Tokyo, 5th edn, 1986.

Japan Statistics Bureau, *Japan Statistical Yearbook*, Management and Co-ordination Agency, Tokyo, 1993.

JETRO, *Business facts and figures*, Nippon 2001, annual.

Kadowaki, Atsushi, 'Seikatsu Suijun Kenkyu no Suii to Seikatsu Shi', *NIRA*, 1985, February.

Kanamori, Hisao, *Sengokeizaino Kiseki*, Sairon Keizai Makusho Chuo Keizai Sha, Tokyo, 1990.

Kaneko, Masuru, Seifutii Netto no Seiji Keizaigaku, Chikuma Shobo, 1999.

————, *Hann Keizaigaku*, Shinshokan, Tokyo, 2003.

Kato, Haruhiko (ed.), *Nihon Keizai no Ashidori*, Zaikei Shoho-Sha, Tokyo, 2001.

Kawakami, Hajime, *Binbo Monogatari*, first published by Kobundo, Tokyo, 1917; reprinted by Iwanami Shoten, Tokyo, 1965.

Kawano, Hiroyuki et al., *Gendaino Gyosei*, Gakuyo Shobo, Tokyo, 1983.

Keizai Kikaku cho/Naikaku-fu (Economic Planning Agency till 2001 to be incorporated in Naikaku-fu, Cabine Office in 2002).

Keizai Hakusho (till 2001)/Zaisie Hakusho (since 2002), Government Printing Office, Tokyo, annual since 1953.

————, *Kokumin Seikatsu Hakusho*, Government Printing Office, Tokyo, frequent publications since 1956, 1956a.

————, *Showa 31-nendo no Kokumin Shotoku*, Government Printing Office, Tokyo, 1958.

————, *Kokumin Shotoku Baizo Keikaku*, Government Printing Office, Tokyo, 1961.

————, *Kokumin Shotoku Tokei Nenpo*, Government Printing Office, Tokyo, 1976a.

————, *Kokumin Seikatsu Senko do Chosa no Enkaku to Chosa no Kouzo*, Government Printing Office, Tokyo, 1978.

————, Research Bureau, *Shiryo Keizai Hakusho 25-enn*, Nihon Keizai Shinbun Sha, Tokyo, 1982.

————, *Kokumin Seikatsu Senkodo Chosa*, Government Printing Office, Tokyo, frequent publications since 1981, 1981.

Keizai Koho Center, *Japan: An International Comparison*, Japan Institute for Social and Economic Affairs, Tokyo, annual.

Kodansha Encyclopedia of Japan, Kodansha, Tokyo, 1983.

Kim, P.S., *Japan's Civil Service System*, Connecticut, Greenwood Press, 1988.

Kimmoth, E.H., *The Self-Made Man in Meiji Japanese Thought: From Samurai to Salary Man*, University of California Press, Berkeley, Los Angeles and London, 1981.

Kirschen, E.S. et al. (eds), *Economic Policy in Our Time*, North-Holland, Amsterdam, 1964.

Koike, Kazuo, 'Human resource development', in Yamamura Kozo and Yasuba Yasukichi (eds), *The Political Economy of Japan*, Stanford University Press, Stanford, CA, 1987.

———, 'Nihon Kigyo to Chiteki Jyukuren', in Itami, Keisuk et al. (eds), *Nihon no Kigyo Shisutemu*, Yuhikaku, Tokyo, 1993.

Kokumin Seikatsu Suijyen Chosa, NIRA, Tokyo, 1984.

Kokumin Seikatsu Suijyun Bunseki, NIRA, Tokyo, 1985.

Kokumin Shotoku Baizo Keikaku Shiryo, NIRA, Tokyo, 90 vols, 2001–2.

Komiya, Ryutaro, 'Three Stages of Japan's Industrial Policy After World War II', Discussion Paper, 92-DF-13, MITI, Research Institute, Tokyo, 1992, mimeo, 1988.

———, 'Josetsu', in Komiya et al. (eds) *Nihon no Sangyo Seisaku*, Tokyo University Press, Tokyo, 1997.

——— et al. (eds), *Nihon no Sangyo Seisaku*, Tokyo University Press, Tokyo, 1984.

——— et al. (eds), *Industrial Policy of Japan*, Academic Press/Harcourt Brace Jonanovich Press, Tokyo, 1988.

Kosei, Rodo-sho (ed.), *Heisei 13-nen Bann, Koyokanri no Jittai*, Romu-Gyosei Kenkyu-yo, Tokyo, 2001.

Koshiro, Kazuyoshi, *Sengo 50-nen, Sangyo, Koyo, Rodo-shi*, Nihon Rodo Kenkyuu Kiko, Tokyo, 1995.

Kumazawa, Makoto, *Nihon no Rodosha Zo*, Chikuma Gakugei Bunko, Tokyo, 1995.

Lane, Robert, *The Market Experience*, Cambridge University Press, Cambridge, 1991.

Lewis, W. Arthur, *The Theory of Economic Growth*, George Allen & Unwin, London, 1955.

Lindblom, Charles, L. 'The Sociology of Planning, Thought and Social Interaction', in Bornstein, M. (ed.), *Economic Planning, East and West*, Ballinger Publishing Co., Cambridge, MA, 1975.

Leys, W.A.R., 'Ethics and Administrative Discretion', *Public Administrative Review*, vol. 3, 1943.

Mabuchi, Masaru, 'Gendai Kanryo no Koeki-kan', *Kikan Gyosiei Kanri Kenkyu*, no. 40, December 1987.

Makoto, Kumazawa, *Nihonno Rodosha-zo* (1995), 3rd edition.

Masamura, Kimihiro, *Sengoshi*, Chikuma Shobo, Tokyo, 1986, 9th print, 2 vols.

———, Nihon Keizai, *Suitaiwa Sakerarerunoka*, Chikuma Shobo, Tokyo, 1997.

———, *Zusetsu Sengoshi*, Chikuma Shobo, Tokyo, 1997, 3rd print.

Matsushita, Keisuke, *Seisakugata Shiko to Seiji*, University of Tokyo Press, Tokyo, 1991.

McClelland, D.C. *The Achieving Society*, The Free Press, New York, 1961.

Migdall, T.S., *Weak State and Strong Societies*, Stanford University Press, Stanford, CA, 1988.

Mikuriya, Takashi, 'Senji Sengo no Shakai', in Nakamura, Takafusa (ed.), *Keikaku Ka to Minshu Ka*, Iwanami Shoten, Tokyo, 1989, Nihon Keizaishi, vol. 7.

Minami, Ryoshin, *The Economic Development of Japan*, Macmillan, Basingstoke, 1986.

Miwa, Ryoichi, *Nihon Keizaishi*, Hoso Daigaku Kyoiku Shinko Kai, Tokyo, 1989.

Miwa, Ryoichi, *Nihon Keizaishi, Kindai,* Nihon Hoso Shuppan Kyokai, Tokyo, 1989.

Miwa, Yoshiro, *Nihon no Kigyo to Sangyo Soshiki,* Tokyo University Press, Tokyo, 1990.

Miwa, Ryoichi, *Nihon Keizaishi, Kindai,* Hoso Daigaku Kyoiku Shinko Kai, Tokyo, 1987, 3rd print.

Moriya, Tomokazu, 'Itantoshite no Senshin Koku Hakusho', in Kanamori, Hisao (ed.), *Sairon Keizai Hakusho, Sengo keizai no Kiseki,* Chuou Keizai Sha, Tokyo, 1990.

Murakami, Yasusuke, 'Sengo Nihonno Keizai syste', *Yomiuri Economist,* 14 June 1982.

———, *Hankoten no Seiji Keizaigaku,* Shinpo Shikan no Tasogare, Chuo Koron Sha, Tokyo, 1992, 2 vols.

Muramatsu, Mineo, *Sengo Nihonno Kanyro-sei,* Keizai Shinpo Sha, Tokyo, 1981.

Muramatsu, Mineo, *Nihon no Gyosei,* Chuokoron Sha, Tokyo, 1994.

Najita, Tetsuo, *Japan: The Intellectual Foundations of Modern Japanese Politics,* Chicago, The University of Chicago Press, 1974.

———, *Visions of virtue in Tokugawa Japan: The Kaitokudo Merchant Academy of Osaka,* University of Chicago Press, Chicago, 1987.

Nakamura, Takafusa, *Nihon Keizai, Sono Seicho to Kozo,* University of Tokyo Press, Tokyo, 1968.

———, *The Postwar Japanese Economy,* University of Tokyo Press, Tokyo, 1981.

———, *Showa Keizaishi,* Iwanami Semina Books, Tokyo, 1986.

———, *Showa Shi,* Toyo Keizai Shinpo-sha, Tokyo, 1993, 2 vols.

Nakano, Minoru, *Nihongata Seisaku Kettei no Henyo,* Toyo Keizai Shiopo Sha, Tokyo, 1986.

Nakayama, Ichiro, *Wagamichi Keizaigaku,* Kodansha Gakujyutsu Bunko, Tokyo, 1979.

Naramoto, Tatsuya (ed.), *Kinsei Nihon Shi Kenkyu,* Kawade Shobo Shinsha, Tokyo, 1965.

National Personnel Authority, 'The Civil Service System', in Tsujii, Kiyoharu (ed.), *Public Administration in Japan,* University of Tokyo Press, Tokyo, 1984, chapter 5.

NHK, Yoronchosa Jo, *Nihonjinn no Shokugyokan,* NHK, Tokyo, 1979.

Nihon Keizai Shinbun under the column entitled 'Watakushino Rirekisho', 26 November 2003.

Nishikawa, Shunsaku, *Edojidai no Political Economy,* Nihon Hyoron Sha, Tokyo, 1989.

Nishikawa, Shunsaku and Abe, Takashi, 'Gaisetsu', in (eds), *Sangyo Ka no Jidai,* Iwanami Shoten, Tokyo, 1990, Nihon Keizaishi vol. 4.

Nishio, Masaru and Muramasu, Mineo (eds), *Koza Gyosei Gaku,* Yuhikaku, Tokyo, 1995, vol. 2.

Nishioka, Koichi, 'Kakushin', *Nihon Keizai Shinbun,* 26 July 2004.

Ookawa, Kazushi and Rosovsky, Henry, *Japanese Economic Growth,* Stanford University Press, Stanford, CA, 1973.

Otake, Hideo, 'Kankyo Gyosei nimiru Gendai Nihon no Seiji Kenkyu', *Chuokoron,* September 1982.

Ohokouchi, Kazuo, Kuraitanima no Jiden, 1979, pp. 91–111.

Oka, Yoshio, *Kindai Nihon no Seijika*, Iwanami Shoten, Tokyo, Dojidai Library, No. 15, 1990.

Okimoto, Daniel, I., *Between MITI and the Market: Japanese Industrial Policy for High Technology*, Stanford University Press, Stanford, CA, 1989.

Ookubo, Yukio (ed.), *Shinsotsu Mugyo*, Toyo Keizai Shinpo Sha, Tokyo, 2002.

Ono, Goro, *Jissenteki Sangy Seisak Ron, Nihon no Keikenkara no Kyo'kun*, Tsusho Sangyo Chosa Kai, Tokyo, 1992.

Ota, Souichi, 'Jyakunenn Shitsugyo no Saiken to sono Keizaiteki Haikei', in Genda, Yushi, et al., *Risutora to Tenshoku no Mekanizumu*, Nihon Hyoron Sha, 2002.

Otake, H., 'Kankyo Gyosei ni miru Gendai Nihonseiji no Kenkyu', *Chuokoron*, September 1982, pp. 82–112.

Otake, Hideo, '1955-nen no Seiji Taisei', *UP*, August 1996.

Pusey, Michael, *Economic Rationalism in Canberra: A Nation-Building State Changes its Mind*, Cambridge University Press, Melbourne, 1991.

Putnam, R.D., *The Comparative Study of Political Elites*, Englewood Cliffs, NJ, 1976.

Redding, S.G., *The Spirit of Chinese Capitalism*, de Gruyrter, Berlin, 1990.

Saito, Osamu, 'Rodo', in Odaka, Konosuke et al. (eds), *Nihonkeizai-no 200-nen*, Nihon Hyoron Sha, Tokyo, 1996.

Sakai, Takatoshi, 'Gaisetsu', in Sugihara, Shiro et al. (eds), *Nihon no Keizai Siso 400-nen*, Nihon Keizai Hyoronsha, Tokyo, 1990.

Sawa, Takamitsu, *Shijo Shugi no Shuenn*, Iwanami Shinsho, Tokyo, 2000.

Schubert, G.A. Jr, 'The Public Interest in Administrative Decision-Making: Theorem, Theosophy or Theory?', *American Political Science Review*, No. 2, June 1957.

Sekiguchi, Sueo and Horiuchi, Toshihiro, 'Trade and Adjustment Assistance', in Komiya, R. et al. (eds), *Industrial Policy of Japan*, Academic Press, Tokyo, 1988.

Sheridan, Kyoko, *Emerging Economic Systems in Asia*, Allen & Unwin, St Leonard, NSW, 1998.

———, *Australian Economy in the Japanese Mirror*, Queensland University Press, St Lucia.

———, 'Japan Towards 2000', Management Briefings, Graduate School of Management, University of Adelaide, vol. 1, no. 3, December 1993.

———, *Governing the Japanese Economy*, Polity Press, Cambridge, 1993.

———, 'Political Economy in Post-war Japan – Preliminary Notes', *Australian Journal of Public Administration*, vol. 53, no. 3, 1994.

———, 'Nihon Jin no Seikatsu, Manzokudo to Keizai Seisaku no Kadai', Horitsu Kagaku Kenkyuu Jo Nenpo, July 2002.

Shinbo, Hiroshi and Saito, Osamu (eds), *Kindai Seicho no Shido*, Iwanami Shoten, Tokyo, 1989, Nihon Keizaishi, vol. 2.

Shindo, M., *Gyosei Shido*, 7th edn, Iwanami Shinsho, Tokyo, 1995.

Shiroyama, Saburo, *Kanryotachino Natsu*, Shincho Sha, Tokyo, 1980, 18th print.

Slaiman, E.N., *Politics, Power, and Bureaucracy in France: The Administrative Elite*, Princeton University Press, NJ, 1974.

(1995), Social Policy Bureau, *National Survey on Life style Preferences, Fiscal Year 1995, 'Perceptions of an Affluent Society'*, Government Printing Office, Tokyo.

(1999a) Kokumin Seikatsu Kyoku, *Kokumin no Ishiki to ni-zu*, Government Printing Office, Tokyo.

(1999b) *PLI (People's Life Indicators)*, Government Printing Office, Tokyo.

Sogo Shinji Den Kanko Kai, *Sogo Shinji Den Kanko Kai*, Tokyo, 1988, 2 vols.

Stretton, Hugh, 'An intellectual public servant', *Meanjin*, vol. 5, summer 1991.

Sugihara, Shiro, *Nihon no Ekonomisto*, Nihon Hyoron Sha, Tokyo, Ekono Books 6, 1984.

Takemura, Kennichi, *Nihon no Shorai, Maekawa Report no Tadashii Yomikata*, Tokyu Agency, Tokyo, 1986.

Takeuchi, H. *Senbatsu Shakai*, Kosai-do, Tokyo, 1988.

Tanaka, Kazuaki and Okada, Akira, *Chu'o Shocho Kaikaku, Hashimoto gyokaku ga Mezashita 'Konokuni no Katachi'*, Nihon Hyoron Sha, Tokyo, 2001, 3rd print, Policy Studies Series.

Taylor, Charles, *Sources of the Self: The Making of the Modern Identity*, Cambridge University Press, Cambridge, 1989.

Thurow, Lester, *Head to Head: The coming economic battle among Japan, Europe and America*, Nicholas Brealy Publishing, London, 1992.

———, *The Future of Capitalism: How Today's Economic Forces Shape Tomorrow's World*, Allen & Unwin, Australia, 1996.

Tinbergen, J., *Economic Policy: Principles and Design*, North-Holland, Amsterdam, 1967.

Tsujii Kiyoaki (ed.), *Public Administration in Japan*, University of Tokyo Press, Tokyo, 1984.

Tsusho Sangyo Sho (now Keizai Sangyo Sho, often abbreviated Sangyo Sho [Ministry of Economy and Industry]), (1971) *70-nendai no Tsusho Sangyo Seisaku*, Sangyo Kozo Shingikai, MITI, Tokyo.

———, *Tsusho Sangyo Sho 30-nen Shi*, Tokyo Tsusho Sangyo Chosakai, 1979.

———, *80-nendai no Tsusan Seisaku Bijon*, Tokyo Tsusho Sangyo Chosakai. 1980.

———, *Kyozonteki Kyoso heno Michi*, Tsusho Sangyo Seisaku Kyoku, Tokyo, 1989.

———, *90-nendaino Tsuusan Seisaku Bijyon*, Tsusho Sangyo Chosakai, Tokyo, 1990.

———, Rodo Jikan no Eikyo ni kansuru Kenkyuu Kai Hookoku Sho, 1991, mimeo.

———, *Tsusho Hakusho, Tsusho Sangyo Sho*, Tokyo, 1992–.

———, 21-seiki no Sangyo Kozo, Sangyo Seisaku Kyoku, Tokyo, 1994.

———, Kigyo Soshiki no Sin Choryu, Sangyo Chosakai, Tokyo, 1995.

———, Sozoo-Kakushingata Kooporeeto Shisutemu, Tokyo, 1998.

———, 200-nen Sekai no Enrugi-Tenbou, Keizai Sangyo Chosa Kai, Tokyo, 2001.

———, Akaruku, Hatarakiyasui Shokuba Kankyo o Mezashie, Chusho Kigyo Cho, Tokyo, 2003.

———, Aratana Keiei Kakushin Kigyo no Soushitsu ni Mukete, Kyuushuu Keizai Sangyo Kyoku, Tokyo, 2004.

———, Shinsangyo Sozo Senryaky, N Report, Keizai Sangyo Chosakai, Tokyo, 2004.

Tsutsui, Kiyotada, *Ishibashi Tanzan-Jiyu Shugi Seijika no Kiseki*, Chuo Koron Sha, Tokyo, 1986.

Tsuru, Shigeto, '"Keizai Hakusho" Dai Ichigo ni tsuite no Kaiso', in Kanamori, Hisawo, *Sengo Keizai no Kiseki*, Chuo Keizai Sha, Tokyo, 1990.

———, *Japan's Capitalism, Creative Defeat and Beyond*, Cambridge University Press, Cambridge, 1993.

Tsusan Sho (abbreviation of Tsusho Sangyo Sho, MITI, now Keizaisangyo Sho, METI), *Kyozonteki Kyoso eno Michi*, Tsusho Sangyo Chosa Kai, Tokyo, 1989.

————, *80 Nendai no Tsusan Seisaku bijyon*, Sangyo Kozo Shingikai, Tokyo, 1980.

————, *90 Nendaino Tsusan Seisaku Bijyon*, Tsusho Sangyo Chosa Kai, Tokyo, 1990.

————, *International Trade and Industrial Policy in the 1990s – Toward Creating Human Values in the Global Age*, Tsusho Sangyo Chosa Kai, Tokyo, 1990.

————, 'Rodo Jikan Tanshuku no Eikyou ni kansuru Kenkyuu Kai Hokoku', Sangyo Seisaku Kyoku, 1991, mimeo.

————, *MITI Handbook*, Japan Trade and Industry Publicity Inc., Tokyo, 1992.

————, *Tsusho Sangyo Seisaku Shi*, Tsusho Sangyo Chosa Kai, Tokyo, 1993.

————, *Souzoteki Kakushin no Jidai*, Tsusan Shiryo Chosa Kai, Tokyo, 1993.

————, 'Sozo teki Sangyo Soshiki no Kouchiku', Sangyo Kozo Shingi Kai, Tokyo, 2001, mimeo.

Uchino, Tatsuro, *Japan's Postwar Economy: An Insider's View of its History and its Futue*, Kodansha International, Tokyo, 1983.

University of Tokyo, Shakaigaku Kenkyujo (ed.), *Gendai Nihon Shakai*, 3rd edn, University of Tokyo Press, Tokyo, 1992.

US Department of Commerce, *Japan, The Government – Business Relationship, A Guide for American Businessmen*, Washington, DC, Government Printing Office, 1972.

Vogel, E.F. (ed.) *Modern Japanese Organisation and Decision-Making*, 4th edn, Tokyo, Charles F. Tuttle, Tokyo, 1975.

Wolferen, K., *The Enigma of Japanese Power – People and Politics in a Stateless Nation*, Macmillan, London, 1989.

Yamada, Katsuhisa, *Tsubasa no aru Sozo*, Tshushosangyo Chosakai, Tokyo, 1988.

Yamazaki, Hiroaki and Kitsukawa, Takeo, *'Nihonteki Keiei' no Renzoku to Danzetsu*, Iwanami Shoten, Tokyo, 1995.

Yano, Tsuneta Kinen Kai (ed.), *Nihon Kokusei Zue*, Tokyo, annual.

Zaimu Sho (formerly Ookura Sho, Ministry of Finance), 'Nihongata Keizai Shisutemu: Saiho' Kenkyuukai Hokoku Sho, Tokyo, 2002.

Index

Note: 'n.' after a page reference indicates the number of a note on that page.

administrative guidance (*gyosei shido*)
    138–9
    electric furnace steel-making
        industry   139–43
    evaluation   144; intellectual
        approach   144–7; responsible
        behaviour sought in
        industry   147–51
    LPG, sale of   143–4
administrative Platonism   89–90,
    96
administrative rationalism   89
administrative realities   89, 90
agricultural sector, performance   76
aims of economy   223–4
alienation of people at work   228–9
All Japan Trade Unions
    (Nikkeiren)   76, 77, 78
amakudari (heaven-descending)
    system   123–30, 159, 238–9 n. 6,
    240 n. 6
Anpo US–Japan security pact
    237 n. 24
anti-pollution measures   101, 228
Australia   116
authoritarianism   67
automobile industry   158–60, 187–9

balance of trade surplus
    case study   159, 161
    and life satisfaction   200
    smaller government, move
        towards   80–1
Bank of Japan   122
Banno Junji   166
bargaining power of the workers, and
    industrial development   48
black market   19
Booth, Charles   51
Boulding, Kenneth   46, 61, 63, 150
building boom   153–4
bureaucratism   128–9, 136, 242 n. 14

Cabinet Office (Naikaku-fu)   15,
    235 n. 16

capital
    needs   49, 55
    retained   48
    surplus accumulation of   65–6
capitalism
    Fukuda's views   54
    Kawakami's views   51, 54
car industry   158–60, 187–9
centrally planned communist society,
    planning approach   144, 145
chemical industry   11, 88
childbirth, death of mothers and
    babies at   48
China   72
Communist Party   182
commuting time, reduction
    of   185–6
competition, excessive (*kato-
    kyoso*)   188–9
Confucianism
    and inequalities   53
    iron and steel industry   149
    move away from   153
    Shooin *see* Yoshida Shooin
construction boom   153–4
consumption, personal   46–7, 64, 181
cooperative arrangement
    (*kyosei*)   159
'corporate men'   216, 219–21
'corporate soldiers' (*kigyo
    senshi*)   217
cottage industries, modernization
    of   9–10

'Damn the GNP' movement   200
deferred payment system   48
demographic issues   27
Depressed Industry Law (1978)   140
deregulation
    Keizai Hakusho   23, 24
    Koizumi government   238 n. 1
    national economy, planning
        of   23, 24, 30, 33
disease and illness   49
dual production structure   74

economic adjustment policy   75–80,
    157–8
'economic animals'   216, 221–2
economic development, and life
    satisfaction   193–5
    contentment levels   195–201
    quality of life   201–10
economic freedom   62, 66–70
    economization ethos   216, 223
    'freeter' syndrome   207–9
    lifestyles   206, 208
    volunteer works   206–7, 208
economic growth
    economic adjustment policy   75,
        78, 79
    economic society, establishment
        of   7
    Fukuda's evaluation   52–4, 55, 67
    industrialization   11, 12, 13, 44
    Japan as No. 1: 22–3
    Kawakami's evaluation   50–2, 53,
        54, 55, 189
    Keiza Hakusho   20–2; *see also under*
        Economic Planning Agency
    and life satisfaction   195–6, 197,
        199
    MITI administrative officers   100,
        101–2; case studies   114, 116,
        128, 129, 135, 175
    planning   61–3
    road to   72–5
    skewed industrial structure   71–2
    smaller government, move
        towards   26–30
    sources   12–13
    speculation boom   23–6
    standards of living   46–7, 48, 56,
        64, 65
economic justice   62–3
Economic Planning Agency (EPA)
    case studies   122, 138, 142, 181,
        185
    economic adjustment policy   77
    establishment   31–2
    Keizai Hakusho   15–18, 22–23, 25
    satisfaction survey   195
economic society, establishment
    of   3–4, 7–10
    early experience   4–7
economic stability/instability
    MITI administrative officers   101
    national economy, planning   24
    oil crises   156
    people's concerns about   62

Economic Stabilization Board   69
economic thought, development
    of   4–7
Economic White Papers *see Keizai
    Hakusho*
economization ethos   214–23,
    225–6
education and training
    economic society, establishment
        of   8–10
    for entrepreneurialism and
        individualism   30
    industrialization through
        people   10
efficiency
    Japan as No. 1: 22–3
    Keizai Hakusho   21
    MITI administrative officers   100
    smaller government, move
        towards   26–30
    speculation boom   23–6
egoism   221
electric furnace steel-making
    industry   139–43, 145, 146, 147
Emergency Economic Policy
    (1947)   69
employment system
    high economic growth, road
        to   72–3, 74–5, 125–6
    lifetime employment *see* lifetime
        employment system
    origins   233 n. 17
    promotion *see* promotion practices
    and quality of life   102–3, 104
    and standards of living   48, 61
    see also labour market
Engel's coefficient   56
England *see* United Kingdom
entrepreneurialism
    and economic growth   64, 72,
        75
    MITI   116, 117
    national economy, planning
        of   30
    and quality of life   101
    smaller government, move
        towards   81
Environment Agency   120
environmental issues   75, 101,
    204–5, 227–8
EPA *see* Economic Planning Agency
European Union   160
exports
    of cars   158–60

importance to the promotion of
industries 88
international competition 28, 77;
administrative guidance 139
Keizai Hakusho 22
National Income-doubling
Plan 74
promotion 74
smaller government, move
towards 80–1
see also balance of trade

family life 202–3, 204
farming methods 5–6
feudal system
economic society, establishment
of 4–5, 7
inequalities 53
foreign aid programmes, lack of 8
foreign direct investment by
Japan 22, 23, 200
France
case study 160–2
labour's share in total value
added 50
working hours 177, 182
freedom of speech, wartime
suppression of 56
free market 24, 30
freeter syndrome 207–9
Fujibayashi Keizo 56–7
Fuji Steel (later Nippon Steel) 114
Fukuda Tokuzo 52–4, 55, 67
Fukuzawa Yukichi 210, 223
full employment 73, 74

Galbraith, John K. 194
Germany
economic planning 46
Fukuda 52
labour's share in total value
added 50
working hours 177, 181
globalization 106
green revolution 163
gyosei shido see administrative
guidance

Hallo Work 245 n. 13
han initiatives 6
Harvard Law and Business
Schools 105
Hashimoto Ryutaro 28, 29
Hazama Hiroshi 167, 217

health, and life satisfaction 201–2,
204
heavy industries
government control 55
Industrial Bank of Japan 88
industrialization through
people 11
Hong Kong 163, 165, 166, 167
household supply industries 118–19
housing policy 185–6
human resources
economic adjustment policy 78
economic society, establishment
of 3, 8–10
economization ethos 216–17
industrialization through 10–14,
44–5, 62
National Income-doubling
Plan 74
Thurow's views 163
hyperinflation 236 n. 13

ido promotion system 129, 137,
138, 142, 162
Iida Tsuneo 63
Ikeda Hayato 73, 113
illness and disease 48
imports 80–1
see also balance of trade
indicative planning 64, 75
case study 146
economic freedom 70
Indonesia 116, 121
Industrial Bank of Japan 88, 114–15
industrialization
capital-scarce labour-surplus
economy 44–5
economic society, establishment
of 3–4, 8–10
MITI 115–16, 121, 136, 138,
166–8, 187–8
through people 10–14, 44–5, 62
standards of living 46, 48–9, 50
working hours, reduction of 187
industrial sector, productivity 76
'industrial soldiers' (*sangyo senshi*)
216, 218–19
industrial structure, skewed 70–2
inflation
economic adjustment policy 76–7
hyperinflation 236 n. 13
Keiza Hakusho 19
National Income-doubling
Plan 74

inflation – *continued*
    oil crises   156
    skewed industrial structure   71
    toleration of   62
infrastructure
    National Income-doubling
        Plan   74
    Vision Policy for the 1970s   79
innovation   20, 30
    see also entrepreneurialism; research
        and development
intellectual approach to problem
    solving   144–7
internationalization   22
iron industry   148–9

Japan National Railways   30
JETRO   160
jitan proposal   169–70, 174–90
job creation   69, 70

K., Mr (type A officer)   231
    career path   152–62
    observations made in Asia   162–5
    writing industrial policy   166–8
Kaitokudo   6
karo-shi syndrome   219
Kasumigaseki government   117, 121
kato-kyoso (excessive competition)
    188–9
Kawakami Hajime   50–2, 53, 54, 55,
    189
keisei saim (political economy)
    approach to economic
        studies   6, 53, 68
Keizai Antei Honbu   69
Keizai Hakusho (Economic White
    Papers)   34–43
    economic freedom   69–70
    and economization ethos   217,
        221, 222
    Japan as No. 1: 22–3
    observations and lessons   31–2
    policy cycles   18–20
    speculation boom   23–6
    structure and work
        mechanism   15–18
    welfare economy, growth towards
        a   18–22
Keizai Kikaku-cho *see* Economic
    Planning Agency
Keynesian thinking   237 n. 14
kigyo doryoku (management
    effort)   144

kigyo senshi ('corporate
    soldiers')   217
Kimmoth, E.H.   13
Kirschen, E.S.   17
Kobe earthquake (1995)   206
koeki (in the public interest)   87, 88,
    89–90, 91, 221
    characteristics of interviewees   93,
        105–6; case studies   123–30,
        134, 152, 155–6
Koizumi government
    deregulation, promotion of   238 n. 1
    discretionary decision making,
        evaluation of   90
    Keizai Hakusho   235 n. 16
Kokumin Seikatsu Senkodo Chosa see
    Satisfaction Survey
Korean War   31, 56
Kuwait   143
kyosei (cooperative arrangement)   159
Kyoto Protocol   228

labour market
    administrative guidance   138–19
    economic adjustment policy   75,
        77–8
    economic freedom   67, 69, 70
    jitan proposal   174–5, 179, 180–1,
        183
    job creation   69, 70
    National Income-doubling
        Plan   74
    stability   62
    standards of living   57
    women's opportunities   205
    see also employment system
labour protests   73
labour unions   76, 77, 78
lean production methods   12, 187,
    219
leisure time   169–70, 182–90, 234 n. 25
    smaller government, move
        towards   81
Lewis, Arthur   12, 49, 63
life expectancy   49, 202
lifestyles, and economic
    freedom   206, 208
lifetime employment system
    and *amakudari* system   241 n. 9
    case study   114
    decline   203
    and life satisfaction   246 n. 11
    positive evaluation of   80
    and quality of life   102, 103

Lindblom, Charles 144–5, 151
liquefied petroleum gas (LPG), sale
    of 139, 143–4, 148, 150–1
living standards *see* standards of living
loans, low-interest 48

M., Mr (type C officer) 111, 230
    career path 113–17
    family, schooling and university
        days 111–13
    post-Ministry career in
        business 123–30
    work experience 117–23
Maekawa Haruo 237 n. 36
Maekawa Report 32, 170
MITI 99
    smaller government, move
        towards 80, 81
Makoto, Kumazawa 166
management effort (*kigyo
    doryoku*) 144
management style
    Allied Authorities' influence on 55
    economic adjustment policy 78
    economic society, establishment
        of 9
    industrialization through
        people 12
    Japanese Management
        System 218
    national economy, planning 20, 28
    retained capital 48
    security for employees 62
    working hours 183
man-made resources *see* human
    resources
market-led liberal democratic society,
    planning approach 144–5
Marxist thinking 68, 237 n. 14
material science revolution 163
mechanization of cottage
    industries 10
Meiji Restoration
    challenge, size of 79
    economic society, establishment
        of 4, 9
    Fukuzawa 210
    humanistic economy 245 n. 3
    Shooin's influence 126
merchants 6
METI *see* Ministry of International
    Trade and Industry
militarism 67
Ministry of Construction 87, 174

Ministry of Economy and Trade and
    Industry *see* Ministry of
    International Trade and Industry
Ministry of Education 30, 172–3
Ministry of Employment 174
Ministry of Finance (MoF) 115, 120,
    121, 122
    staff 86, 239 n. 8
Ministry of International Trade and
    Industry (MITI, later METI)
    Consumer Goods Industries
        Bureau 121
    diversity of employees 239 n. 7
    economic adjustment policy 76,
        75, 78–80
    employment structure 238 n. 4
    female recruits 135
    Industry Policy Bureau 121
    interviews with administrative
        officers 82–4, 98;
        characteristics 91–8;
        'economic objective', in search
        of an effective 98–104;
        emerging types among 'young
        recruits' 104–6; *koeki* 89–90;
        procedure 85–6; samples
        and meetings 84, 107–8;
        self-assessment 86–9
    K., Mr (type A officer); career
        path 152–62; observations
        made in Asia 162–5; writing
        industrial policy 166–8
    M., Mr (type C officer) 111; career
        path 113–17; family,
        schooling and university
        days 111–13; post-Ministry
        career in business 123–30;
        work experience 117–23
    N., Mr (type C officer) 131–2;
        administrative guidance
        evaluated 144–51; career
        path 132–44
    O., Mr (type B officer) 169–70;
        jitan proposal 174–82;
        personal background 171–4;
        working hours, reduction
        of 182–90; senior
        positions 238–9 n. 6;
        Sozoteki Kakushin no Jidai
        101; Vision Policy for the
        1970s 77–8; Vision Policy
        for the 1980s 78, 80, 100;
        Vision Policy for the
        1990s 100, 103–4

Ministry of Labour   138, 177
Ministry of Transport   88, 115
MITI *see* Ministry of International
   Trade and Industry
Mizuho Financial Group *see* Industrial
   Bank of Japan
modernization
   cottage industries   9–10
   investment   49
   Keiza Hakusho   20, 31–2
   standards of living   46
multinational enterprises   8, 163

N., Mr (type C officer)   131–2, 230–1
   administrative guidance
      evaluated   144–51
   career path   132–44
Naikaku-fu (Cabinet Office)   15,
   235 n. 16
Naikoku Chosa-ka   16
Najita, Tetsuo   98, 99
   bureaucratism   128, 136, 242 n. 14
Nakasone Yasuhiro   80, 81
Nakasone Yasusuke   26–7, 28
Nakayama Ichiro   68, 72, 73, 79
national economy, planning of the
   growth and efficiency   22–30
   Keiza Hakusho   15–22, 34–43
   observations and lessons   31–2
National Income-doubling Plan
   (1960, *Shotoku Baizo*)   57, 72,
   73–4, 79, 218–19
   case studies   113, 114, 130, 174
natural environment   75, 101,
   204–5, 227–8
neoclassical economics   237 n. 14
Netherlands   181–2
new entrants   71
'new type of people'   209–10, 223
Nikkeiren (All Japan Trade
   Unions)   76, 77, 78
Nippon Steel   88, 114, 148
'Nixon shock'   139
non profit organizations (NPOs)   206

O., Mr (type B officer)   169–70, 231–2
   jitan proposal   174–82
   personal background   171–4
   working hours, reduction
      of   182–90
oil crises   212, 227
   case studies   138, 143, 144, 156–7;
      working hours, reduction
      in   176, 183

'corporate men'   219, 220
economic adjustment policy   75,
   79, 80
Keiza Hakusho   20
national economy, planning
   of   20, 27, 29, 31
Ookita Saburo   237 n. 25
Ookubu Toshimichi   9

pay *see* wages and salaries
Peace Police Law (1923)   56
peasants
   economic society, establishment
      of   5, 6, 8–9
   industrial development   48
Pigou   52–3
Pilot pen workers   11–12, 167
planning
   economic society, establishment
      of   3, 4, 7
   industrialization through
      people   11, 13
policy cycles   18–20, 26
political economy (*keisei saimin*)
   approach to economic
      studies   6, 53, 68
pollution   101, 228
poverty
   and economic development   48
   elimination of   227, 229–30
   in England   50–1
   Fujibayashi's views   56–7
   Kawakami's views   50, 51
Priority Production Plan (1947)   69
privatization   30
productivity, labour
   economic adjustment policy   75
   industrial development   48
   and quality of life   102–3
   and wage increases   76
   and working hours   175, 178–9,
      184
promotion practices
   case study   120–1, 128, 137, 138,
      143, 162
   deferred payment system   48
   ido   129, 137, 138, 142, 162
   and motivation   63
   seniority-based   80
   and working hours   184
public administration
   economic adjustment policy   75
   and standards of living   60
public budget   28, 29

public holidays 185
public hygiene 49
public interest *see koeki*
public investment 74
public protests 73
Pusey, Michael 239 n. 10

quality control 12, 220, 221
quality of life
    aim of economy 223–4
    and economic development 48
    Keiza Hakusho 21, 31
    leisure time and activities 81
    and life satisfaction 201–9
    MITI administrative
        officers 100–3, 170
    and natural environment 228
    smaller government, move
        towards 81
    vs. standards of living ix, x, 79
    World War II 56

Reagan administration 28
research and development 74
    see also innovation
responsible behaviour among
    competitors 144, 147–51
retained capital 48
retirement 241 n. 9
role of economy 224
role of government 203–5, 224
Rowntree, Seebohm 51

salaries *see* wages and salaries
samurai 6, 126–7
sangyo senshi ('industrial
    soldiers') 216, 218–19
satisfaction in life 193–5, 220, 221
    contentment levels 195–201
    quality of life 201–10
    role of government 224
Satisfaction Survey 195–210, 212
savings
    forced 49
    and life satisfaction 205
    smaller government, move
        towards 81
Schubert, Glendon 89, 91, 93
Second World War *see* World War II
self-help
    and life satisfaction 204
    and self-advancement
        mentality 13, 30
seniority-based promotion 80

services sector, performance, 76
share market, World War II 55
Shimomura Osamu 72, 73, 79
Shooin, Yoshida 126–7
shortages during oil crises 156
Shotoku Baizo (National Income-
        doubling Plan, 1960) 57, 72,
    73–4, 79, 218–19
    case studies 113, 114, 130, 174
shunto 77, 237 n. 30
smaller government, move
        towards 26–30, 33, 80–1
    Keiza Hakusho 21, 23
Smith, Adam 7
social dumping 182
Sozoteki Kakushin no Jidai 101
Special Survey Committee 66, 66–9
speculation boom
    national economy, planning 23–6
    standards of living 65–6
speech, wartime suppression of
        freedom of 56
standards of living 60
    capital-scarce labour surplus
        economy 44–50
    case study 129
    economic adjustment
        policy 74–80
    economic development
        evaluated 50–4
    economic objectives and
        government planning 59–63
    economic society, establishment
        of 4–7
    high economic growth, road
        to 72–5
    and life satisfaction 201
    national economy, planning 24
    planning experience 66–80
    post-World War II 64–6
    promotion of economic freedom,
        search for 66–70
    vs. quality of life ix, x, 79
    skewed industrial structure 70–72
    smaller government, move
        towards 80–1
    transformation of economy 54–8
steel industry 148–8
    case study 139–43, 145, 146, 147
    centrality to Japan's industrial
        basis 88
    labour-intensive design 233 n. 14
Sweden 217
Switzerland 217

Taisho period   218
tariffs   8
taxation   186
   concessions   48
technology   20
Thatcher administration   28
Thurow, Lester   162–3
'Time for Innovative Creation'
   (*Sozoteki Kakushin no Jidai*)
   101
Tokugawa period   245 n. 3
Tokyo Electric Corporation   115
Tokyo University   86, 104, 239 n. 7
   case studies: Mr K.   154–6, 157,
      158; Mr M.   112, 113–14, 115;
      Mr N.   135, 136; Mr O.   173
trade unions   76, 77, 78
training *see* education and training
transport policy   185–6
Tsuru Shigeto   66–7
turnover of businesses   71

underemployment   70
unemployment   70
   freeter syndrome   207–8
'unequal treaties' trading
   condition   8
United Kingdom
   free market   24
   Fukuda's views   52
   Industrial Revolution   7
   Japanese example   27
   Kawakami's views   50–1
   Keizai Hakusho   21
   national economy, planning   21
   public deficits   28
   smaller government, trend
      towards   21, 28
   Thatcher administration   28
   working hours   182
United States of America
   Anpo security pact with Japan
      237 n. 24
   automobile industry   159–60
   balance of trade with Japan   159,
      161
   'corporate men' in Japan   219
   economic planning   61
   economic resources, capacity to
      produce   215
   free market   24
   Japanese example   27
   Keizai Hakusho   20, 21, 217
   Korean War   31, 56

   management skills   20
   national economy, planning   20,
      21
   Occupation Authority   236 n. 12
   pressure on Japan   22
   production techniques   20
   public deficits   28
   Reagan administration   28
   smaller government, trend
      towards   21, 28, 30
   technology   20
   views on Japan   234 n. 9
   working hours   177, 182
   World War II   236 n. 8
urbanization   48, 49

value, creating   166–8
value-added production
   structure   74
value systems   150–1
Vietnam   164–5, 166, 167
Vision Policy for the 1970s   78–9
Vision Policy for the 1980s   79, 80,
   100
Vision Policy for the 1990s   100,
   103–4
volunteer works   206–7, 208

wages and salaries
   economic adjustment policy   76,
      77–8
   and life satisfaction   199, 200,
      203
   and quality of life   103
   standards of living   46–7, 48, 49,
      50, 58
   and working hours   175, 176,
      180–1, 183, 184
welfare economy
   economic adjustment policies
      79
   and family life   203
   Fukuda's views   53–4
   growth towards a   20–22, 23, 31,
      32
welfare systems, post-World War
   II   56
White Papers, Economic *see Keizai
   Hakusho*
whole-industry perspective on
   problems   145
will to economize   12, 49, 63
work ethic   167
   see also economization ethos

working hours
  and life satisfaction   199
  reduction   169–70, 174–90
World War II
  economic freedom   66
  economization ethos   215–16
  high economic growth, road to   73
  transformation of economy   54–6

Yawata Steel (later Nippon
  Steel)   114
yen, value of
  administrative guidance   139
  national economy, planning
    of   23, 28

Zaibatsu   55